The New Spirit of Hospitality

Tourism Security-Safety and Post Conflict Destinations

Series editors: Maximiliano E. Korstanje and Hugues Seraphin

Since the turn of the century, the international rules surrounding security and safety have significantly changed, specifically within the tourism industry. In the age of globalisation, terrorism and conflict have moved beyond individual high-profile targets; instead, tourists, travellers and journalists are at risk. In response to this shift, the series invites authors and scholars to contribute to the conversation surrounding tourism security and post conflict destinations.

The series features monographs and edited collections to create a critical platform which not only explores the dichotomies of tourism from the theory of mobilities but also provides an insightful guide for policymakers, specialists and social scientists interested in the future of tourism in a society where uncertainness, anxiety and fear prevail.

Tourism Security-Safety and Post Conflict Destinations explores research approaches and perspectives from a wide range of ideological backgrounds to discuss topics such as

- Studies related to comparative cross-cultural perceptions of risk and threat
- Natural and human-caused disasters
- Post-disaster recovery strategies in tourism and hospitality
- Terror movies and tourism
- Aviation safety and security
- Crime and security issues in tourism and hospitality
- Political instability, terrorism and tourism
- Thana-tourism
- War on terror and Muslim-tourism
- The effects of global warming on tourism destinations
- Innovative quantitative/qualitative methods for the study of risk and security issues in tourism and hospitality
- Virus outbreaks and tourism mobility
- Disasters, trauma and tourism
- Apocalyptic theories and tourism as a form of entertainment

Editorial Advisory Board

Tzanelli goes beyond the co-ordinates of contemporary cultural theory to contextualise a new "atmospheric" ethos in tourism markets. All of this grounded in a Marxist appreciation of the relation of space to labour and, perhaps the most innovative focus of the book, on the notion of worldmaking borrowed from Hollinshead and deployed here to organise the appearances (another mode of spirit, etymologically justified in Marx's terminology) of tourism in case studies. As cases, however, these studies are saturated in an astute appreciation of theoretical confluence, from Derridean spectres and hospitality to Hardt and Negri's Empire, to Boltanski and Chiapello, Žižek, Sewell, that guy Hutnyk and the classics – Hegel, Nietzsche, Arendt

The book narrates a necessary movement from crisis to justice, designing places for care and reviving a new hospitality in an always open-ended inquiry. It will allow you to travel to your own conclusions, taking or leaving the many stops on the way as possible swelling-places or refreshment. Theoretical tourism has rarely been done with such vigour. A fabulous, fun, and flagrantly phantasmagoric read.

–John Hutnyk, Ton Duc Thang University, Vietnam

The New Spirit of Hospitality is a much-needed breath of fresh air in the current and mainly normative fields of travel, tourism, and hospitality studies. Tzanelli disturbs the normative premises on which much tourism and hospitality research are predicated to make space for imaginations whereby the represented can manage their representations, and destination design is co-developed with more just digital technologies. Zooming in on 'film-induced' or 'cinematic tourism' Tzanelli problematises the production of truthfulness and justice to unveil discomforting rifts between what is sustainably and justly possible and attainable, and for whom. Such discomforting conclusions are bound to push the boundaries of knowledge creation in tourism and hospitality studies.

–Dorina-Maria Buda, University of Essex, UK

The New Spirit of Hospitality: Designing Tourism Futures in Post-Truth Worlds

BY

RODANTHI TZANELLI

University of Leeds, UK

United Kingdom – North America – Japan – India – Malaysia – China

Emerald Publishing Limited
Emerald Publishing, Floor 5, Northspring, 21-23 Wellington Street, Leeds LS1 4DL

First edition 2023

Reprints and permissions service
Contact: www.copyright.com

British Library Cataloguing in Publication Data
A catalogue record for this book is available from the British Library

ISBN: 978-1-83753-161-5 (Print)
ISBN: 978-1-83753-160-8 (Online)
ISBN: 978-1-83753-162-2 (Epub)

INVESTOR IN PEOPLE

The future world may be a murky world, but it is one that we have to enter, interrogate and hopefully reshape. It should be a direction of travel for fateful analyses of social life within this new century.

John Urry, What is the future? *2016, Polity, p. 192.*

For Majid

Table of Contents

List of Figures and Tables   *xiii*

List of Abbreviations   *xv*

About the Author   *xvii*

Acknowledgements   *xix*

Introduction   *1*

Chapter 1   Representation, Presence and Public Culture   *19*

**Chapter 2   From Cultural Worldmaking to Structural
               Technomorphism in *Zorba the Greek* Tourism**   *37*

**Chapter 3   From *Borat* Post-tourism to Market Post-truth:
               Kazakhstan's New Spirit of (In)Hospitality**   *73*

**Chapter 4   Spirited Edgeworks: *Breaking Bad's* (In)Hospitable
               Worlds of Soft Crime**   *101*

**Conclusion: Undoing the Cinematic Tourist Provenance,
               Designing Viable Futures**   *133*

Bibliography   *141*

Index   *179*

List of Figures and Tables

Chapter 2

Figure 1.   The Moment Basil Meets Zorba for the
First Time.   45

Figure 2.   The Beach of Stavrós, Akrotíri, Crete.   48

Diagram 1. A Map of Conceptual Connections and
Process-Driven Placemaking as Worldmaking.   71

Chapter 3

Figure 3.   Glod Is a Roma Village in the Commune of
Moroeni, Dâmbovița County, Romania.   90

Chapter 4

Figure 4.   A Map of the Key Locations in Albuquerque
That Featured in *BB*.   113

Figure 5.   Jesse's RV, With Its Peculiar Ventilation System,
Is Today a Site of Tourist Fascination.   118

Figure 6.   The Notorious *Los Pollos Hermanos*.   120

Figure 7.   *The Candy Lady*, Old Town of Albuquerque.   124

Figure 8.   Cooking Meth at The Candy Lady, Old Town
of Albuquerque.   125

Figure 9.   *Breaking Bad* Merchandise at a Gift Shop in
the Albuquerque International Sunport.   126

Chapter 2

Table 1.   International Tourist Arrivals in Greece During
the Period 1954–1990.   49

Table 2.   International Tourist Arrivals in Greece as a
            Percentage of All International Tourist Arrivals
            Worldwide During the Period 1960–1995.   50
Table 3.   Hotel Bed Capacity in Greece, on Crete and
            on Rhodes.   51
Table 4.   Growth of Hotel Bed Capacity on Crete and
            Rhodes and in Greece Over the Period 1970–1990
            Compared to the Base Year of 1964 (Base Year
            Value = 100).   68
Table 5.   Growth of Overnight Hotel Stays on Crete and
            Rhodes and in Greece Over the Period 1970–1990
            Compared to the Base Year of 1970.   69

List of Abbreviations

ABQ	Albuquerque
BB (TV series)	*Breaking Bad* (dirs. V. Gillingan, M. Slovis, C. Bucksey, T. McDonough M. MacLaren, A. Bernstein, R. Johnson, C. Bucksey, B. Cranston, J. Renck, P. Gould, S. Winant, C. Haid, J. Shiban, T. Shauz, B. Hughes, G. Mastras, S. Catlin, F. E. Alacalá, T. Brock, T. Hunter, J. Dahl, J. McKay, P. Medak, P. Abraham, P. Slade, 2008–2013)
Borat 1 (film)	*Borat: Cultural Learnings of America for Make Benefit Glorious Nation of Kazakhstan* (dir. L. Charles, 2006)
Borat 2 (film)	*Borat Subsequent Moviefilm: Delivery of Prodigious Bribe to American Regime for Make Benefit Once Glorious Nation of Kazakhstan* (dir. J. Woliner, 2020)
DMO	Destination Marketing Organisation
IAEA	International Atomic Energy Agency
US	United States (of America)
USSR	Union of Soviet Socialist Republics
ZG (film)	*Zorba the Greek* (dir. M. Cacoyannis, 1964)

About the Author

Rodanthi Tzanelli is Associate Professor of Cultural Sociology and Director of the Mobilities Area in the Bauman Institute, University of Leeds, UK. She is a social and cultural theorist with particular interest to hybrid mobilities (tourism, travel, migration, social movements and new technologies) as well as the representational contexts of contemporary crises such as climate change, consumption and capitalism. Her work on cinematic tourism is widely regarded in studies of popular and public culture. She is the author of numerous critical interventions, research articles, chapters and 15 monographs, including *Space, Mobility, and Crisis in Mega-Event Organisation: Tokyo 2020 Olympics' Atmospheric Irradiations*, published with Routledge (2022).

Currently she is Visiting Independent Scholar at Ce.Mo.Re., Lancaster (Department of Sociology) and member of the International Advisory Board of Global Studies (University of Urbana Champaign). She also serves on the editorial board of six journals, including *Cultural Sociology* and the Emerald book series *Tourism Security-Safety and Post Conflict Destinations*. In addition, she is Critical Reviews Editor for *Tourism, Culture & Communication*, one of the Chief Editors for *Hospitality & Society* and Website Coordinator for the Research Committee 50 (Tourism) of the International Sociological Association.

Acknowledgements

This book draws on, but theoretically and empirically updates, a series of sole-authored and co-authored articles, managed by me between 2013 and 2021. A big thanks goes to my co-authors, Majid Yar, Maximiliano Korstanje and Dimitris Koutoulas, who were not involved in the development of these materials to a uniform thesis but were contributors at the time of the articles' development. The original articles were published in the following formats and academic journals.

Tzanelli, R., & Yar, M. (2016). Breaking bad, making good: Notes on a televisual tourist industry. *Mobilities*, *11*(2), 188–206. https://doi.org/10.1080/17450101. 2014.929256

Tzanelli, R., & Korstanje, M. E. (2020). Critical thinking in tourism studies. *Tourism, Culture and Communication*, *20*(3), 59–69. https://doi.org/10.3727/ 109830420X15894802540133

Tzanelli, R., & Koutoulas, D. (2021). Zorba the Greek's tourism worldmaking: Gendering Cretan place identity and Greek memory through film. *Tourism Critiques: Practice and Theory*, *2*(2), 170–194. https://doi.org/10.1108/TRC-02-2021-0003

Tzanelli, R. (2021). Tourism worldmaking and market post-truth: Borat's new spirit of capitalism. *Tourist Studies*, *21*(4), 596–614. https://doi.org/10.1177/ 14687976211019909

Permission was granted by the journals' publishers (Routledge, Ingenta, Emerald & Sage, respectively) to reproduce the articles' content in part or in whole. Content Development Editor, Lydia Cutmore, and in-house image designer, Mike Hill, deserve a thanks for their support in bringing this project to completion. This monograph is recognised as one of the RC50 (International Tourism), International Sociological Association 2023–2027 key publications.

Introduction

Travels to Post-truth Worlds

The principles of perspectival judgement – what we associate with the proposition: 'truth is in the eye of the beholder' – permeate the transdisciplinary imagination. Some philosophical constituencies adhering to the rules of irrealist analysis may push this envelop under the methodological door of neoliberal pluralism, whereas other may attempt to tame reality proliferations by reducing events to facts allegedly 'hard to dispute'. Be as it may, scholars and scientists with respect for justice tend to undercut ultra-pluralist arguments by testing their rigour in practice. Enacting purposeful cognitive travels through various 'world versions', or scenarios of what is valid as real and/or just, they reach a conclusion that crowns one perspective as more accurate than the rest.

This book does not just interrogate what is real but proceeds to problematise what is just, where context cannot afford a singular perspective on justice. Specifically, it interrogates both in the hypermobile contexts of image-induced tourismification, which sets in motion mobility injustices (as per Sheller, 2018b). The 'gist' of this challenge is to evaluate the role of designing such locales at both aesthetic and ethical levels without reducing research to an exercise in moralist judgement. In this respect, the book cannot be categorised as a (critical) realist or traditional irrealist exercise, and its conclusions are bound to disturb those who operate on normative constants. I myself often found some of my conclusions hard to accept, as they provided no comfort concerning the rift between what is possible, what is transparently attainable and what is just and for whom. However, discomfort can facilitate a broader horizon of expectation for research on tourism and hospitality. To this end, I will not feign a scholarly or activist identity as the saviour of the disenfranchised. Discomfort arises from the complexities of what different groups can access and afford as identifiable capabilities so as to be socially recognised and therefore attuned to the demands of contemporary societies. Therefore, different affordances to social and cultural mobility must be treated as objective variables, rather than a preference embedded in the researcher's social and scholarly stance (Elliott & Urry, 2010, p. 10; Sheller, 2020, pp. 2–3). Normative fixities may also paralyse scholarly excellence. Hence my decision to prioritise an appraisal of the limits to justice in

The New Spirit of Hospitality, 1–17
Copyright © 2023 Rodanthi Tzanelli
Published under exclusive licence by Emerald Publishing Limited
doi:10.1108/978-1-83753-160-820231001

designing as a process involving too many voices and forms of action to avoid cacophonies and misunderstandings.

I commence my investigations with the hypothesis that we have entered a new era of tourism and hospitality mobilities. The era is characterised by problems pertaining to the *representation* and *presence* of animate entities, including human groups, in the public spheres of tourism. In political theory, the right to 'be present' refers to the right to autonomy, freedom in self-determination and equal treatment in spheres of social and cultural interaction (Castoriadis, [1975] 1987). However, in this book, it also means the right to follow different flourishing pathways – to achieve a becoming (as a citizen, a community, an agent) outside predetermined planning (Nussbaum, 2011; Sen, 2009; Sheller, 2012). 'Representation' also means more than the right to political advocacy in a world saturated by media forms and artforms as well as different styles of mediation. Above all, it means to be in control of the ways one appears to others, in public and private contexts. Of course, this is only possible when both communication styles and the infrastructural management of the platforms on which representations occur are managed by the represented – a ludicrous imaginary of possibility in our neoliberal worlds (Lehman-Wilzig, 2004; Ohlsson et al., 2017; van Dijck, 2009). Viewed from the perspective of an emergent heritage for places, the institution and management of mediatised tourism introduces questions of 'heritage valorisation, from the top down to the bottom up' in selective ways by its 'respective promotors and advocates' (Muzaini & Minca, 2018, p. 3). This is an ethical minefield, as the design aspects are bound to transform power relationships and identities (Agarwal & Shaw, 2017; Brandellero & Janssen, 2014; Schiavone et al., 2022).

Clearly then, the book does not develop a media and communications thesis. Above all, it interrogates the styles in which tourism and hospitality analysis approaches public spheres in contemporary image-based popular cultures. Tourism and hospitality are fields in which debates on presence and representation run wild because tourism and hospitality industries often become implicated in both debates in global capitalist networks (Fletcher, 2011). As Jamal (2019) has recently evidenced, all classical political philosophies of recognition and advocacy do not just find comfortable application in tourism and hospitality analysis but also the very field's complexities bear the potential to modify their core theoretical assumptions. My niche focus on 'film-induced' or 'cinematic' tourism also connects to a second proposition: ultimately triggered by the urge to renovate concept design, the double crisis of presence and representation is sustained by a proliferation of what is just, true and real, with various effects for the work of those interest groups involved in the production of truthfulness, justice and reality in hospitality and tourism. To explore this, I provide examples from three interest groups in film tourism design: common labour in hospitality industry; distinguished artists and tourism designers and the administrative agents of film heritage hotspots.

Not everything in this hypothesis is entirely new. For example, marketing the properties of hosting lands, cultures and their people as unique ('immutable') commodities has been a major theme in critical tourism analysis (Sheller, 2004). The original key studies range from those on 'staged authenticity' (MacCannell, 1973, 1989) to mainstream political economies of tourism development (Bianchi, 2018;

Britton, 1982), and systems theory applied to post-colonial contexts of tour-ismification (Cohen, 2001, 2002). Outside the field of tourism, I can point out Hut-nyk's (2004) caustic satire of contemporary academic scholarship's travel ethos, from which he does not exclude himself; this finds its highpoint in the ways he approaches both Hardt and Negri's (2004) and Derrida's (1981) treatment of the Third World and class politics, to which I return below. In agreement with these early theses, I highlight a basic contradiction: on the one hand, the 'new spirit of hospitality' pro-moted by the digitisation and cinematic advertising of tourism destinations releases identities, populations and environments from their geographical and political isolation, but on the other, it robs their communities of their ability to communicate cultural diversity on their own terms.

This paradox of immobility and paralysis in terms of rights within multiple cultural mobilities of image and destination advertising is by now well docu-mented in tourism and hospitality theory (Korstanje, 2018a; Peaslee, 2010; Tza-nelli, 2007a). Few scholars proceed to explore how the changes affect the professionals who produce aesthetic renditions of other home territories as tourist destinations. Often, an assumption that *they are* the industries for which they work brings the analysis to hasty conclusions. The trick is to disambiguate pro-fessional travel biography and intentionality from the structural expectations of labour, which lead to unwanted applications of the work of such designers in absentia (Desforges, 2000; Tzanelli, 2013a). Let us not speak of *individuals* on this, as a Popperian methodologist would, but about the post-industrial condi-tions of creativity – the forces of market discourse that do things to people and their environments when operationalised by particular institutions. Lapointe (2021) suggested that instead of reiterating in tourism abstracted approaches to stakeholders, we may consider bringing to the fore the significance of *territoire* as the intersection of physical place and social relations; it is such intersections that reveal how place and cultural representations are controlled and by whom. Likewise, Ek (2011) noted that urban tourism operates on design principles, which out-define and replace traditional politics with 'governmental practices that leave little room for public influence and participation' (2011, p. 169). Promoting human worlds and environments as auratic properties for the tourist gaze, the new abstracted ethos of hospitality can turn the playful, hopeful and oft revolu-tionary values of wellbeing upheld by tourism designers and local or international labour into profit-making tools with various consequences for planetary futures.

I repeat that it may be naïve to attribute the 'problem' exclusively or partially to those who design, without acknowledging that their labour is entangled in networks of power over which they may not have enough influence to change the way things work (Freudendal-Pedersen, 2020, pp. 24–25; Temenos & McCann, 2014, pp. 578–579). Therefore, I refute the idea that institutions (the state or local administration) or powerful individuals 'do' things outside discursive fields – instead, they become carriers of action pathways they may occasionally modify. My study's critical-analytical premises problematise a 'principles document' drafted between 2017 and 2018 by the coordinators of the Design Principles Network to deliberate on real issues affecting practitioners in the design sector at large. I use this manifesto only as a starting point to reflect upon and deconstruct processes of what I call 'worldmaking' in tourism after a number of arguments, including Keith Hollinshead's (2008, 2009a, 2009b). As a mediated production of tourism destinations, cinematic-tourist worldmaking carries the seeds of further ad hoc social change, for better or worse. Nicely relaying critical theory's warnings about the problems generated by media advertising, the 'Principles Document' states that:

> ...the people who are most adversely affected by design decisions—about visual culture, new technologies, the planning of our communities, or the structure of our political and economic systems—tend to have the least influence on those decisions and how they are made (The Design Justice Network Principles in Costanza-Chock, 2020, p. 6).

Even critical theorists, who for some public sociology groups do not do 'public engagement', develop a soft spot for advocacy, which could blind their judgement. At times advocacy can harbour crypto-fundamentalist arguments in a pedagogical vocation that should not always legitimise itself on the basis on action-as-agency. By this I refer to a tendency to silence unwanted scenarios: the ways good and self-serving goals may become implicated in the outcome of such advocacy in equal stead, modifying its nature; the way institutional power may remove actual agency from resurgent networks, recruiting from its disaffected members for different development projects; the fact that localities may never engage with the 'activist cause', because they are more interested in short-term gains from tourism development, which harm some. In favour of a neat case study, such deviations, which may reveal that victims are also victimisers, or central decision-making harms less the disenfranchised than activist intransigence, are airbrushed. In short, research in tourism and hospitality may benefit by closer inspecting the processes implicated in the *events* leading to the finished product and situations: design*ing*, instead of design (Jensen, 2013; Jensen & Morelli, 2011).

There is an isomorphism between the complexities involved in human harm, and the ecological/environmental neglect many overdeveloped tourist destinations suffer in late capitalist networks. Unlike my previous major publications on cinematic tourism design and natural environments (Tzanelli, 2018a), here I focus on the monetisation of human nature by tourist businesses that draw upon cultural industrial productions, mainly films. As much as the natural environment will take a back seat in my analysis, technology, especially digital technologies, will dominate my analysis of hospitality's 'new spiritedness'. The choice is based on the fact that epistemic approaches to cinematic tourism cannot avoid acknowledging the role of steering media in the development of destination design (Munar, 2016). There is one extra issue for which to account in scholarly movements for principled design, which further muddies the waters: it has been noted that the ways the ethno-religious systems of 'post-colonial *cosmoi*' feed into generic discourses of cultural difference, do little to acknowledge their radical untranslatability in Western thought (Chakrabarty, 2000, p. 75). The same observation can extend to the social practices that inform their everyday life. In some of the book's case studies, we will observe how this error is lifted out of hostile political approaches to 'pluriversality' or many-worldness (Escobar, 2018; Reiter, 2018). Where the co-existence of many worlds of wisdom and action in planetary politics is treated as a governmental nuisance, certain scholarly approaches to managing cultural diversity in cinematic tourism development may refuse to enact different reality scenarios in design (Clark & Szerszynski, 2021, pp. 150–154; Law, 2015, p. 130).

Admittedly, running multiple world-versions in speculative design is a major undertaking. A heuristic methodological tool/constant is necessary to facilitate the illumination of what is specific to place and its cosmos/oi, and what is feigned as such by post-industrial governance. Even this proposition can be problematised, if we consider that such installations often become integrated into organic narratives of place and culture, thus ultimately becoming versions of the native and the indigenous. The trick is to not assume seamless transitions from pluralism in cultural production to a symbolic-interactionist utopia of hosts, who enjoy the post-industrial change in which they are thrown. This is a rookie methodological error, based on the reduction of context into text: in real life, change that transforms infrastructural and political forms without consent and fast, can cause real harm. Therefore, this constant/tool has to be emplaced early on in the process of designing (that is, when this integration is yet to happen). At the same time, for a book claiming a planetary perspective, the partial cannot promise objective vision (Haraway cited in Clark & Szerszynski, 2021, p. 51). However, as much as contextualising may breed partiality in some studies, it can prevent an unwanted explosion of scales (Morton, 2018, p. 110) that leads to unworkable phenomena in the social and human sciences. There in no way we can comprehend the 'Hyperobjective' or temporally and spatially inoperable whole, beyond its topicalised manifestations (Morton, 2013, p. 15; Tzanelli, 2021a, pp. 9–10). The spatio-temporal specificity of my own research design justifies both my contention that we deal with phases of tourism worldmaking, and the need to deal with *évènements*, short-span events or phases of design as 'field blocks'. This is methodologically significant for two reasons: first, each of these 'phases' has its own politics and cultural logic; second, what is designed within each of them is predominantly *atmospheric* – a term I unpack below.

Through post-phenomenology, which in this book becomes a medium of networked atmospheres, I endeavour to expose the nature of contingency in tourism design: (a) through the *effects* of different actors and actants in designing (i.e., communities of 'technopoesis' or informed/expert making – Hand & Sandywell, 2002), but also (b) the affective consequences such assemblances have in hospitality contexts. Materialist phenomenology and post-phenomenology generate stories about those (f)actors who act on the social and natural worlds in blocks/phases. On the one hand, 'nature' features in my work as a key metaphor in the design of film-tourism destinations by localities, tourism organisations, the tourist state and tourism experts (i.e., 'the nature' of things and humans). On the other, its material dimensions are demoted to symbols that obscure its vital properties as a network of environments, ecosystems and natural habitats. To return to Ek's (2011) thesis on the formation of advertising 'post-poles', cities in which techniques of governance have replaced political life, at stake in cinematic-tourism design is not regional economic development, but the nourishing of planetary solidarity (see also Clark & Szerszynski, 2021, p. 81). By the same token, planetary solidarity can be maintained in critical scholarship only if scholars manage to shift analysis from systems of production to what Latour (2018, pp. 82–90) has termed 'systems of engendering' – nourishing not just humanity, but all terrestrial living forms/beings. Still, in some respects, this book is a diary of the Anthropocene, narrated (as usual) by those who 'innovate' (like *nova -us, coené* means novel): human actors (*ánthropoi*). To explain the signifi-cance of such decisions, I provide some key referents to the book's conceptual map.

The Techno-Anthropocene and Structural Technomorphism

In previous work (Tzanelli, 2015, 2017, 2018, 2021), I approached the Anthro-pocene through the lens of climate change and the progressive release of funda-mentalist assumptions about the alleged bio-social makeup of different human groups. The post-colonial condition featured prominently in such analyses, whereas the effects of technological innovation were mostly presented as auxiliary tools to capitalist organisation. In this book, I revise this thesis, in a call to decolonise the social-scientific imagination from assumptions regarding causality in the generation of new tourism markets. The new argument replaces the post-colonial with the technocratic, rather than technological sphere, while stressing the latter's centrality in the playfulness of cinematic tourism leisure. Hence, 'technocracy' as the prevalence of organisational forms features in the book's studies as both a mode of business in hospitality and tourism services and a style of consuming filmed landscapes in a sequential manner organised via new technologies (Dann, 1996).

This oxymoron, which is also implicated in the acceleration of technological instillations in tourism sites, suggests that climate change scholarship featuring the Anthropocenic paradigm lacks an essential component in its analyses, which may help science to mitigate the uncertainty of disasters: a focus on the modes of cognitive re-organisation that facilitate such installations in the form of theme parks (Sorkin, 1992). Consequently, I will discuss how the 'techno-Anthropocene' (Jensen, 2022) has been with us as a cinematic tourist vision for a while in more embryonic stages than those proffered by post-phenomenologists (e.g., Ihde, 1990, 2022; Verbeek, 2005). In the same vein, I will explore the 'structural tech-nomorphism' such visions of leisure impose: the morphing of populations, land-scapes and environments via new and old technologies at both material-semiotic (i.e., the cultural image of tourist destinations) and bio-cultural ends (i.e., the classification of different identities). Taking place in the minds, bodies and hearts of hosts and guests, this technomorphism remains entangled with technological processes of image-making, spatial-cultural modification and eventually also biopolitical refashioning or a novel management of the ethnocultural blueprint of localities and their labour mobilities by the nation-state and international markets (see also de Sousa Santos, 1995, 2007; Scribano, 2021). The literature on connections between tourism and films or TV series is vast and not at the centre of this book's investigation. Also, where so-called 'film-induced tourism' may be a process of marketing, destination imaging and motivation to visit filmed locations (Beeton, 2015, pp. 21–22), what I have termed 'cinematic tourism' (Tzanelli, 2007a, 2013a) focusses on a critique of the entrepreneurial governance of new urbanism, which hosts laboratories of tourist fascination (Bauriedl & Strüver, 2011, p. 170). Indeed, over the last two decades, film tourism or film-induced tourism has developed into a subject area, in which a variety of issues are explored, including fandom and pilgrimage (Geraghty, 2019, pp. 208–211; Reijnders, 2011, pp. 113–114), destination management planning (Lindström, 2019), labour conflict (Tzanelli, 2013a, pp. 53–62) and strategic destination development (Wray & Croy, 2015). The question of sustainability seems to cut across all these themes, as there have been scholarly voices questioning the longevity of interest in such niche tourism (Beeton, 2016; Kim et al., 2017; Macionis, 2004), but also the factors determining it (Thelen et al., 2020). There has been less interest in the sociocultural modus vivendi rather than economic consequences and impacts of such development for the filmed destinations that must host diverse tourism mobilities (see critiques in Buda, 2015; Mostafanezhad & Promburom, 2018; Tzanelli, 2018a).

The scarcity of rigorous research into such issues seems to reflect the disciplinary orientation of film-with-tourism analysis, which prioritises the development of business – regardless of whether this focusses on community growth or fandom – over social-scientific critical analysis, which may even question the promotion of such tourism mobilities per se. A limited number of scholars with significant contributions in the field talk about the need for 'social exchange theory' (Thelen et al., 2020, p. 292) – a term, which can involve disparate and potentially conflicting sociological and anthropological methods and perspectives, all of which were never used in relevant studies. And, whereas such research is not uncritical or lacking in analytical depth, it deploys critique as a means to a particular end: to develop a sustainable business agenda with limited (but arguably, suitable for the agenda) epistemological tools.

The difference rests in my shift from either marketing strategies or community development as such to the varied effects the cinematic tourist project's utopian core may have on populations and the environment. Significantly, the programmatic statement of the 1990s 'New Urbanism' was materialised in 'Celebration', a green community prototype built in Florida at the edges of the Disney estates. The vision of this design dated back to the beginning of the 1950s, when Walt Disney himself spoke of a collectivist blueprint, involving housing his corporation's workers, and thus endorsing a new orderly and clean community lifestyle framed by organisational structures (AlSayyad, 2006, p. 212).

Not only is Disney's vision the opposite of heritage as a natural process of producing communal rules, rites and futures but also a strategy of sabotaging collective action as both the outcome of *Gesellschaft* (for lovers of classical sociology see Tönnies, 2001) and multitudinal agency/actancy (for lovers of contemporary theory see Deleuze, 2002; Hardt & Negri, 2004). Action and agency/actancy are replaced with the organisation of a systemic blueprint, which in the wrong mouths and minds can mutate into an ultra conservative discourse on fundamentalist communitarianism (Scribano et al., 2019). Evidently, then, I view the Techno-Anthropocene as an era in which processes of making community are filtered through organisational design – or rather, *designing*. However, organisation itself can also include quotidian action – different layers of practical assemblages of discourses and cultural sensibilities, that produce tourism worlds (Muzaini & Minca, 2018, pp. 1–2; see also Sandywell, 1996, pp. 410–412).

Worldmaking and Atmospheres

Designing is a key factor in the production of this book's epistemo-ontological hypothesis as a mitigator of unpredictable actions. In fact, the notion of world-making facilitates an important methodological link. Because I inflect manifestations of reality through different tourism and hospitality actors, I compose worldmaking's intrinsic scholarly meaning from different but compatible arguments in different disciplines and subject areas. This compatibility is not only scalar (from micro to macro agents, structures and situations in global contexts of cultural and economic mobility) but also epistemologically complementary (from variations of realism to situated constructivism – Barkin, 2020; Bartucci et al., 2018).

Epistemologically it is possible to argue that one can arrive at a conclusion as to how things are in contexts of tourism design (realism) through an analysis of different and even conflicting constructions of it (Tzanelli, 2020a). Thus, Nelson Goodman's (1978) approach to worldmaking as the nomothetic activity of a community of artists, who produce their own version of what is aesthetically real and plausible is compatible with Hollinshead's (2008, 2010) and Hollinshead and Suleman's (2018) gradualist/pluralist approaches to worldmaking. Where Hollinshead (2009a) spoke of a group of 'false' imaginative activities 'to purposely (or otherwise unconsciously) privilege particular dominant/favoured representations of peoples/places/pasts within a given region, area, or "world", over and above other actual or potential representations of those subjects' (2008, p. 643), Goodman (1978) had suggested that each 'world' is valid in its own right as a concerted-collective human activity. These cultural manifestations of worldmaking also have political extensions, which are distributed across different populations and social groups: for example, Swain's (2009) argument on world-making intelligence suggests the act of making new realities as a variation of critical cosmopolitanism (Delanty, 2009). This proposition is compatible with Hollinshead and Suleman's (2018) argument that the enunciative potential of worldmaking can benefit living worlds.

Scholarly uses of the concept also embrace urban studies as a variation of globalisation studies in an 'ongoing art of being global' (Ong, 2011) outside policy domains (Baker & Ruming, 2014). The concept's uses in political theory as an informal variation of what others call 'worlding' (Roy & Ong, 2011), or the process of becoming part of the grand projects of modernity through small acts of participation in the commons of the city (Arendt, 1958), inflects Hollinshead's (2009b) split between the state's authority/authorship in tourism and the tourism designers' and tourismified populations enunciations of identity (forms of 'tourism agency'). Hutnyk (2022) approaches such 'worldings' from the perspective of a comparative urbanist methodology, which bears the potential to accommodate different voices in inherently heteroglossic urban environments/ fields.

The term has ample potential to incorporate traditional decolonial approaches on resistance to dominant forms of belonging and thought as a mode of inter-rogation of their authoritarian validity – what Peirce (1896, pp. 415–519) dubs 'an attempt to develop categories from within'. Chapter 2 partly attempts such an analysis from the perspective of hospitality, which problematises du Bois' ([1899] 1903) thesis on double consciousness. However, the book's thesis addresses themes broader than those adhering to concerns about race or traditional decolonial studies scholarship. Its Techno-Anthropocenic focus interrogates the ways old and new technologies both rediscover old and build new semiotic constellations/representations of place and culture (Goodman, 1978, pp. 8–15). Renditions of worldmaking in media theory adopt a particular constructivist approach, whereby symbols and forms shape how individuals and communities shape reality, and not the other way around (Nünning & Nünning, 2010, p. 9).

To summarise then, the study views 'worldmaking' as a *multi-scalar process of designing* places, lifeworlds and cultures that is unevenly distributed across different agents and actants in the fields of tourism and hospitality. Below I expand on how the very diversity of such constructions organises publicness and privateness in politics, society and culture around the world. But before that it is important to dedicate a few words to phenomena that develop between public and private contexts: the worlds that manifest in the activities of communities and institutions and which are intentionally or unintentionally enshrouded in atmo-spheric discourses. Before they develop their discursive form in tourism design, these fragments of communication lack cross-cultural recognition; ironically, when they achieve this, they are perceived of as 'faux' renditions of place (Hol-linshead, 2009b). The passage from experimental 'being' (an existential approach to reality) to constructivist belonging (to international markets) allegedly 'kills' their authentic patina (on existentialist and constructivist approaches to authen-ticity see Moore et al., 2021; Wang, 2001).

This introduces the study of atmospheres. As intersubjective happenings, atmospheres actualise in encounters between humans and the material natural worlds 'out there' (Nünning & Nünning, 2010, p. 11) – in this respect, they are the effects (or after-effects) of symbol interpretation. A cross-disciplinary excursus reveals two major approaches to atmospheres, one borrowing from phenome-nology and aesthetics (Böhme, 2016; Griffero, 2014; Schmitz, 2016), and the other from ecology and praxeology (Kazig et al., 2017; Thibaud, 2014). Although in cinematic tourism symbols adhere to the cultural politics of visual perception, my analysis of atmospheres extends to the invisible world of affect to interrogate responses to rapid tourismification and uneven distribution rights to design destinations (Anderson & Ash, 2015). The latter often connects affects to real action on cultural forms and spaces, including the makeup of communities and landscapes (Anderson, 2015). As such it generates links between micro-social/ cultural and macro-social/cultural events – note that one of the first uses of the term is attributed to Marx's address to crowds during a meeting to mark the fourth anniversary of the Chartist *People's Paper*. In this address, he begins to articulate what becomes a central theme in this book: an attempt to grasp the connection between material places, and the spaces of affect as a form of labour (Marx cited in Anderson, 2009, p. 77). All three case-study chapters take a close look at the affective extensions of tourism worldmaking on cultural landscapes to not just explain how late capitalism alters heritage narratives but also uncover the vicissitudes of affective labour involved in this process. At this stage, it is more important to deliberate on the post-phenomenological nucleus of atmospheric designing: the very 'spirit' on which contemporary hospitality is organised in cinematic tourist sites and sights.

The New Spirit of Hospitality

The idea of spiritedness is often connected to the Christian heritage, and more generally to forms of religious world heritage. The Hegelian critique of Kant, which informed philosophical approaches to tourism (Fennell, 2009), can be seen as a milestone in analysing what is spirited in this book's case studies and why. For Hegel, humanity commits the ultimate crime 'within the orbit of life' (Hegel, 1977, p. 230) when crime is approached as a perspective 'in the now' of life, not the noumenal sphere. The crime to which Hegel refers is the denial of freedom to others: what breaks 'unified life' (Hegel, 1977, p. 229) and thus communal vitality. In Hegel's thesis, we find the beginnings of the functionalisation of fate, which proved to be the most useful tool in the justification of capitalist expansion. Renditions of this crime in socio-philosophical arguments are intrinsically connected to well-established disciplinary discourses. Accordingly, Weber (1985) used of the term 'spirit' to relay the rationalisation of belief in the modern commercial cultures of the West rooted in Protestantism, whereas Campbell ([2005] 2018) argued that by masking spending habits as individual freedom, the romantic tradition provided consumerism with an ideological rationale. Rationalisation is an aspect of this newness, which ties intelligent design to the progressive ethos of modernity (Fuller, 2018). The newness is also recorded in the post-modern turn separately from religious or generally metaphysical thinking as a gateway into multiple ways of knowing (Bingel, 2010). However, due to their 'generative function' (Ricoeur, 1995, p. 37), the genres of religious heritage fed into the ways capitalism ordered its creative ethos and reproductive rationale. Even in late capitalist domains of creativity, we will find stylistic traces of religious formulas (Barber, 2003; Ritzer, 2010, 2019).

Both creativity as originality and commercial reproduction are value-ridden processes in scholarly critiques of contemporary tourism markets (Cronin, 2004, 2018). Because the new spirit of hospitality markets things, ideas and even values, its (re)presentational qualities do not prioritise truthfulness, justice or equality: tourism and hospitality have to sell, so a degree of construction is always involved in the system of tourism and hospitality mobilities (Iwashita, 2003). However, the novelty of new hospitality's spiritedness also refers to the immateriality of exploitation in the sector's labour systems (Lazzarato, 2004, 2011, 2013), as well as its co-option of different 'natures' (of human culture and behaviour and natural habitats alike) in a game of commercialised abstraction (Tzanelli, 2013b, 2022b). To invoke a revised Hegelian conclusion, an intelligent design of tourist desti-nations is the first ground-constituting act of the power of choice that destroys unified life: the moral nature of communal law. This nature, stands for a unified spirit, often preserved not just by localities but also the nation-state itself (Smith, 1999) as 'a myth-symbol complex that stretches into state institutions to help give semi-official status to particular aspects of culture … at the expense of other visions' (Hollinshead, 2009a, p. 530). I must add that 'intelligent' can at times be interpreted as 'smart' (digital) design, and caution readers that I do not accept the Hegelian parable as the best practice or an absolute ideal. Finally, I must add that a state-focussed model of myth-making is in need of updating to take on board the networked nature of contemporary capitalism.

It must be stressed that the rational goals of the new spirit of hospitality feed on the hauntological aspects of heritage. By this I mean that even previously unknown filmed places will enter heritage design as ideal types to address the goal-orientated 'needs' of tourist markets and the nation that 'sells'. To speak of 'interpellation' grasps only some aspects of the process, but in what follows, I do use a revised Althusserian thesis. I seek ways to tease out of Derrida's spectrology (Derrida, 1994, p. 146; Derrida & Dufourmantelle, 2000) the ways that difference (including embodied presence) is subjected to the production of a faux spiritedness that is then used to promise brighter futures (Derrida, 1994, p. 30). To specify: while branding filmed landscapes, environments and human populations as spectacular heritage, such spiritedness may remove the actual specificity of their roots and routes (indeed, this may also involve turning their diverse roots and routes into a single tarmacked highway for globetrotters to walk effortlessly). The presence of such spectres in Techno-Anthropocenic networks seals the absence of voice of certain groups – a theme also noted by others in contexts of class struggle (Hutnyk, 2004, p. 103) and the new digital networks of hospitality-catering (Germann Molz, 2018, pp. 230–232). The consequences of this vanished pres-ence are felt in the politics of cultural representation at large: at stake is first and foremost how truths and realities are shaped in my studied cinematic tourist fields.

Post-truth in Cinematic Tourism Mobilities

The term 'post-truth' is connected both to the public cultures of twenty-first century political journalism and some scholarly debates on relativism and post-modernity. More recently, this scholarly use in political theory expanded to incorporate the development of new cultural practices in communication tech-nologies by different categories of digital platform users (Salgado, 2018). From an existentialist perspective, entanglements of truth-making with value concern both the consolidation of what is real in the 'will to power' and the human gift of fabulist creativity in the form of design (Nietzsche, ([1873] 2020). The latter refers to the human gift and ability to create truthful versions of the world through metaphor and myth. Weber (1958) usefully distinguished between facts and values in the social scientist's search for truthful contexts, whereas in a similar vein, Hannah Arendt (1972) spoke of de-factualisation as one's inability to distinguish fact from fiction in contradistinction to deliberate falsehood in politics. Although we can trace fragments of Hollinshead's (2009a) 'mythomoteur' in all these arguments, he cites Michel Foucault, Michel Pêcheux, Homi Bhabha and Nelson Goodman as his primary sources of inspiration. Unlike Arendt's Weberian-Marxist approach to truth fabrication as a manifestation of hyper-rationalisation, he considers tourism worldmaking as the effect of discursive enunciations by the state and its tourism designers, as well as acts of counter- or dis-identification with them by the tourismified populations. The Foucaultian influence is crucial also in John Urry's (1990, 2002; Urry & Larsen, 2011) ground-breaking 'tourist gaze' thesis, according to which the professionalisation of tourism produces truths in the form of ocular/cognitive discourses about tourist destinations, cultures and their people.

In this book I attempt to harmonise paradigmatic conflicts across different arguments in the rich interdisciplinary tradition of 'post-truth'. For example, I borrow from Luc Boltanski and Laurent Thévenot's (2005) approach to justification because it partly furthers my post-phenomenological/experiential argument on the ways truth emerges in atmospheric discourse. I repeatedly stressed my preference for a process-driven approach to particular cases of cinematic tourismification, which can accommodate the study of ontologies from an epistemological point of view (see also Susen, 2016). In fact, Goodman (1978, p. 6) leads this process-driven debate when he concludes that even when the design of new worlds (of tourism, in this book) promotes the erasure of their substance (i.e., they turn into functional objects for advertising), the scholar needs to ask how they were made and unmade. Additionally, I ask: how can we test these worlds' making? How can they be known? My answer shifts emphasis on the networked nature of truth-making in contemporary societies (DeLanda, 2006; Latour, 1987, 2005) and thus a process-driven approach to what emerges as reality and truth.

I find no use in propositions that scholars can 'recover' an alleged 'First World' of reality or truth – on this I agree with Goodman's (1978, p. 7) suggestion that this is the work of theologians. In the following chapter, I also clarify that, as an investigation into the problematic aspects of 'publicness' and 'privateness' in contemporary life, my research seeks ways to transcend the epistemological rupture plaguing 'public sociology' manifestos. The latter do not resolve ideological polarisations between 'scholastic' and 'common-sense' conceptions of the world, even though both modes of knowing and doing struggle to escape the neo-managerialist ethos of institutional sociology (Sussen, 2016, p. 199). As I explain in Chapter 1, the split between an allegedly elitist and an allegedly democratic approach to knowledge and its design for others also applies to the workings of institutional managerialism in this book's cases of cinematic tour-ismification. The shift from a concerted post-industrial varnishing of reality to its vanishing as a coherent category of being connects to cinematic tourism's func-tionalist ethos, but the results and the very process of de-spiritedness merit careful examination. Needless to add that what scholarship may approach as function-alism, the tourist may view as or turn into a creative pursuit. My proposition is highly eclectic and synthetic in critical ways: like Hollinshead's, it borrows from subaltern studies (feminist and post-colonial methodologies – Mignolo, 2009; Rose, 1993; Thambinathan & Kinsella, 2021), without making their subject matter its central theme; philosophies of science and technology (Barad, 2007, 2010), without turning either into the core problematic in its analysis and visual, urban and film studies (Degen & Rose, 2022; Rose, 2012), without replicating their methodological priorities. Also, like several other scholars' observations on the production of truth in mobility regimes (Jensen, 2016, 2019; Urry, 2000), its institutional and discursive repertoires interrogate the nature of agency within systems (Hutnyk, 2000, 2004).

At this point, I must return to the main question posited/generated by my epistemological tenets: Do I really have access to the events leading to the pro-duction of the 'tourist stage', or just to the discourses that contributed to it? And are these discourses/events coherent happenings outside my cross-disciplinary pursuits and the socio-political context in which I was educated? Such ques-tions add a new layer of 'worldmaking', both as a process of events unfolding 'out there' and one constructed in synergy with me as a 'knowing subject' (Tzanelli, 2020b, p. 16). The tourist and media experts and their expertise are mediated by me, a scholar in search of what really 'went on back then'. From the perspective of the scholar, as this book's events unfold, versions of what is real or true become eliminated as non-viable versions of how the world and society really are. What commences as an 'irrealist' exercise (that is, a proposition that not only many versions of reality are available to us relative to the positionality of those who uphold them but also that all of them should be recognised as valid in their own right – Goodman, [1968] 1999) may produce a para-realist conclusion (Rose, 1999). In this conclusion, many propositions are invalidated not in relation to who upholds them, but what type of situations they create: unliveable, unjust and exclusionary. However, at this stage, research begins to flirt with ethics that may ignore the aesthetics of pleasure in contexts that are designed for rest and well-being. This issue is addressed mainly in Chapter 4.

The Cinematic Exopolis

To recapitulate, the new spirit of hospitality has turned post-human mobilities, involving technologies, landscapes, nature and humans into images for general public dissemination and consumption. The digital and cinematic channels of such representations proliferate truths about the tourist destination, its labour and even heritage value. This circulation of post-truths is designed alongside the tourist destination itself, implicating professionals, and unskilled labour in the workings of neoliberal designing. It is important to clarify where these processes really take place and whether they have any ontological consequences at the level of conceptual categorisation.

Degen and Rose (2022) explain how the new urban aesthetic is based on the generation of atmospheric portfolios that sustain cultures of fascination. Developing the view on contemporary cities as laboratories of spectacularised complexity that incorporates aesthetics, emotions, lived experience, power structures and governance, Cronin (2010, pp. 1–7) and Schmid et al. (2011, p. 7), bring into focus a tension between invisible and visible worlds of art, labour and consumption. Although the worlds of tourism design I will present in specific chapters mostly aspire to modify filmed places to visit outside the big urban centres, designing is infrastructurally based on metropolitan centres. This trend is concomitant with the development of world cities to both golden standards of aesthetic excellence and financial centres, in which technological and representational flows are managed (Markin, 2012; Sassen, 2001, 2013).

Although the spiritedness of this designing portfolio is 'discovered', or invented by urban centres, it is instilled in the filmed geographical outposts, which develop into exurban extensions of the cinematic tourist machine. Thus, truth regimes in tourism development are tied to urban/metropolitan centres, which attract revolutionary designers (Boltanski & Chiapello, 2018). A what we may call 'geodesic process' commences (MacKenzie, 2017), whereby the designing urban centre's production labs are connected via new technologies to the less developed places, which designers are asked to prepare for the tourist gaze. This earth (*geo*)-folding-and-binding (*dénō*) process eventually transforms the spectacularised outposts into an extension of the neoliberal ethic of mobility (Alderson & Beckfield, 2004). This is what I call an *exopolis* or exotic cultural topos, materialised as a filmed place, loved, and visited by strangers, but often excluded from the decision-making strongholds of the infrastructural centre (on this see also Hutnyk, 2000, pp. 218–220).

Davis (1990) used Los Angeles's 'studio system' representations as a stylistic metaphor of the city's counterfeit urbanist realities of exclusion amidst illicit alliances with other urban centres and the accumulation of ideological capital (Davis, 1990, p. 21). Based on the antithetical imperative of sunshine spirituality and bright intellectualism on the one hand, and the dystopianism of anti-myth *noir* on the other, the metaphor reappears in accounts of other major urban nodes that function as laboratories of fascination. Hutnyk (1996) couples Davis' metaphor with observations on the 'new educational and editorial apparatuses' mobilised to map new locations (Derrida in Hutnyk, 1996, pp. 30–31). Such apparatuses effectively replace social bonding with organisational modes of content editing (Hutnyk, 1996, p. 197), to facilitate the consolidation of mental geographies of prejudice. Where Davis views the migrant and working-class areas of Los Angeles as 'junkyards of dreams', I concentrate on what happens when the 'geological and social detritus' of *exopolitan* cinematic-tourist regions gives way to 'designer living' (Davis, 1990, p. 375). At the same time, unlike Davis and Hutnyk, I prioritise the effects that the blended re-designing of virtual and natural environments on real exopolitan sites (see also Soja, 2000 on the virtual makeup of cities).

Such blended styles of design do not favour direct depictions of the shocking reality of social violence, on the contrary, they airbrush them. To turn their visual and digital properties into methodologically useful events, I stress how the design itself displaces social and environmental 'ugliness' to the invisible domains of affect – a magical realist technique of filmmaking adaptation (Bowers, 2004, pp. 110–115). Indeed, if processes of urban 'cinematisation' favour cognitive automatism that is conducive to consumer capitalism (Roberts, 2012a), the 'auto-navigation' facilitated by digital locative media separates the realities of the map from the practice of mapping altogether (Roberts & Cohen, 2015). As a result, exopolitan design legitimises the development of novel carceral contiguities: it enables the tourismified filmed domains to function as zones of exception in which privileged forms of consumer citizenship thrive (Sheller, 2020, p. 36). We cannot treat these exopolitan formations exclusively as zones of entertainment. Much like the ontological properties of the Archipelagos (Vannini et al., 2009), they are fabrications of macro-scalar events, and thus subjects of study in a cultural-political economy of hospitality (Sheller, 2018a).

Events and Mobilities Design

The very construction of *exopoles* is an experiment that sets in motion a series of events that may relocate spiritedness outside regimes of consumption (in reactions to them), or within tourist *communitas* (among cinematic tourist fans, who create alternative ways of experiencing destinations – Ziakas et al., 2022). Nevertheless, such spiritedness is not a Hegelian figment or a straightforward Bourdieusian trade of symbolic capital for networks (as per Boltanski & Chiapello, 2018; Larsen & Urry, 2008). The experiment's atmospheric artifice (i.e., the re-designing of locales after sequels of cinematic imaginaries – Reijnders, 2011) is primarily based on the dissolution of what some may consider as a form of 'primordial reality' into a series of 'events' (Žižek, 2004, p. 664). Upon its commencement, all social groups affected by this process respond to the experiment's force to change life in emotional styles, which by turn produce new spirited events. Otherwise put, the impetus for the design of cinematic tourism mobilities is its capacity to sustain endless emergence (e.g., Deleuze, 1990; Stengers, 2000). As much as the material dimensions of new cinematic tourism destinations may be more fixed, their capacity to produce new worlds of tourism and thus also new forms of hospitality/ hospitableness lead to performative proliferations of identity and action for an undetermined period of time (Sewell, 2008, p. 526).

To unpack these entanglements of material creativity and tourism staging with affective action, we need a good understanding of classical and contemporary event theory. Pyyhtinen (2007, pp. 111–112) is right to trace event dynamics in a shift from Simmel's emphasis on the dissolution of substance into function, to the de-substantialised processes of systems, such as that of capitalism. However, the systemic paradigm does little to explain the elasticity with which humans as bodies and emotions respond to systemic impositions (i.e., changes in their life-worlds – on this compare Habermas (1989) with Jensen (2021)). Setting the Hegelian paradigm aside once again, then, I introduce in critical tourism theory reflections from the new mobilities paradigm on the eventisation of social and cultural life (Hannam et al., 2016; Sheller, 2018b).

Events analysis originally used a macro-sociological synthesis of Charles Tilly's (2003) research on systemic violence and Theda Skocpol's on 'experimental temporality' (Skocpol, 1979, p. 36). Both thinkers emphasised the importance of comparative research to understand the ways in which an essential component in local/global social change emerges: a self-conscious, autonomised and organised revolutionary group. Given the clear influence from symbolic interactionism, post-phenomenology and systems theory, today the new mobilities paradigm's proponents move in the opposite direction: towards the event. It is not coincidental that events theory thrives in mobilities publications, as socio-geographical approaches to events inform their epistemic basis. The studies involve the ways in which the now is lived by the researcher while they attempt to resolve its place in what may come (Revil, 2014, p. 517; Schindler, 2020, pp. 102–103).

However, Tilly's and Skocpol's theses are still important – if anything, they are echoed in Hardt and Negri's (2004) suggestion that a 'multitude' residing different sites in a globalised ecumene rises to give voice to collective disaffection with the exploitative workings of the 'Empire' of capitalism. Unlike Hardt & Negri's thesis, they do not acknowledge that in contemporary contexts, change necessitates virtuality to bring such groups together (DeLanda, 2002; Deleuze & Guattari, 1987). Also, unlike the *Annales* School thesis on the systemic significance of the *évènement*, their work does not embed events into a multi-causal analysis of planetary change enough (Sewell, 1990). Of course, as much as this facilitates a temporal mapping of events, the events' material core is produced by a system that has enmeshed other social systems and now affects natural ones: capitalism. World capitalism supports the disorganised, complexly networked, post-national nature of economic, cultural and political flows of our planet (Lash & Urry, 1987, 1994). The end beckons not just the workings of capitalist (infra) structuration but crucially the ways the paradigm's epistemic community analyses crises. Otherwise put, the 'Empire' has featured in mobilities research on revolutionary formations across the social and cultural spectrum – from common labour and migration movements to resurgent discourses propagated by the distinguished creative classes (Buscema, 2011; Tzanelli, 2016). But it has not informed the ways the new mobilities paradigm acts as a multitude (Tzanelli, 2022b) – and the same goes for critical tourism analysis (Tzanelli, 2022a). Mobilities and critical tourism studies scholars need to devise ways to construct a genealogy of abstraction (of crises) that networks all the way down to their own multitudinal action, and the individuals that sustain it (Hutnyk, 2004, pp. 136–138), without falling into traps set by Popperian methodological individualism (Geertz, 2000, pp. 16–17, 164–165). This epistemic model is eminently transferable to the subjects of their study (see for example Michael, 2022, pp. 4, 6, 11–12).

Thus, 'events' in this book carry a heavier analytical weight than that called for in an examination of the design of cinematic tourism. As part of an epistemic apparatus facilitating the study of contemporary mobilities, they allow critical tourism and mobilities scholars alike to record the impacts of capitalism in the spatio-temporal organisation of culture and social interaction. Following from this, I consider the cinematic *exopolis* as a non-place of consumption (Augé, 2008), which facilitates a heterochronia: it activates other-temporalities or multiple temporalities in which myth and reality blend and space is taken over by fabricated versions of time (Harvey, 1982, 1989). The *heterochronias* of capitalism are not equivalent to the *tiempos mixtos* of post-colonial analysis, which narrated the meeting of native and settler times in coherent ways (Nederveen Pieterse, 2019). Much like the unsettling rhythm of feedback loops in climate change (Urry, 2011a, p. 164), the *heterochronias* of capitalism meddle events and local experiences in unpredictable ways to produce marketable cinematic tourist locations. For this reason, only, I cannot analyse post-truth without post-phenomenology: crafted from events that facilitate better fabrication of actual occurrences, the making of post-truths tends to resemble the making of cinematic tourism landscapes in capitalist temporalities.

The oscillation between the events and the small temporalities that define this study's cases of cinematic tourismification and the scholar's virtual engagement with them is not a methodological error. As a speculative study of 'the now' of crises of representation and presence, such oscillations question the ways *public sociologies of the event* are produced. This type of sociology is refracted in my work from transdisciplinary perspectives to suit the needs of tourism and hospitality, two subject areas drawing on such blended knowledge (Korstanje et al., 2016). Several attempts to transduce and thus suspend unhelpful disciplinary boundaries featured behind the attachment of prefixes such as 'post', 'trans', 'a', 'inter' and 'non', conveying the centrifugal tendencies of tourism and hospitality studies as journeys (Graff, 2015; Korstanje et al., 2016; Munar et al., 2016; Tzanelli, 2022a, 2022b). I am convinced that my centrifugal method will not prevent me from drawing on sociological resources along the way as still valuable conceptual tools.

With this in mind, Chapter 1 forms an attempt to resolve where the 'post' of my epistemic tools fits in the ways publicness is discursively formed in different academic fora. The 'trans' is already embedded not specifically in tourism analysis, but the potential of travel metaphors to tell transdisciplinary stories about tomorrow (Brown, 1977, pp. 90–91; Czeglédy, 2003, p. 17; Geertz, 1973). This is in itself a rendition of worldmaking that attempts to inflect the panoramas of now-ness and then-ness through small, situated points of view (epistemological, methodological and 'graphic', including ethnographic and netnographic). In many respects, the first chapter discusses the role of virtuality in public cultures of hospitality and tourism, by examining how their scholars' geodesic approach to modes of judgement and analysis is a reaction to crises *évènements*.

Chapter 1

Representation, Presence and Public Culture

Crisis and Publicness in Perspective

The book's subtitle prompts readers to consider what the chains of (de-)spirited production and consumption in cinematic tourism do to planetary futures in an age of uncertainty, natural and human-made disasters and risks. I make two suggestions regarding the study of the spirit of hospitality in respect to tourism mobilities: the first stresses that it draws its power from networking in digital channels and through image proliferation. The proliferation itself assists in the concealment of the origins of the images, which, more often than not, cannot provide evidence regarding the material conditions of their birth (Baudrillard, 1973; Lash & Urry, 1994). To explore the complexity of this transformation, we must develop digital and audio-visual epistemological and methodological capacity in the field of tourism studies and beyond in disciplines such as sociology, geography, anthropology and even philosophy. The second suggestion argues for a more refined analysis of human action and agency, as well as its polemical limitations in a world networked formally by powerful capitalist networks on the one hand, and informally through communal norms and values on the other (Escobar, 2004; Hassard & Law, 1999; Latour, 2005; Law & Mol, 2002). Any apparatus, including the tourism and hospitality apparatuses, must first produce the subjects that they govern (Agamben, 2009, p. 11) – the tourist and the host. The two systems of belonging and networking feed into the spirit of hospitality in various ways, producing resistance or constraints to individual freedom, wellbeing and safety.

The mobile apparatus of this new hospitable spirit is essentially centrist: capitalocentrist, Eurocentrist, Western-centrist and Anthropocentrist. Its implication in the circulation of money-values is also often reflected in an epistemological certainty on which critical scholars hold fast in dominant theories of inequality and immobility. Even the most outstanding theses in the discipline of sociology and political-cultural economy consider capital as a universal source of power, thus coupling the universal geopolitical dominance of economic flows with the normative basis of dominant geo-cultural codes and cosmologies. As a result, designing methodologies of emancipation never escapes the travelling pod of what sociologists discuss as 'modernity' (Latour, 2018). Unfortunately, many such

The New Spirit of Hospitality, 19–35
Copyright © 2023 Rodanthi Tzanelli
Published under exclusive licence by Emerald Publishing Limited
doi:10.1108/978-1-83753-160-820231002

materialist critiques of development do not consider how the immaterial worlds of emotions and creativity continue to exist in some cultural systems next to the Western Frankenstein of 'immaterial labour' (Seigworth & Greggs, 2010).

Boltanski and Thévenot's (2006) methodological sojourns already warn us that the ensnaring of the crisis of presence in regimes of representation is *experienced* by the common people who possess common sense. Contrariwise, common sense is *applied* by the scholars, who study them. I do not refute here that this division of labour is essential for ethnographic and theoretical research. My concern is that in some sociological studies of publicness, it may inflict a form of tokenisation upon the studied groups. The tokenisation mediates certain agendas concerning what social research is supposed to do, so certain styles of research that their authors do not wish to dub activist, or regenerative in utilitarian ways are demonised as not helpful to those in need. We must disambiguate notions of 'public culture' in the study of tourism and hospitality from what Buraway (2005, 2008) sees in vocational and yet activist 'public' sociology. This proposition connects to my concluding reflections in the Introduction on the transferable nature of multitudinal action from modes of activism to modes of scholarship – a simile introduced in Thomas Kuhn's (1970) analysis of the structure and thus nature of scientific revolutions. We can find better ways to acknowledge that the critique of critiques forges an active – or what Sheller (2014) calls 'live' – sociology that does not need to 'prove' its rigour in the political field beyond its power to produce reflective analysis. The latter is far from being an a-political action because it always partakes in debates that modify collective imaginaries of what is to come, protects the core of hopeful experimentation and gives people a reason to act in sensible ways. I would also suggest that these two propositions are followed by the promotion of a fresh portfolio of a reflexive intra-action in a network of human-non-human voices (Barad, 2007, 2010).

It is my contention that a live sociology does not mute forms of past (re)action to crisis but learns instead to archive them in ways that nourish planetary futures – an activity that is repeated when and as necessary to avoid trapping it into the system of discourse/power/knowledge. To engender all terrestrial life, a live sociology needs to create its own 'Critical Zone': a field in which we can consider how all or at least the most dominant positionalities in crises struggle 'for legitimacy and autonomy against countless other concerned parties that have contradictory interests, and all of which possess other bodies of knowledge' (Latour, 2018, p. 80). Historically, the very idea of the 'public' and the 'private' stand at the centre of the crisis of presence. From the outset, their differentiation was anchored on political, cultural and social processes guiding the programme of modernity: individuation and the pursuit of self-interest in the context of an increasingly more complexified division of labour; family as the core of individual labour and urbanisation and the emergence of the socially detached human subject (Brown, 1987, pp. 38–39). However, not only does Habermas's ([1962]1982) argument on the demise of the public sphere due to society's penetration by the state and markets, and Sennett's (1977) concomitant thesis of the human subject's loss of moral compass in modernity reiterate the very oppositional qualities of public-private but also they hide their geopolitical and psychic specificity. Publicness forges in them a universalist moral code, as it becomes attached to other equally heavily foundational theses on transparency, meritocracy and the likes. We must not forget that conceptions of the public sphere acquired legitimacy through their attachment to rigorous intellectual conduct in European modernity, and civility in its American version (Escobar, 1999, 2001). Significantly, neither of these dominant arguments accepts the nature of privacy as a source of the self and identity (Sheller, 2012; Tzanelli, 2008, 2022b); neither explicitly addresses the lack of intersectionally informed enunciations of publicness and privateness (Nakano Glenn, 2007, p. 214) and neither proceeds to explore the pluralisation of public and private situations and spheres in contemporary hypermobile contexts (Sheller & Urry, 2003).

Tourism is the realm of social and cultural visibility, as well as staged atmospheres for hungry eyes with disposable income (Urry, 1990, 2002). Not only are travel activities, the tourism system and hospitality as a practice and norm organising public spheres but also they participate in aesthetic adjudications pertaining to the audio-visual narrative content of the films to which they become geopolitically bound (Tzanelli, 2015). Issues of class scratch only the surface of a deep intersectional wound, which malforms and pollutes global solidarities with racism, sexism, disablism and more. Hospitality on the other hand cuts across the domains of the public and the private, destabilising a series of binaries: visibility vs. invisibility, materiality vs. immateriality, image vs. atmosphere, reason vs. emotion and work vs. labour. With these observations in mind, I purport that publicness stands at the heart of an epistemic crisis in tourism and hospitality studies, which is paradoxically concealed behind the selection of the subject matter in these academic areas: contemporary crises in tourism and hospitality (Cheer et al., 2021; Gössling et al., 2021; Korstanje & Séraphin, 2020; Lew et al., 2020; Tzanelli, 2021a, 2021b, 2020c). My critical appraisal of this paradox will be facilitated by a juxtaposition of Burawoy's (2004) 'public sociology', which was developed through actual travels across the world (Nichols, 2017, p. 317), with Keith Hollinshead's (1999b) approach to 'public culture', which was based on both actual travels and contemplative post-colonial critique. I contend that the idea of a 'live (tourism) mobilities' (Sheller, 2014) reveals that both approaches are built on stylistic ethics, which should not be conflated with normative judgements. The situated enunciation of these styles can be considered as both part of a new reading of the critical cosmopolitan project (Delanty, 2009) via the twin poles of non-human actancy (technology and nature) and a post-cosmopolitical statement, which prioritises the agency of networked scholarly communities (Urry, 2000).

Burawoy's (2004) ISA Presidential Address (Burawoy, 2005) opens with Walter Benjamin's metaphorical use of Klimt's 'Angelus Novus' as the psychomotor of history: a drive towards the future in the presence of a pull to the past. Burawoy (2005, pp. 4–6) builds his analysis around conceptions of crisis – or rather crises. These are related to a succession of changes in political systems, which also drove a collapse of old thought structures. His main task is to address the relevance of sociology in a world that races to the future, with reference to the vocation's public role. He notes the following 'trends' in the discipline: (1) a clash between the conservatism of commonplace structures of thought and action and the move of sociology to left-wing radicalism, (2) the presence of multiple public sociologies addressed to different publics, (3) an internal division of labour within the discipline (policy sociology, professional sociology and critical sociology), (4) an elaboration on internal complexity (i.e. for whom is knowledge produced and to what ends?), (5) a differentiation between the internal division in the discipline (critical, policy and so forth), and the biographical trajectories of its members (who may move into other professional sectors), (6) the increased 'pathologisation' of sociological positionalities due to the scholars' exclusive focus on particular audiences, (7) the instrumentalisation of reflexive knowledge, which appeals to political tendencies to capitalise everything, (8) a concomitant stratification and validation of knowledge within the discipline through the consolidation of institutional hierarchies (i.e., elite universities vs. regional or local institutions), (9) the global domination of the discipline by particular cultural trends (i.e. Anglophone sociology as the golden standard), (10) a positivist division of disciplines, which leads to hierarchical evaluations of their public voice and the suppression of interdisciplinarity and (11) a move towards 'partisanship' in the name of 'real' social groups with 'actually existing' problems.

Although in practice there are overlaps between these positionalities, the thesis on the 'division of labour' appears to drive hierarchies of complexity in the overall analysis, which develops against universal processes of capitalist accumulation and rationalisation. Indeed, when placed in contexts pertaining to the organisation of subject areas, such as tourism studies, a utopian collaborative division of labour in them gives way to a demotion of theory to an auxiliary pursuit. But let me first return to the division of labour in Burawoy's analysis. There, he distinguishes the role of policy studies from that of public sociology, stressing that the sociologist's vocation involves their pursuit of a dialogical engagement with the public (Burawoy, 2005, p. 11).

Elsewhere, Burawoy (2008, p. 10) explains that critical sociology specifically is supposed 'to examine the foundations—both the explicit and the implicit, both normative and descriptive—of the research programs of professional sociology'. This definition already feeds into what he recognises as 'public sociology proper': without it, publics are faced with a series of opaque statements which we find in the programmatic statements of populist political parties. In this respect, the 'partisanship' factor in point 11 is transferred to the uses of criticality as the basis of publicness, but this use is not acknowledged as such. This concealment appears in genealogies of tourism studies: the newer generation of critical tourism studies scholars are often trapped between the push to prove the utilitarian value of their studies and the recognition that the public sphere has transformed into the fragmented pluralised playscape of consumer capitalism (Bianchi, 2018; Hannam & Diekmann, 2016; Korstanje & Seraphin, 2020; Mostafanezhad, 2017). Publications by scholars belonging to the 'Academy of Hope' both exemplify critiques and amplify this entrapment between utilitarianism and critique, but not discuss it as such, as this would contravene the pedagogical objectives of the paradigm. Suddenly, the domain of the 'private' is equated with the teaching university, in which scholars cater on knowledge for particular groups: students, who may enter the 'real' professional world 'out there' to 'truly' influence situations.

We are in the domain of institutions and the way they work. Note that Burawoy's public sociology is also filtered via state education 'where faculty bear the burden of huge teaching loads' (2005, p. 20). Although such associations may not do justice to the scholarly context in which Hollinshead's (1999b) thesis develops, they still help us to understand how public scholarship can advance a critical tourism mobilities paradigm that turns private/privatised problems into the gist of critique of public sociological critiques. Hollinshead's key source is Donald Horne's *Intelligent Tourist* (1992), a book whose theme he approaches as 'a matter of authority, authorship and reliability ... in social science', due to 'the socio-political constructive power of the ... themes of tourism' (Hollinshead, 1999b, p. 268). The trope of social and cultural construction cuts across Burawoy's and Hollinshead's approaches – where Burawoy (2005) draws on Charles Wright Mills' (1959) approach to imagination, Hollinshead (1999b, p. 269) focusses on scholarly deliberations on the generative role of interactive performances between hosts and guests to achieve the 'arrestive communication' of culture. However, Hollinshead also provides a clearer critique of the Eurocentric entelechies purported by the certainties of immobile statist imaginaries of identity than Burawoy, who primarily puts such critiques to practice in American contexts. His starting point is the presence of a 'skilled legerdemain of tourism', which tourism practitioners use to manufacture 'preferred versions of public culture' (Hollinshead, 1999b, p. 267). Hollinshead concludes that behind the expert's intelligence may hide both interpellation of their studied cultures and a critical reflexivity constrained by their profession (for tourism professionals) and vocation (for tourism scholars). In fact, the critique of Eurocentricity-as-immobility of spirit leads Hollinshead to a conclusion shared with theorists from the new mobilities paradigm: 'travelling' and 'seeing' are essential 'conveyors of meaning about the realities by and *within which people live*' (1999b, pp. 269–270).

At this stage, it is important to capture the geopolitical panoramas in which both theses develop – for, as another two prominent contributors to public sociology, Steve Fuller (2006, p. 7) and John Holmwood (2010, pp. 649–650) stress, public sociologies are products of the new circumstances in which they emerge and thrive. Burawoy's 'public sociology' is a backlash to the ways modern American academia was institutionally formed: its twentieth-century post-Keynesian profile was the product of an intensive neoliberalisation of American education, which mirrored the country's disorganised capitalist modes of engagement with world markets (Delanty, 2001, pp. 124–126). As Lash and Urry (1987, pp. 81–82) note, the widespread discourse of American exceptionalism was filtered through processes of social neo-stratification that, past the 1960s revolutionary milestones, turned a 'prematurely sizeable service class' into a political force that both contested the brutality of capitalism and structured it anew in new styles of largely immaterial labour. In the environments of instrumentalist neoliberal expansion that promoted invention and innovation as pathways to achievement resurgent academics searched for new styles of public engagement, to not just articulate new scholarly agendas but also propagate them to wider audiences for maximum impact.

It is easy to miss the irony in all this, which is based on trading one form of instrumental functionalisation for another. As far back as the 1962 ASA Conference on 'The Uses of Sociology', public and applied sociology would be conflated with as absurd experiments as boxing intellectual discourse into clinical sociology, thus filtering the discipline's relevance through institutional imperatives based on production returns (Lazarsfield et al., 1967) – the basis of Foucault's critique of 'biopolitics' (Foucault, 2010). Becoming part of the mass was the new critical way of *doing* what matters: maximum reach could translate to maximum social value. In this respect, the American version of the public intellectual formed the perfect replica of the American spirit of DIY achievement through hard work, rather than the social privilege that came with European cultural capital. Behind this version of publicness hides the 'American Everyman' with his good intentions and know-how ethos, pursuing the utopia of the American dream (Morley & Robins, 1995, p. 80).

Here is the core of the paradox: the zone of intimate culture 'conceived in opposition to powerful images of an idealised West (or conceivably some other political pole) and affording a refuge from such imposing formalities' (Herzfeld, 2005, p. 53) seems to stylistically guide such dominant models of public sociology. I stress 'stylistically', as behind the style's subversive irony hides a degree of structural-institutional imitation. Note how Hays (2007, pp. 82–84) worries that hierarchical compartmentalisation in the discipline will demote public sociology to a second-class subject, divesting it of its ability to mend society's moral fibre. What this statement does not highlight is Hays' American brand of publicness, which is geared towards a particular form of professional conduct. In reality, when scrutinised in a decolonial style, this vision of public sociology can be understood as a critique of heavily theoretical continental modes of public engagement.

As I explain below, a sustained genealogy of tourism studies reveals a historical split between the soft, contemplative analyses of European cosmopolitan thought, and the hard, activist portfolios of non-Western post-colonial academies, which may even view contemplative analysis with contempt for its lack of use-value (Tzanelli & Korstanje, 2020). The critical–moral hue of the 'tourist gaze' (Urry, 1990) chimed naturally with Hollinshead's (1999a) early suggestion that tourism is in contemporary consumption sites the eye of a 'softer power', barely sensed and understood by its customers and obligingly adopted by disempowered host destinations, that enact agency by modifying structures of consumer exoticisation. As Bianchi (2009) put it, tourism studies appear to be torn between the promises of the catch-all market and cultural studies' softer focus on discourse analysis. Both Bianchi (2009) and Edensor (1998, 2002, 2005b) beautifully explained how nation-states often promote tourism as a fertile ground for development, while overlooking the political consequences of their fancy programs: elimination of ethnic difference and the intensification of class conflict in home territories. Bianchi suggested that even tourism scholars tend to overlook in their work the diachronic nature of material asymmetries created by global capitalism in its latest mutations.

In the discipline of sociology, today the need to reach large unspecialised publics may also lead not to the hierarchical demotion of the subject, but its disciplinary de-specialisation – a note that can also apply to tourism and hospitality studies (Tzanelli, 2022a). Burawoy's sophisticated version of public sociology still falls prey to institutional biopolitics – so much so, that some have dubbed his manifesto a way of 'branding' the discipline (Agger in Nichols, 2017, p. 317). The new mobilities paradigm steps into this controversy to mediate the conflict through understandings of multitudinal action (Hardt & Negri, 2004). This action is guided by a camaraderie that does not always fall under the ambit of institutional action; nor does it prioritise it over contemplative models of critical intervention. The strength of the new mobilities paradigm is its reflexive virtuality, which will hopefully be preserved as the paradigm becomes more institutionalised across the world. In fact, the original thesis of the paradigm's founders, John Urry and Mimi Sheller (2003, p. 117) on 'public life', comfortably fits into Burawoy's (2005, pp. 7–9) definition of the second trend of public sociology. However, as the paradigm developed its epistemological portfolio, it embraced the fourth version of public sociology, which highlights disciplinary and world complexities.

As an essentially biopolitical phenomenon, publicness guides such debates, which have always oscillated between understandings of biology or inheritance, and legacy. Fuller (2006, pp. 41–42) makes a crucial observation on the origins of academic institutions in the artificial and temporary mode of associations that we find in companies. Where folk biological approaches to belonging are primarily based on blood bonds, corporate ones entertaining legal protection, such as the higher educational institutions, forge artificial bonds that transcend the particularities of place and culture. It is the future of such forms of guild consciousness, originally known as *universitas*, that is at stake in Burawoy's vision of publicness and Hollinshead's understanding of associative identity in tourism scholarship (see also one of his last collaborative essays on 'postidentity': Hollinshead & Vellah, 2020).

Although submerged to this day under layers of pragmatic vocational justification, the institutional version of publicness rests on a performative contradiction: it recruits intellectual labour to support and justify 'common sense' and does so in the name of equality and justice, without necessarily promoting intellectual excellence. Often, the latter is murdered at the expense of a 'democratization of knowledge' (Light, 2005). Specifically in tourism and hospitality studies, this murder is re-enacted in dominant genealogies of both subjects as both activities and norms, respectively, as well as modern industrial organisations. To refer to Burawoy's ninth version of public sociology, both tourism and hospitality as subject areas and industries are not always 'provincialised' to address particular problems, and when they do, they may prioritise the delivery of 'results' over scholarship. Especially the film-tourism industry moves in this functionalist direction, enhancing the new spirit of hospitality, which does not merely exploit land resources as spectacular landscapes, but enmeshes its human custodians into the post-industrial rationale of 'cultural landscaping'.

My critique of the demotion of stylistic ethics to a non-consequential private business can be connected to what John Urry's (2000, 2016, 2017) viewed as the subject area's 'direction of travel'. A call to adopt directionality also guides Sheller's (2014) discourse of 'live sociology', Burawoy's (2005) deliberations on sociology's Benjaminian futurity and Hollinshead's (1999b; Hollinshead & Vellah, 2020) call for a worldmaking project that addresses glocal concerns beyond Eurocentrist tourist development. Although I dub my approach in this book 'critical', I maintain that its objective is to design public futurity, therefore an elective possibility to appeal to different publics, as it is incrementally released in different public domains. At the same time, I refute the label of policy-making and celebrate contemplative judgement. My aim is to evaluate possibilities, while resisting plausible and the probable targeted by approaches 'that claim to be neutral' (Stengers, 2010, p. 57). My understanding of criticality is emplaced within understandings of reflexivity, not as an individualistic 'sport', but what Sandywell (1996) calls 'our material involvement within a larger whole, of being connected to larger constellations of experience, being involved with others and exemplifying that involvement in the course and conduct of our own practices' (Sandywell, 1996, pp. 415–417; Sandywell & Beer, 2005). Sandywell's axiological thesis on thinking-as-conduct is not disconnected from what tourism practitioners do and how tourism and hospitality scholars think and what they argue. On the contrary, it brings centre-stage some constellations of critique. It invoke a Benjaminian image-metaphor of mobility, which also guided Cresswell's (2001, 2010) thesis on the life and direction of purposeful movements or mobilities, including those of tourism and hospitality. As a reflexive technique designed to promote research that stays true to the 'complexities of the concrete' (Sandywell & Beer, 2005, unpaginated), the constellation is a predecessor of event theory.

There are two forms of constellations that I follow in the following two sections: the first is a Foucaultian presentation of events (a genealogical organisational 'story-journey'), marking the development of academic criticality in tourism and hospitality studies. The second applies to the particular case studies I develop in the book to exemplify the ways the new spirit of hospitality produces faux worlds of cinematic tourism.

Critical Tourism Studies Scholarship 'Events' and Directions of Travel

The faux phantasmagoric hue of the worlds of cinematic tourism I visit in the three chapters of the book, their atmospheric patina, invites the proponents of the projects of public sociology and public culture to 'provincialise' knowledge about tourism and hospitality. Inevitably then, my attempt to be 'critical' will embrace the axiological realm of tourism mobilities, as well as their adjacent hospitality rituals and customs to provide an intricate analysis entwining cultural activity with socio-political structures in the form of *problématiques* (Hollinshead, 2009b; Sheller & Urry, 2004). However, my axiology will be an analytical journey to judgement about how people act. For the readers who do not have access to the first leg of my journey, *axioō* (ancient Greek: ἀξιοῶ-ῶ) means to *gauge* [facts] (first meaning) thus *demanding* access to a/the truth (second meaning), not deliver normative ultimatums.

In their attempt to answer questions of genealogy, tourism scholars have often borrowed from Michel Foucault's ruminations on the 'order of things' and Thomas Kuhn's (1970) structural approach to the birth of scientific paradigms (Dann, 1997; Echter & Jamal, 1997; Wearing et al., 2005). Such exercises have consolidated the recognition of tourism as part of Enlightenment's programs of knowledge expansion – 'tourism' has to be in quotes, given controversies concerning its universality and elitist juxtaposition with 'travel'. Established sociological approaches to the European birth of 'tourism' relate tourist activity to cultures of eighteenth century aristocratic and nineteenth century middle-class *loisir* centring on luxurious rural lifestyles and travel (Franklin, 2009).

Concomitant studies of urban modernity as a cage for humans, who, in reacting to everyday pressures, began to take more trips to exotic places and romanticise the outdoors and its alien cultures, further refined the triptych Europe–episteme–tourism: touring began to signify learning and performing, apprehending and moulding otherness in recognisable forms (Tzanelli, 2015). The study of urbanite modernity has also usefully acknowledged how overlaps between industrial and colonial expansion questioned the modernity of tourism/travel itself, pushing its birth back to the epistemic pursuits of colonial administrators, affluent Oxbridge 'Grand Tourists' and adventurous artists, eager to delve into the mysteries of the Orient through travel (Brodsky-Porges, 1981; Towner, 1984, 1985). To date, in as famous theses as Urry's (1992; Urry & Larsen, 2011) 'tourist gaze', the birth of tourism is genealogically dichotomised between the slow pace of the Grand Tour outside and within European territories and the fast pace of Western industrial mobilities in the European North.

This split may help us to understand an analytical oscillation between the axes/axiologies of pragmatism and uncompromising moralism in critical tourism studies. In reality, 'critical tourism studies' has been an umbrella for a constellation of paradigms, including that inspired by Urry's (1992, 2002; Urry & Larsen, 2011) Foucauldian 'tourist gaze'; the new mobilities paradigm that uses Foucault more sparingly and eclectically (Sheller & Urry, 2004), preferring Actor–Network Theory instead to examine tourism mobilities (Cohen & Cohen, 2012, 2015; Cohen & Cohen, 2019; Hannam et al., 2006); the 'Academy of Hope', which ditches such antihuman traditions in favour of post-Marxist repertoires on 'transmodern ethics' (Ateljevic et al., 2013); the 'tourism/tourist imaginaries' Castoriadis-inspired argument (Salazar & Graburn, 2016), which focusses on interplays between the structural and agential forces governing representations of place, culture and people and the post-humanist turn that studies the impact of climate change on leisure mobilities such as tourism, as well as their hospitality extensions and implications (Grimwood et al., 2018).

'Critical turn', 'critical thinking', 'critical action' and increasingly 'post-disciplinary knowledge' have become common usage terms for researchers of the same object of study (Ateljevic et al., 2013): the advent of capitalist domination over humans and earth, or what Moore (2016) called the 'Capitalocene'. Where capitalism advances, axiologies slide into normative crevices: Ateljevic et al. (2013) discussed the power of international corporations to create new consumption patterns, streamlined into citizen pools with little knowledge on tourism ethics. Echoing Dussel's (1985) transmodernism, they invite us to adopt more creative pedagogical designs to illuminate the contradictions of global capitalism and its ideological scaffoldings. Such a proposed critical programme challenges old positivist paradigms still in place in school curricula, which train students to adopt morally vacant economic models of thought and tend to demote alternative forms of knowledge to peripheral trivia (Tribe, 2001).

Thus, critical thinking has taken multiple applications within tourism studies. While Bramwell and Lane (2014) embraced criticality to rethink new all-encompassing models of sustainable tourism, Chambers and Buzinde (2015) stressed that current critical theorising does not decolonise tourist scholarship. To remember sociologist Husseyn Alatas' suggestion that native minds are held captives by Western episteme (e.g., Tzanelli, 2015, 2020), scholarly criticality has not provided an epistemological perspective on tourism, which legitimises the cosmologies of marginalised world communities. Perhaps for the new twenty-first-century critical tourism paradigm, 'radicalism' in terms of learning tools, stands between soft and hard modernising repertoires, and this is what Fullagar and Wilson (2012) baptised as 'critical pedagogy' (Huang, 2008; Sheldon et al., 2008; Tribe, 2007). But an axiological genealogy may prove that more thinking work is necessary, as even critical pedagogies can 'demand' results and justice before better gauging what appears in the form of 'indisputable facts'.

Tribe (2007) nicely unpacks where the crevice emerges: he argued that the critical study has evolved through tourism's twin legacy of borrowing concepts from the Frankfurt school and the objective to establish good governance and management in fields of practice. He also pointed out that managerialism tends to prioritise profit-making and consumer satisfaction over ethical transformative praxis. In unison, Wilson et al. (2008) stressed that criticality is more of 'a contested idea', as what it means tends to be overdetermined by the fieldworker's, tourism practitioner's or scholar's methodological and epistemological priorities. They employed the term 'critical approach' instead to connect critical pedagogy to epistemology and methodology. But if this is the case, then a critical approach should be employed in practically transforming the ways tourist industries function in a reflexive and just way, so that they produce equally self-reflexive tourist subjects and happy, rather than 'alienated', workers, others argued (Korstanje, 2017; Lapointe & Coulter, 2020; Lapointe et al., 2020; Lin et al., 2018; Roelofsen & Minca, 2018; Tzanelli & Korstanje, 2016). Belhassen and Caton (2011) stressed that such a silent revolution (both 'soft' and 'hard' in its modernising styles, as per my analysis) necessitates the advocation of more constructive critical management styles. In sharp contrast to what some scholars believe, critical management studies can be understood as a fresh movement oriented towards challenging dogmatic management ideologies.

It has been repeatedly argued that one of the main obstacles in the realisation of this programme is indifference towards adopting self-reflexive and critical pedagogical curricula for training scholars and practitioners (Belhassen & Caton, 2011).

But what does this really entail? Pritchard et al.'s (2011) 'hopeful tourism' (p. 947) has a similar ethico-practical basis, which attacks unhelpful negativity in academia and business contexts, understandably affected by late modern pressures. Ever since the Critical Tourism Studies Conference (2005), 'hopeful tourism' has advocated pro-justice portfolios based on indigenous empowerment, as well as policies fighting social inequality. Like the aforementioned scholars, Pritchard et al. (2011) promoted a manifesto that properly engages with philosophical debates in tourism, thus aspiring to bridge the field's theory gap, dismantle the established prejudices and stereotypes in dominant discourses in and about tourism and provide a nurturing environment 'to reduce the isolation experienced by interpretative and critical researchers in a field where objectivity, generalisation and distance are the norm' (Pritchard et al., p. 213; Mair & Raid, 2007).

Let me backtrack here to bring Tribe's comments on criticality into a better genealogical focus: the picture of 'hard modernity' forged by capitalist forces painted by scholars such as Boorstin (1962) and Ritzer (2019) is both symmetrical and complementary with the 'soft modernity' of contemplation and community building that was originally propagated in the subject by anthropologists such as Nelson Graburn and John Eade. Soft approaches to modernity honed a modernising perspective, befit for those who believe in pilgrimage as a method of awakening conscience a-la Zygmunt Bauman (1996a, 1996b). Softness and hardness articulate the two antithetical poles of contemporary action theories, social theorist Hans Joas ([1996] 2005) explains. Unfortunately, he adds, hard activism has been favoured in scholarship at the expense of contemplative action – a note also provided by Ritzer (2019) in a recent interview. The 'hard modernity' of critical tourism studies sought to restore faith in Frankfurt School's Weberian–Gramscian–German idealist critique of commoditisation by revolution (Korstanje, 2018b; Krippendorf, 1986). Though essential in the partition of human activities between work and leisure in Western and European societies, especially after the institution of paid holidays as a universal right (in 1948), 'hard modernisers' stellar contribution in the field was to refuse to treat tourism as a universal value. However, it would be incorrect to say that the 'soft modernisers' of the Baumanesque type were less important. Eade became an international name in the study of South Asian diasporas in his later career in urbanite contexts of virulent British racism, while promoting a mobilities approach to pilgrimage (Coleman & Eade, 2004) still in use two decades after his first major collaborative publication in the field. Eade's pilgrimage studies moved from the cultural realm to political–economic ones, especially in contexts of military and political tourism, thus updating agendas in another budding academic niche: thanatourism and dark tourism (Coleman & Eade, 2018).

Young Graburn (1977) became known as a contributor in Valene Smith's *Hosts and Guests: An Anthropology of Tourism*. It is important that his debut connects to a landmark publication that contributed both to tourism and hospitality studies. Next to Dennison Nash's attack of tourism as a form of imperialism, Graburn nominated tourism a 'sacred journey', making 'life worth living' (p. 22). Graburn communicated with Fennell's (2006) later philosophical explorations of different registers of wellbeing in tourism and travel, and Caton's (2012) pragmatic suggestion that tourists have to prioritise their own mental integrity and health against moral calls to do virtuous things for the community. Graburn's impressive now magnum opus spanning four and a half decades also interrogated the complexities of hospitality, community advocacy and situated ethics as part of a 'just tourism' agenda (Bunten & Graburn, 2018). Significantly, in terms of methodology, early anthropological contributions to such complexities introduced critical–hermeneutic phenomenologies borrowing from semiotics, Marxism and even the 'phanerology' (i.e., perception of totality in the mind) of Charles Saunders Peirce (Belhassen & Caton, 2009). The latter was perfected in Mac-Cannell's (1976) work on tourism as an activity and industry thriving on sign-posting landscapes and cultures. But note how MacCannell's (2012) more recent work has also conveyed the ethical complexities of ocular consumption in heritage sites, thus treading now the fine line between soft and hard modernising approaches in the field. So, 'soft modernisers' in critical tourism analysis are very important for the promotion of a balanced perspective, which does not discard phenomenology in favour of materialism.

The rise of corporate tourist expansion to world peripheries, especially in the context of war conflicts such as that in Vietnam, has been pivotal to such original interrogations of tourism's business ethics. The American scholarly contingent of the 1960s and the 1970s was bred in the Marcuse-led style student revolutions that pronounced the modern human a one-dimensional being. Such anthropological tourist worldmakings also critiqued the totalisation of notions of human, stressing the plurality of human inheritances, commitments and experiences in tourism and hospitality settings (Hollinshead et al., 2015). In the second half of the twentieth century, American tourism academia and its European counterparts began to question their own scopophilic and positivist managerial portfolios more systematically. The 'first wave of critique' produced a reflexive shock, leading to denigrations of tourism as an offshoot of cultural illiteracy, insensitivity to the other and pathological attraction to consumerism. Soon enough, however, a 'second wave' washed away such indiscriminate guilt to constructively forge new ethical agendas on tourism business practice (on cultures of critique see Boltanski & Chiapello, 2018).

Today, the moral and pragmatic nexus of tourism and hospitality is more prevalent in critical tourism analysis, if still underdeveloped in some key respects. It is important not to lose sight of the fact that a large portion of the produced knowledge comes from Marxist-inspired theories, which once considered tourism as a mechanism of indoctrination and cultural alienation (Ash & Turner, 1976; Enzensberger, 1974; MacCannell, 1976). These studies did not discuss the epistemological limitations of economic aetiologies in tourism – a position that was radically altered by cultural theorists. Instead, critical thinking turned attention to the role played by First World constructions of Third World peripheral exoticism, rejecting the hierarchical organisation of different cultures on a single civilisational schema for the benefit of tourism business. In such theses, a single 'tourism industry' deploys considerable resources to construct an exploitative platform, on which homogenised 'non-Western natives' are commoditised and consumed (Britton, 1982; Shepherd, 2002).

Because the twin colonial and capitalist axes of the 'tourist gaze's' oper-ationalisation produced ways of doing business, it was repeatedly regarded by critical scholars as an ethically questionable premise from which one can tour the world. As new generations of critical tourism geographers, sociologists and anthropologists note today, occulocentric practices organise new (decentralised) 'economies of signs' (Lash & Urry, 1994), in which tourist products, locations and experiences are externally designed by experts and consumed by clients (Mosta-fanezhad et al., 2016). The critique is then directed both to the designers of tourism and the consumers of these product-bundles: a new 'aesthetic reflexivity' surfaces in such environments of production and consumption to both preserve and contest Enlightenment rationality (Lash & Urry, 1994). Thus, aesthetically reflexive tourism experts as agents make tourist worlds, by negotiating the geographical and psychological borders between civilised and wild zones (Kor-stanje, 2012). Controlling and mitigating the impacts of external risks in tourism business allows for the expansion of capitalism in such wild zones, which serve as adventure playgrounds for tourists.

To better focus this axiological vision/journey, I place the 'Academy of Hope' between Hollinshead's and Jamal's early attempt to give voice to marginalised indigenous populations (Hollinshead et al., 2009; Jamal, 2019; Jamal & Hol-linshead, 2001). Much like the 'hopeful tourism' scholarly contingent's work, Jamal's work enunciates problems belonging to the European traditions of critical cosmopolitanism (Delanty, 2009) – sadly, employed very little in the field (for exceptions see Swain, 2009; Tzanelli, 2018a, 2020). However, such manifestos centre on human actors as agents attempting to modify large structures. From the late 1990s to early 2000s, the new mobilities paradigm (with its own 'critical mobilities' branch) breathed new life into debates concerning just design of tourism by employing new methodological and epistemological tools from Complex Adaptive Systems and Actor–Network Theory. In this paradigm, 'sys-tems' comprise more or other-than-human actants that propel different types of human performance/agency in tourism (Hannam et al., 2006; Sheller & Urry, 2004). The call to respect the environment and nature as actants in enlarged systems of life connects both to the post-human turn and to sustainability in tourism business. Post-humanism calls for critical re-evaluations of 'the basic unit of common reference for our species, our polity and our relationship to the other inhabitants of this planet' (Braidotti, 2013, p. 2): the human subject, earth's main ruler and destructive force.

This re-evaluation put under scrutiny the damage inflicted by both colonial systems of violence on human populations and indigenous environments and capitalist systems of uncontrolled expansion at the expense of vulnerable groups, including women, disabled and racialised populations (see notion of 'Capital-ocene' above). The post-human manifesto looks to humanity's and earth's futures: it thinks of sustainability 'for those to come' (Kumm et al., 2019). This call's temporal methodologies connect to 'hopeful tourism's' in terms of respon-sibilisation, but do so from a softer modernising perspective, befit for those who believe in pilgrimage as a method of awakening conscience a-la Bauman (1996a, 1996b). It seems natural to have a contribution to these debates by Cohen (2019), but also exciting new publications by critical tourism scholars, bringing together 'hard' evidence on issues of ecological neglect and exploitation (Córdoba-Azcárate, 2020; Mostafanezhad & Norum, 2019).

An examination of scholarly genealogies of hospitality yields its own epistemological conclusions about the nature of social and cultural realities in which it takes place. First, deliberations that centre on hospitality's social dimensions are more deeply rooted in distinctions between public and private spheres than tourism analysis', because they tend to interrogate the commercialisation of privacy in the material and phenomenal form of the 'home' (Lashley, 2000; Lynch & MacWhannel, 2000). Second, they prioritise the intersubjective and cross-cultural nature of mutuality and reciprocity in acts of hospitableness (Heal, 1990), as well as the agency of the labouring human subjects that 'enunciate' or shape social and cultural realities (Mennel et al., 1992; Selwyn, 2000). Third, they shift focus from processes of consumption to the production of material and immaterial worlds of tourism, borrowing from anthropologies of gift and giving (Burgess, 1982; Tefler, 1996, 2000) Albeit still placing notions of generosity and recognition in the marketplace (e.g., Heal, 1990), such early scholarly explorations of the normative basis of hospitality adumbrated twentieth-century hospitality scholarship's use of Jacques Derrida's phenomenological heuristics.

Such heuristics facilitated a shift to ontologies of homemaking, in which some scholars saw an 'anti-scientist' (read: anti-positivist) approach to research, endorsing hermeneutics (Botterill, 2000, p. 189). However, they also reinforced some binary constructions of the subject in the form of public/private, marketplace/home, knowledge/experience and so forth (Still, 2006). It helps to highlight that the binarisms are embedded in European social thought's formal split between epistemology and phenomenology in the 1970s (Jay, 1994), as well as critical theory's self-perceived social mission to save society from the abyss of ignorance. The programmatic move of hospitality studies to the axiological world of giving and receiving also fostered in the new mobilities paradigm continuations between the 'politics of mobility' (Cresswell, 2001) and the 'ethics of hospitality' (Derrida, 2000). However, against erecting boundaries between tourism and hospitality, mobilities studies scholars would stress the *circularity of discourses* on both sides and the activities they enclosed (Germann Molz & Gibson, 2007; Veijola et al., 2014).

The change signalled a transformation of theories of 'network sociality' (a-la Wittel, 2001) into conceptions of 'network hospitality'. The new generation of hospitality scholars is using network theories (Germann Molz, 2014), in combination with a strong agenda on emotional and affective engagement between hosts and guests. This agenda is applied to communications in digital environments (Månsson, 2015; Månsson et al., 2020) and by considering new technologies as the new social intermediaries in the organisation of on-site hospitableness (Bialski, 2011, 2012, 2013). However, to date, the collapse of the scholarly-conceptual boundary between tourism and hospitality is an unfinished process. The established methodological heuristics of travel (i.e., 'the journey' as a methodological metaphor) in critical tourism analysis continues to stumble upon ideas of homeliness as a fixed ethical milestone. Indeed, thinking about mobile hospitality as an intellectual pursuit (e.g., Friese, 2004; Kaufmann, 2000; Lynch et al., 2011; Still, 2004, 2006) brings into dispute ontologies of scholarship that draw legitimacy from moral registers of action. Such moralisations prove to be a dangerous sham, concealing the foundational support of certain categories of action and being (e.g., being a host) as absolute.

It is pertinent to remind readers where the present book stands in all these controversies: I take cognisance of the analytical content of genealogies of tourism and hospitality studies, embedding both in social, cultural and political theory. However, I argue that their engagement with capitalism's earlier mutations must be advanced with a dispassionate critical examination of more recent techniques of agency-neutralisation or amplification in tourism and hospitality events, network tourismification (via new technologies) and acts of hospitableness drawing on post-human tools in novel managerial environments. All in all, I maintain that the Techno-Anthropocene produces post-human 'landscapes' of consumption for the tourist gaze that enmesh the old games of environmental modification and neglect with new technologies of (human) absence. I will return to issues concerning the futurity of scholarly virtuality as an imaginary of movement-action in the conclusion.

The Structure of the Book

Not all my case studies here can stress all the epistemo-ontological discrepancies addressed above, so the analysis of different angles of action, actancy and agency is distributed across chapters. In some cases, I will have to follow the cues of capitalist domination over the ways societies, institutions and individuals act. But there will also be traces of previous or co-habiting practices of 'doing' society and hospitality in the contemporary enclaves of tourismification I explore. Simultaneously, such practices are revealed as happenings in which natural habitats should be recognised as legitimate actants, but are not, as their field of action is taken over by techniques of representation and technologies of presence. It is also worth remembering that in this brutal world, only human voices are listened to, whereas the primary 'capital' of tourism, nature, is not. In fact, the idea of a seamless network of distinctions across any society in the era of globalisation refutes the reality of subject-object mobilities. All I can do is account for how different actors act in different fields of local, international or interpersonal engagement to preserve the modicum of sociality and camaraderie.

Chapter 2 discusses the development of film tourism in Crete from the release of the award-winning *Zorba the Greek* (dir. Michael Cacoyannis, 1964) to date. Because it covers long temporal stretches, I approach cinematic tourism design in a 'genealogical' fashion, seeking to explain how *ZG*-inspired tourism on Crete ended up being more than about the film itself due to historical contingency. I provide some data on tourism growth to fill the auspicious gap of organised information on hotel expansion and tourist traffic on the island between 1964 and 1990, as well as interviews with *ZG* director Cacoyannis and music composer Mikis Theodorakis to establish their creative involvement in tourism design. I argue that the *ZG* tourism niche did not draw on Cretan landscape's romantic sublime as such; instead, it ended up borrowing from an embodied version of transgressive Greek masculinity that knows how to enjoy life to the fullest. The case, I argue, partook of a network of sociocultural and capitalist interests extending beyond the island's global advertising as a tourist destination and generating new problems with a particular form of labour mobility: it encouraged many female visitors to form casual sexual affairs with Greek men known as *kamákia* during their holidays on Crete – a phenomenon that began with the film itself and declined due to the threat of AIDS. This embodied and gendered place-image informed the growth of sex tourism across the country as a special form of tourism worldmaking that then fed back into notions of Greek identity. However, the technomorphic development of tourism mobilities in recent years would wipe the affective labour of sex workers from tourism advertising, sanitising the tourismified locations and modern Greek natures-landscapes alike.

Chapter 3 enhances the argument on structural technomorphism through a contextual interrogation of the connection between the aesthetic and ethical principles that end up informing the engineering of national hospitality in media platforms. Now affording concrete cross-cultural comparisons through two master and several other examples, I explain how the design conforms to the rationalised rules of the new spirit of hospitality, which mobilises romantic ideals of individual freedom to sell landscapes and exotic cultural characters. The technomorphic model is primarily exemplified in the chapter through the phased design of tourism mobilities out of two films with virulent sexist and antisemitic content centred on the journeys of the fictional Kazakh journalist Borat to the United States: *Borat: Cultural Learnings of America for Make Benefit Glorious Nation of Kazakhstan* (2006, dir. L. Charles) and *Borat Subsequent Moviefilm: Delivery of Prodigious Bribe to American Regime for Make Benefit Once Glorious Nation of Kazakhstan* (2020, dir. J. Woliner). Unlike the previous chapter, which emphasises the role of unplanned contributions to the new spirit of hospitality by tourism labour, this chapter examines the ways in which distinguished designers become implicated in the workings of capitalist structuration of leisure.

It is suggested that common assumptions regarding solid continuities between social and aesthetic privilege and 'tourism/tourist agency' are wrong. Both film artists and tourism designers in the *Borat* 'business of tourism' (Dann, 1996) display varied degrees of agency and creativity in the process of making *Borat* art and tourism. However, their intentions, motivations and visions are manipulated to different ends by cultural-industrial apparatuses and the Kazakh tourism authority (nation state). Better developing the argument on 'cinematic tourism' in 'film-induced' tourism's stead, which necessitates the development of 'event theory', the chapter deliberates on the contingent nature of capitalist growth. It is argued that by merely considering the ways the phased development of *Borat* mobilities conforms to contingency and is indifferent to the welfare of disenfranchised social groups, we miss the panoramic picture of tourism development. Instead, we must acknowledge how the networked nature of design produces maps of mismatched agencies that conform to the principles guiding the digital mapping of seamless landscapes. In *Borat's* case, such mapping cannot be examined by having recourse to post-colonial theory or racist flares in post-communist contexts alone. As a novel post-Anthropocenic magma of mobile 'objects', the mapping is a form of action, exceeding the objectives of a 'serious leisure' game (Stebbins, 1992). Mapping supports networks of shifting alliances in pursuit of profit-making and cultural-political recognition alike (but also antagonistically to each other). Unfolding against a background of Sacha Baron Cohen's devastating cinematic satire that produces its own harms and critiques of corruption in equal measure, the magma merits dispassionate contextual analysis prior to drawing any normative conclusions about the actors and agents involved in its phased events.

Chapter 4 explores emerging intersections between the consumption of mediated popular culture and the real and imagined topographies within which these representations are framed. Through an examination of the 'televisual tourism' centred around the successful TV series *Breaking Bad* (dirs. V. Gillingan, M. Slovis, C. Bucksey, T. McDonough M. MacLaren, A. Bernstein, R. Johnson, C. Bucksey, B. Cranston, J. Renck, P. Gould, S. Winant, C. Haid, J. Shiban, T. Shauz, B. Hughes, G. Mastras, S. Catlin, F.E. Alacalá, T. Brock, T. Hunter, J. Dahl, J. McKay, P. Medak, P. Abraham, P. Slade, 2008–2013), I scrutinise the multiple modes of sensorial and embodied travel experience enjoyed by fans of the show as they consume their way around the show's sites, scenes and tastes in the city of Albuquerque. This exploitation of media textuality through fan tourism is centred upon a carefully managed commodification of crime, criminality and transgression. The chapter mobilises spectacular methodologies of design based on atmospheres of thrill, normative/nomothetic risk (i.e., use of illegal substances that erode the human character) and bodily danger to revise the concept of 'edgework' as voluntary risk-taking by consumers of the story and its criminal characters and situations. Such consumption is actualised through adventurous role performance in visitations to filmed *Breaking Bad* locales as someone, who invests in variations of 'metempsychotic' (adopting the soul of another person) and 'metensomatic' (performing another character's role) engagement with drug crime and its monetary seductions.

The auratic qualities of such topographies inform the design of 'dangerous mobilities' and consumption of criminal plots in safe ways. Auxiliary to this commercialisation is the geographical, post-colonial and cultural-industrial marginality of the cinematic background of this design. However, again, the structural technomorphic logic of designing tourism out of fictional crime displays a strong element of contingency in the ways different tourism agents ally and thus in how tourism develops in context. In this respect, race and the post-colonial condition have to fit into a much larger picture of metropolitan-peripheral development of urban design that facilitates disparate aesthetically reflexive mobilities for 'soft edgeworkers' or 'flâneurs of crime'. The chapter's principal 'tourism agents' are now split between local administration developing tourism, private cinematic tourism-orientated business and the popcultural fans who perform *Breaking Bad* tourism in creative styles. I conclude by exploring the epistemological value of voluntary performance in transforming both tourists and hosts into controversial actors or true agents in such new image-based capitalist networks.

Chapter 2

From Cultural Worldmaking to Structural Technomorphism in *Zorba the Greek* Tourism

Zorba the Greek and Cretan Placemaking: Memory Habits and Tourist Souvenirs

Place is the product of a network of memories suspended in competing narratives (Ricoeur, 2004, pp. 116–117): who says what about its qualities and histories exert influence on the basis of social status, cultural development and political contingency. In the tourist trade, placemaking is even more stringently subjected to such rules. Crete, the first case study of this book, is such an example: the release of the internationally successful film *Zorba the Greek* (dir. M. Cacoyannis - henceforward: *ZG*) in 1964 introduced the barren landscapes and traditional culture of this Greek island to global audiences – something that would subsequently lead to an influx of especially, but not exclusively, European tourist clientele in a land with no infrastructural basis to sustain mobilities of such a scale. Crete ended up standing for something different from its allegedly original character, which was as much a native fictional construct as its imported anthropomorphic *ZG* brand. After this film, Cretan land transformed into a tourist landscape (Urry, 2004), a manufactured picture postcard which assumed all the characteristics of the film's fictional literary-cinematic hero. This unintended by its makers effect resembles to some extent Hollinshead's (2009b) rendition of 'worldmaking' (2009b, p. 643).

Let us begin with this proposition then: that Zorbas-the-character is an artificial memory token that 'worldmade' Cretan tourism (see also Introduction). Although the demotion of primary (living) to secondary (processed) memory in such worldmaking networks is often rigorously contested by those wanting to fix identity, in late capitalism, it always reforms the ways place is imagined. Thematically, we can distinguish between 'habit memory' or *mémoire-habitude*, and 'distinct recollection' or *mémoire souvenir* (Ricoeur, 2004, p. 24), with the latter projecting an element of artificiality in the public cultures of tourism. Contextually, we can conclude that in touristified locations, memory registers oscillate between customary and embodied practices of placemaking by locals on

The New Spirit of Hospitality, 37–72
Copyright © 2023 Rodanthi Tzanelli
Published under exclusive licence by Emerald Publishing Limited
doi:10.1108/978-1-83753-160-820231003

the one hand, and the personalised, recollective and impressionistic agency of tourist imaginaries produced by industries and tourist visitors on the other (Salazar, 2012). It is dangerously nostalgic to stick to notions of rooted memory of retrogressive content in the era of globalisation, which is dominated by hybridisation. Experiences that form during encounters with strangers bridge Bergsonian dichotomies between entrenched habit (what we acquire at home) and reference to an acquisition (what we collect during travel). The experiential bridge is built on the subject matter of interaction, which makes both (and/or all) parties reflect on their perspectives, producing a shared image of what is supposed to be the past of the visited land (Ricoeur, 2004, pp. 25–26).

If we follow a blended symbolic interactionist/semiotic path, we may recall MacCannell's (1973) established thesis on 'staged authenticity' in tourist settings. I use his semiotic interactionism to strengthen the argument: tourism that connects to combinations of kinaesthetic (embodied practices such as dancing and lovemaking) and audio-visual tropes and practices (moviemaking and watching as well as music-making and listening) partakes in narrative extensions, which enable the emergence of a new 'place identity'. Several tourist destinations have been put on the tourist map by having featured in popular films (Papatheodorou & Karpathiotaki, 2007, p. 2). However, it is clear by now that when exploring tourism as a form of public culture and a rendition of public sociology, I believe that such staging requires much more than thinking in terms of 'front' and 'back' regions of identity performance and placemaking. On the one hand, especially filmmaking adheres to a tertiary revision of memory or *mémoire souvenir*, an afterimage of place that is not fake, only different from its alleged original form. This both produces and revises already existing imaginaries of place and culture in multiple stages or phases (Gravari-Barbas & Graburn, 2012; Stiegler, 2011).

In many respects, *ZG* tourism is an example of the ways place afterimages in popular art enclose embodied memories of affective quality. These affects are capitalised upon by power nodes, which transform them into property to sell. Ironically, in this arduous process of turning a work of art into national or tourist property, the artwork's creators themselves become not just unintended collaborators of the workings of tourism expansion, but non-bodies of capitalism: by the time structural technomorphism kicks in, they have no actual input in tourism worldmaking – if they even did. Following this process from A to Z will expose the complexity of development as a civilising process that endorses mobilities of animate being and inanimate things. The complexity I unpack here considers technologies of filmmaking as sociotechnical assemblages in which 'multiple components play different roles dependent on circumstances, context purpose, needs, affordances, material possibilities, and multiple other contingencies and variables' (Vannini in Jensen, 2022, p. 2). Elsewhere (Tzanelli, 2015), I explored this process under the banner of artistic semio-technologies that release signs in markets hungry for the consumption of what may be perceived as 'authentic'. Enter the Techno-Anthropocene, in which variations of technology condition not just the life we live but also our embodied and disembodied presence in social networks (Jensen, 2022; Tzanelli, 2018a, Chapter 1).

In speaking about process, I will not use Richard Butler's (1980, 2006, 2011) celebrated thesis on the 'Tourism Area Life Cycle', which simply maps in

evolutionary terms the growth, stagnation, decline and fall of a tourism destination. Where I converge with Butler is our mapping of the causes of development, but my epistemological framework and objectives differ significantly from
his: first, I view with suspicion his use of evolutionism, which clashes with my
critical analysis of biopolitics; second, I view tourism mobilities as the symptom of
much broader (than tourism) developmental trends, which bring together what
individual actors do (e.g., hospitality labour) and how this connects to the
imperatives and norms of structural and systemic agents (e.g., nation states and
markets). Here the new spirit of hospitality rears its ugly face by trapping
atmospheric configurations of embodied relations in objects and technologies of
glamour (Thrift, 2010). Otherwise put, at first, the labour of those who catered for
the growing *ZG* tourist market on the island appeared to be an auxiliary
by-product of a movie. However, it would eventually become so vital to the
provision of a specific form of services (*ZG*-inspired sex tourism) that the whole
enterprise would be supported by a capitalisation of affect (Kolehmainen &
Mäkinen, 2021). Only in contemporary renditions of *ZG* tourism mobilities, such
affects have become disconnected again from these sexual subjects, to abstract
placemaking as an enterprise.

Thus, I begin by considering how Greece and Crete in particular developed
their 'network capital' (Larsen & Urry, 2008, p. 93) or tourist 'currency' in
European domains and beyond through successive interpretations of a film, until
the film itself did not dominate as such their promotional strategies. In line with
MacCannell's semiotic interactionism, I intend to show how in these stages, such
strategies were delegated to particular hospitality actors, such as men offering sex
to female tourists: they too were interpreters of the *ZG* phenomenon. Their need
to maintain a sliver of symbolic capital in the capitalist jungle motivated them to
identify with practices of engendering global social relations for Greece as a
tourist destination. Their role in the accruement of emotional, financial and
practical benefit has been significant in the first two phases of *ZG* tourism
development. It may even be argued that they worked as mediators between the
Cretan need to prosper economically and global markets. Their role was, in other
words, not just that of a 'knowing pawn' in the consolidation of the tourist
market's placemaking powers but also its aspiration to turn mobility as such (of
entrenched identity) to a 'government of the market' (Bærenholdt, 2013; Foucault, 1997, 2007, p. 26). Hollinshead's (2009a) thesis and the new mobilities
paradigm (Bærenholdt, 2013; Korstanje, 2017; Lapointe & Coulter, 2020), which
considers how capitalist networks shape the ways tourism is 'done' and therefore
why and how it develops and with what consequences for cultural and political
life through widespread discourses are tools better suited to my analysis than
Butler's model. Both approaches are also in agreement with Giddens's (1991)
approach to self-identity as the product of increased lifeworld structuration in
globalised capitalist networks as this is played out at a personal, and in our case
also interpersonal and global levels (Ashworth & Swatuk, 1998).

Let me apply these ideas: at first, the making of *ZG* was replete with the poetics
of gender, which were used to articulate a Greek politics of belonging to European civilisation and its leisure opportunities, including tourism. Although never

formally colonised by Western colonial powers, Greece experienced an invisible subjection to Western expectations of civility, including in our case the obligation to cater for foreign tourists and adhere to their stereotypical expectations (Herzfeld, 2002). The result in Crete's case has been the elevation of the ordinary poetics of manhood to an internationally mobile ideal of risqué identity (voluntary sexual engagement with foreign female tourists), which 'orientalised' Greekness for practical purposes (Herzfeld, 1985). Such an anthropomorphic development of place identity is common in countries developing a post-colonial national identity and ubiquitously draws on the romantic potential of the border, the hinterland, which is turned into the nation's symbolic centre as tourism and identity scholars argued likewise (Herzfeld, 2005; Hollinshead, 2003). Otherwise put, gender and sexuality begin to serve as a metaphor for blood relations: belonging to the right group of political units in global public spheres. That is why further down the line of this worldmaking process, we will notice a displacement of tourism as a civilising process by structures of hospitality which were in turn informed by frameworks of sensibility (Scribano & Sánchez Aguirre, 2018). Hospitality norms address strangerhood and belonging, activating the biopolitical and technomorphic sorting of identities. When Cretan and other native Greek sexual encounters with foreign female tourists fed into patterns of hospitality, the 'caterers' became more aware of a status inconsistency in their identity vis-à-vis especially that of their female guests. Even further down the line, this awareness would include the fear of personal harm by sexually transmitted disease. This personal fear, which led to yet more changes in the ways a 'masculinised' (that is, European, westernised) Greekness was projected in the tourist marketplace, would continue to collude with the politics of nationalism.

Hence, after *ZG*, Crete, and synecdochally Greece, were subjected to a 'progressive sense of place' (Massey, 1994), through patterned forms of action (Capra, 1997, pp. 7–8) or habits. This involved the operationalisation of an assemblage of ideas of how a place is or should be (DeLanda, 2006; Salazar & Graburn, 2016), a purposeful and strategic gathering of characteristics of 'Cretanness' by different social actors, including the filmmakers, people working in the tourist industry, those flirting with sexual adventure and tourism-related organisations. This assemblage was also affected by representations of identities involved in the making of the film (its primary and secondary heroes and heroines) and those generally defined by their outsidedness to Greek identity (mostly foreign female tourists). The outcome has been a redefinition of Cretan uniqueness through global interactions and mobilities that brought into sharp focus the centrality of gender in Greek identity only to conceal its private core: the fear of exclusion from the revered European centre of world civilisation. Indeed, the fictional Zorba helped Greek and international tourism to assemble a group of mostly transgressive habits associated with intersectional identity (gender, class and ethnicity) and turn them into narratives of authenticity in the marketplace. Habit turned into a souvenir for international tourist clientele that wanted to use this simulacrum of Greek culture as a gateway to a personal transformation – a romantic project that Urry (1990) contrasted to 'mass tourism'. Unlike Urry, I place mass and romantic tourist gazes on a continuum in the middle stages of Zorba-inspired tourism to map placemaking mechanisms.

I used a series of interviews held between 2010 and 2014 by Dr Dimitrios Koutoulas to whom I am indebted for sharing his materials with me. The first two interviews from 2010 were with the creators of *ZG*, that is, the Greek-Cypriot film director Michael Cacoyannis (1922–2011) and the film's score composer Mikis Theodorakis (1925–2021). These structured interviews focused on the making of the film, the social context in which it was shot (1964) as well as its social and economic implications. The interviews helped to construct a clearer picture about the first phase of *ZG*-inspired tourism development. Both artists' contributions to the making of the film eventually connected to the production of an invisible Cretan 'mediated centre' (Couldry, 2000), a bundle of core representations of the island in the form of images and aural signs, mostly revolving around the semiotic potential of the film's central hero.

My reading of the film itself has not been an arbitrary exercise, but one purposely orientated towards its tourist potential, as this was defined by the growing pool of *ZG* tourists. As Rose (2014, pp. 19–20) has stressed, a critical methodology of the image involves careful consideration of three 'sites': that of the image itself (in our case, both Crete as land and landscape and the fictional Zorba hero), the site of its production (Crete as a tourist place) and the sites where this is interpreted by its audiences (for the earlier stages/phases of tourismification, these audiences are purposely reduced to female tourists, not cinematic audiences). Of these three modalities or aspects, I selected the third, which helps us to focus on the social, political and economic relations surrounding the production of the film-image, as well as the institutions involved in it. This social reading enabled me to transition my analysis to the second and third phase of Cretan Greek mobilities. I intentionally removed 'tourism' from this sentence, because when the design of tourism on the island matured, it 'converged' behind a new paradigm of movement of culture, tradition and memory to the marketplace, becoming about more-than-tourism mobilities. This paradigmatic shift from medium-specific content (a novel, a film) towards 'content that flows across multiple media channels, towards the increased interdependence of communication systems, towards multiple ways of accessing media content, and towards ever more complex relations between top-down corporate media and bottom-up participatory culture' (Jenkins, 2008, p. 254) suits better my mobilities approach.

A second round of structured interviews took place in Crete between 2011 and 2014 with veteran tourism industry professionals who witnessed the very beginning of international tourism on the island during the 1960s and the early 1970s. These interviews explored, among others, how *ZG* affected Crete as a tourist destination, as the initial interviews with Cacoyannis and Theodorakis yielded limited information about the tourism impact of the film. This second round of interviews provided a better understanding of *ZG's* contribution to establishing Crete's fame and put the film's impact into perspective with the overall tourist development of the island.

All interviewees were men owing to the dominance of male professionals in senior tourism industry roles at that time. This situation has changed quite dramatically over recent years with the increase in female tourist entrepreneurs and much more women ascending to managerial posts in the hospitality sector (ICAP, 2020). Interviewees included Zacharias and Nikos, both retired hotel managers based in Heraklion, Nikos and Manolis, both hoteliers from Rethymno, as well as Kostas, founder of one of the country's largest hotel groups (last names have been omitted for privacy reasons). Their first-hand testimonies focussed on the impact of *ZG* on Cretan tourism, the profile of the island's first visitors and the advent of large-scale tourism. These interviews yielded qualitative observations that enabled a multivariate analysis of purely quantitative data on the growth of tourism. Aside from the fact that they enabled us to map a continuous growth, they inspired, together with secondary academic research on Greek and Cretan tourism over the same period a phased genealogical model. Much like multidimensional scaling's use in testing hypotheses in tourism studies (Fenton & Pearce, 1988), but unlike its focus on psychological variables, the multimodal method connected individual effects and motivations to macro-sociological questions of social conflict and communitarian violence.

Thus, far from promoting a hard positivist analysis of phased development, I use the Foucaultian notion of market governance of mobilities (Bærenholdt, 2013) as a methodological tool. I use discourse analysis to do justice to the multimodality of the data and explain how my interpretation of the content of individual sets of data contributes to my central thesis on market governance through tourism worldmaking design (Hollinshead, 1999a). I attempt to present a genealogy of such worldmaking imaginaries of place identity for Crete. 'Genealogy' (after Foucault, 1979) suggests exploring the causes and consequences involved in the particular ways Cretan tourism developed over the decades: a transition from how it was affected by to why it was connected to different concerns, including those of sexist prowess and deadly viral mobilities. The phases of assemblage are mapped in distinct ways to examine not just how change followed the usual supply-demand model in film-induced tourism but also examine the implication of global sociocultural, political and biomedical changes on such modifications. I will conclude with some observations on the ways tourism flows intersected with discursive flows on what is considered to be the border and the centre of identity. Such intersections are not studied from a nationalism but a 'tourism imaginary -ies' point of view, as ambivalent repertoires of Cretan and Greek identity, here promoting social change, there regressing to sexist, racist and nationalist visions of belonging to an imaginary West, Europe or global tourism market.

Phase 1: Script, Atmosphere and Tourism Authority

Two of the makers of the film were interviewed during the summer of 2010. Film director Michael Cacoyannis was interviewed in June 2010, about 1 year before he passed away, while the interview with composer Mikis Theodorakis was held one month later. When interviewed, neither Cacoyannis nor Theodorakis had any information to share about Zorba-induced tourism in Greece and on Crete in particular. During the period following the film's release, Theodorakis was busy with his concerts, his seat in Greek parliament for the left-wing EDA party and his presidency at the Lambrakis Youth Movement. He was also travelling to the poorest parts of the country setting up cultural centres. Two years after the release of the film, the military overthrew the Greek government with a coup d'état and Theodorakis, among many others, was imprisoned by the colonels' regime. He was released 4 years later following strong international protests. Even though he did not come across Zorba-inspired tourists in Greece, Theodorakis subsequently met some of them on his international concert tours. He confirmed that there are thousands of people around the world who were inspired to learn the Greek language and history, listen to Greek music, read Greek poetry and visit the country after having watched *ZG*. Cacoyannis, on the other hand, stayed away from Greece for some time, owing to threats against him by some Cretans.

It was difficult to steer interviews with Cacoyannis and Theodorakis towards themes of tourism development, as both focused their answers on the artistic and social aspects of the film. However, filmmaking itself is a form of pilgrimage to the filmed land, which is also both artists' homeland (Tzanelli, 2013a). At this stage, the artists' inheritances undergo radical alterations into hybridised heritage, transforming organic knowledge of place into 'synesthetic narratives': images combined with music in semantic interchanges. Cacoyannis' filmmaking and Theodorakis' music composition should be treated as tertiary revisions of place-memory that draw both on experience and perceived tourist authenticity to relay notions of place/culture (Stiegler, 2011). When examined from this perspective, these interviews can be read as a proto-tourist discourse, a form of worldmaking agency that would eventually feed into Cretan tourism (Hollins-head, 2009a).

Cacoyannis (2010 interview June) recalled how the film was co-financed by himself, Antony Quinn and initially United Artists. However, the latter withdrew, and Twentieth Century Fox stepped in. The deal ensured Cacoyannis absolute artistic freedom to make the movie as he wished. Darryl F. Zanuck of Twentieth Century Fox was ecstatic with this project as it was the first film ever to achieve profitability even before its premiere. It is worth stressing that no Greek authority or private business was involved in financing the production, and nobody had the intent of using the film for promoting tourism. The interviewed tourism industry veterans interestingly noted that before *ZG*, tourism to Crete was of a small scale and limited to affluent and well-educated visitors mostly from Germany and the United States of America coming to the island just for one thing: the archaeo-logical sites of the ancient Minoan civilisation. It was only after the release of Zorba that Crete started to attract sun worshippers and more hedonistically inclined tourists. Theodorakis (2010, interview July) recalled that Cacoyannis asked him to write the soundtrack for Zorba, but it turned out that he needed some music for shooting the dancing scene on the beach. Theodorakis used two existing compositions of this: the slow introduction from his songs *Strōse to strōma sou* and the fast 'Cretan Dance', which he had composed for a ballet some 12 years before, joined together by a bridge. This music was played on the beach for the shooting, but Theodorakis was supposed to replace it with a new piece on the same tempo. It was jointly decided in the studio in Athens, where the artists watched the scene, that the existing music fit perfectly the dance event and decided to keep it.

In an international system of tourist services, blends between Greek Cretan habit and tourist or artistic recollection assembled a grand script of gendered, class and ethnic hierarchy to valorise and exoticise Cretan Greek identity. When I talk about a script, I draw on the ways *ZG's* script promoted Greece's exoticisation in the West, and an entrenched Greek habit of generating gendered and ethnic hierarchies of value at home. On the latter, I draw on Judith Butler's (1990) argument that globally, there is a silent but pervasive agreement on what comprises a sanctioned 'heterosexual matrix'. This matrix is based on what she also calls a 'script', which dictates what passes as acceptable sexual and gendered performance and what is demonised or excluded from society as 'abject' (e.g., ladettes, gay men or lesbians). Humans are socially inculcated in the script: they perform it unconsciously, classifying themselves as male or female. However, Butler's critique of the matrix's heteronormativity is not enough to relay its funnelling in individual tourism performances of joy, nor can it tell us the whole story about the ways tourism markets inflect the script in the form of tourism imaginaries (Salazar, 2009, 2010). As constructivist vehicles of place and belonging, tourist imaginaries not only tend to exceed the fixities of identity but may also lead to its fortuitous stabilisation for profit-making (Salazar, 2013). The movie's valorisation of Cretan Greek identity through the development of Zorba as a character drew on contemporaneous (to its release) debates on masculinity and sexual freedom. Thereafter, the growing *ZG*-inspired tourism in Crete further revised this script to produce a marketable romantic image of gendered Cretan exoticism. This complex alignment between societal norms and values, and national and international tourist markets consolidated the Greek nation's authorial role in tourism (Hollinshead, 2009b; Hollinshead et al., 2009). We should not confuse this with the creative actions of the movie's screenwriter and director, although, admittedly, both were products of their time and projected various social stereotypes in their work unconsciously. Also, movie scripts have to harmonise individual creativity with market demands.

Let us examine the cinematic script and its music, as these informed the first phase of tourism worldmaking. The film is based on the novel of the same title by the Greek author Nikos Kazantzakis (1883–1957). Sadly, there is no space to discuss the intricacies of cinematic adaptation here, but it is important to make two observations: the first concerns the eventual orchestration of Hollywood and tourist industries in selling an exotic version of Greekness to international audiences (Basea, 2015). Thus, in terms of tourism design (Busby & O'Neill, 2006), the film's literary inspiration was demoted to a tool in a process of concerted Orientalisation of place and culture that cannot be attributed to its makers. The second connects to Kazantzakis' interest in relaying in his work Bergsonian notions of 'vital style', the development of an attitude towards life that is as spontaneous as it is inculcated through experience.

The cinematic plot centres around two men: Basil, a soft-spoken intellectual from Britain, who travels to a coal mine on Crete that he inherited, hires Zorba, a

Fig. 1.   The Moment Basil Meets Zorba for the First Time. *Source:* CC BY 2.0, Peter Sigrist, <https://www.flickr.com/photos/psigrist/ 4791438226> via Flickr.

man of all trades, to run the coal mine (*see* Fig. 1). Being constantly challenged by the harsh reality of life and one disaster after another, Basil turns to Zorba for guidance. It is this uneducated man who will show Basil how to overcome his fears and inhibitions to live his life to the fullest (Römhild, 2003). The story culminates in the famous liberating dance to the tunes of *santoúri* (zither or hammered dulcimer) and *bouzoúki* (long necked lute) filmed on the beach of Stavrós, one of the most memorable moments in cinematic history. Cacoyannis turned this simple story into a Greek, rather than Cretan-style philosophical exercise, replete with notions of well-being that we associate with tourism. Both lead actors, Mexican-born Anthony Quinn (1915–2001) as Alexis Zorba and the Briton Alan Bates (1934–2003) as Basil performed their careers' most memorable roles, and the film won three Oscars, including one for Lila Kedrova (1918–2000) in the role of Madame Hortense as Best Supporting Actress. Millions have seen the film; however, even more know its soundtrack and especially 'Zorba's Dance'. Written by the celebrated composer Theodorakis, this emblematic tune became an instant hit and is to this day the most recognisable piece of Greek music.

In an attempt to captivate this Greek-style celebration of life, the film and the music did more than what was intended. As a synaesthetic project that combined music with moving image (i.e., listening and watching to produce a particular appreciation of Cretan Greek character), *ZG's* 'script' brought to life a gendered imaginary of identity. This script was entrenched in everyday Greek socialisation long before the making of the film. The film also invited Western audiences to assume the foreign protagonist's gaze and to exoticise Greece (Basea, 2015). Let us unpack this: the idea of 'well-being' in tourism has been associated with notions of individual fulfilment and collective growth alike (Fennell, 2006). However, its Greek variation, which favours an individualist variation of such philosophies, acquired its own trajectory in the twentieth century, when the country's doors were opened to international tourists. Originally, Greek notions of the good life were mediated through *kéfi* – from Turkish *keyf*, literally state, or individual disposition. *Keyf/kéfi* is an atmosphere of joy, a phenomenological occurrence, the materialist manifestations of which are communicated through embodied rituals.

Here I can return to Kazantzakis' literary interpretation of the work of his academic mentor at Sorbonne, Henri Bergson. Bergson's (1941) thesis in *Creative Evolution* posited *élan vital* or the spontaneous creative force in living organisms, as the main drive for creative growth that leads to higher levels of organisation (Kim, 2017, pp. 181–182). Bergson's focus on laughter translates in Kazantzakis' characterisation of Zorba into *kéfi*, which is relayed in the film to Basil, the alleged 'civilised' recipient, in embodied styles (through dancing). There is a clearer sociological analysis to provide on the significance of such successive forms of 'education' in well-being that connect to my previous observations on place and memory: Ricoeur associates such repertoires with *mémoire-habitude* and sociologist Pierre Bourdieu (1977, 1984) talks about *habit/hexis*, a semi-conscious expression of social identity in linguistic and embodied styles. The term, which cannot be translated accurately in other languages, refers to affects (high spirits, individually experienced eudemonia) externalised in embodied repertoires. Its non-representational/affective qualities can only be communicated through rituals, such as dance, which are nevertheless not identical to this disposition.

In discussing the role of emotions in tourism, Robinson (2012, pp. 33–34) draws on Solomon's (1993, p. 100) observation that emotions structure one's world, while often revealing collective dispositions from an individual perspective. Significantly, Loizos and Papataxiarchis (1991b) note that *kéfi* is part of the practice of male heterosexual self-presentation, 'a state of pleasure wherein men transcend the pettiness of a life of calculation' (Loizos & Papataxiarchis, 1991a, p. 17); 'the spirit of desire that derives from the heart' (Loizos & Papataxiarchis, 1991b, p. 226). A feminist critic would ask who was actually authorised to express desire in the 1960s Greek society, which was yet to experience a culture shock with international tourist mobilities. *Kéfi*, which acknowledged the agency of male desire but punished its female public expressions as 'prostitution' (Lazaridis, 2001, p. 76), had a very ambiguous place in the 1960s Greek society. On the one hand, it was in line with Orthodox sexist nationalism, which thrived under the colonel's junta (1967–1974). On the other, its borderline transgressive ethos opposed the junta's neoconservative agenda, which saw many young men arrested, publicly humiliated and imprisoned by authorities. Many critical artists self-exiled to make art that stayed true to their beliefs, moving with them both entrenched stereotypes and criticism of Greek parochialism (Tzanelli, 2011, Chapter 6). As part of a Mediterranean normative system at the time (Herzfeld, 1980), the dualism of male honour/female shame is negotiated in the film's script in the famous dance scene. The two protagonists' dance performance on an idyllic beach – a quintessential tourist sign – articulates a 'bromance', side-lining female agency: Zorba and Basil become friends of the heart, perhaps a bit too close for the taste of someone who knows nothing about the abrasive mannerisms of Greek machismo friendships. Indeed, Cacoyannis and his peers treaded a fine line between offence and critical representation, by exposing a very real misogynistic attitude in Cretan culture. In contrast to the triumphant reception of *ZG* in the United States of America and across the globe in 1964 and the following years (a reaction conforming to a more general pattern in film-induced tourism development – Beeton, 2006, p. 183), things were different back home. During the shooting, critic Fredie Germanos stressed that 'all Cretans ... wanted the film to be shot in their home village' because it 'will make Crete famous all over the world' (Germanos quoted in Basea, 2015, p. 72). After its release, Greeks, and especially Cretans and the Church, were furious about the way Cretan culture was depicted, particularly in the scenes of the widow's killing and the looting of the dying Madame Hortense (Herzfeld, 2005).

Such reactions, which reiterate the stereotypical script of the hot-blooded native Cretan, match the atmospheric content of the dance routine, making both central to enunciations of romantic travel. Ousby (1990) discussed how the romantic sublime originally involved the development of a highly stylised vocabulary to describe objects of nature and human reactions to them (also Trauer & Ryan, 2005, pp. 484–485). The stylisation of the dance routine is structurally homologous to representations of acts of violence allegedly describing Cretan temper; the two together, help to sublimate the cinematic travel into Greece's Cretan hinterland. The dance routine is the environmental sublime staged in an interactive style. Including the tourist in it as a subject who experiences Cretan-ness, the dance routine conceals the ambivalence of falling in love with a masculinised landscape. The ambivalence of bromance is constitutive of the difficulty to articulate embodied emotions in interpretative styles that neatly differentiate between classificatory playfulness and seriousness in sexual identity – a constant theme in tourism analysis across different cultures (Bruner, 2001; Simoni, 2012; Veijola & Jokinen, 1994).

Transitioning from such representations to embodied travel was not as straightforward. To achieve this, one must return to the role of atmosphere as the roots of a Greek-Cretan imaginary of tourism, which can be objectivised as part of an affective routine (dance, joy), but cannot be captured in perceptive ways as such. The effect this has on a human subject can lead to a 'pathological protest' against it, a counter-discourse of sobriety and seriousness that cancels the original atmosphere's nature (Griffero, 2014, pp. 134–135). This is what Zorba's élan *vital* was destined to become in an increasingly touristified Creta land: an atmospheric rendition of dark heritage, fixed in imaginary renditions of *ZG* landscape: the beach of Stavrós (*see* Fig. 2). Oscillating between a performance site in which

Fig. 2.   The Beach of Stavrós, Akrotíri, Crete. *Source:* CC BY 2.0.
Miguel Virkkunen Carvalho <https://www.flickr.com/photos/
miguelvirkkunen/10409875154> via Flickr.

pasts are re-enacted, and a literary landscape (Rojek, 1993, pp. 136–137), but being neither due to its ethereal quality, Zorbas' *kéfi* would almost literally land on the tables of family tourists as a more authorised script of tourist joy during a visit on Crete. Enter Crete's tourism modernity, which would disperse the value of such black spots across the mushrooming hotels of the island.

First, the lack of relevant statistics from the 1960s makes it quite difficult to quantify the impact of the film on Greek tourism. Data for several years were missing, but Dr Koutoulas kindly attempted to measure key tourism indicators both before and after the premiere of *ZG* (*see* Table 1). The number of international visitors to Greece has been growing constantly since the 1950s. In 1954, there were less than 200,000 tourists coming from abroad, growing by a few tens of thousands each year. In the following years – and after the large international success of several movies that were shot in Greece, mainly *Never on Sunday* (1960, starring Melina Mercouri) and to a lesser extent *Boy on a Dolphin* (1957, starring Sophia Loren) – the pace started to pick up. The largest increase came in 1965 amidst the global Zorba fever. One year later, the international tourist arrivals exceeded for the first time the one-million mark. 1967 was the first year with a decrease in visitors, caused by the military's violent coup d'état to overthrow the Greek government. However, tourist numbers quickly recovered in the following years (with the exception of 1974, a year of political turmoil in Greece and a war in Cyprus) and kept growing throughout the 1980s.

Table 1. International Tourist Arrivals in Greece During the Period
1954–1990.

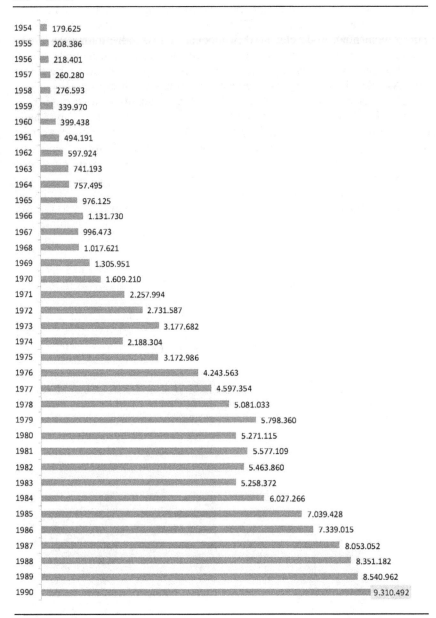

Year	Arrivals
1954	179.625
1955	208.386
1956	218.401
1957	260.280
1958	276.593
1959	339.970
1960	399.438
1961	494.191
1962	597.924
1963	741.193
1964	757.495
1965	976.125
1966	1.131.730
1967	996.473
1968	1.017.621
1969	1.305.951
1970	1.609.210
1971	2.257.994
1972	2.731.587
1973	3.177.682
1974	2.188.304
1975	3.172.986
1976	4.243.563
1977	4.597.354
1978	5.081.033
1979	5.798.360
1980	5.271.115
1981	5.577.109
1982	5.463.860
1983	5.258.372
1984	6.027.266
1985	7.039.428
1986	7.339.015
1987	8.053.052
1988	8.351.182
1989	8.540.962
1990	9.310.492

Source: National Statistics Service of Greece; Greek National Tourism Organisation; Tzanelli
and Koutoulas (2021).

These growing visitor numbers exceeded the average growth rate of international tourism, explaining the rapid rise of the country's market share. Greece amounted to just 0.58% of all international tourist arrivals in 1960. Its market share rose to a record high of 2.2% in 1985 (*see* Table 2). As other countries gained momentum in developing their inbound tourist traffic during the 1990s, Greece's market share started to slip. Evidence portrays Crete as an undeveloped tourist destination, amounting to just 1,392 hotel beds in 1964, the year *ZG* was shot. As pointed out during the interviews with tourism industry veterans, only a small number of Cretan hotels were of Western standards with *en suite* bathrooms. Rhodes, the leading Greek island destination at the time, had a hotel capacity thrice as large as Crete's, yet only 5.8% of the country's total, as most hotels were operating on the Greek mainland (*see* Table 3). That the two films – *Never on Sunday* and *ZG* – were released over this period is not coincidental, but the first major contingency I map in our analysis.

To further elaborate on sociocultural transformation, I need to ascertain what these internationally acclaimed films shared, given their contribution to tourism growth (Tzanelli, 2011). Again, this can be traced back to the embodiment of Greek land-as-landscape for cinematic afficionados, who would soon turn into actual tourists to the country. *Never on Sunday's* narrative arc reversed *ZG's* lesson of spiritual and embodied emancipation. Where Basil is educated in *kéfi* by Zorba, Ilya, a self-employed, free-spirited sex worker, who lives in the port of Piraeus, is subjected by Homer, an American tourist and classical scholar to a compulsory education into restraint and literacy in all things ancient, including the Apollonian habitus of philosophical contemplation. The fact that Ilya is a woman, who celebrates her sexuality, matches the global script of gendered-as-

Table 2. International Tourist Arrivals in Greece as a Percentage of All International Tourist Arrivals Worldwide During the Period 1960–1995.

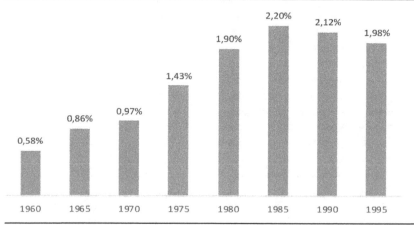

Source: Calculation based on data by UNWTO; National Statistics Service of Greece; Greek National Tourism Organisation; Tzanelli and Koutoulas (2021).

Table 3. Hotel Bed Capacity in Greece, on Crete and on Rhodes.

	Total Greece	Crete	Rhodes	Share of Crete	Share of Rhodes
1964	71.741	1.392	4.174	1,9%	5,8%
1971	135.377	6.440	12.882	4,8%	9,5%
1972	151.420	8.092	15.977	5,3%	10,6%
1973	166.552	9.332	17.233	5,6%	10,3%
1974	175.161	10.079	17.393	5,8%	9,9%
1975	185.275	11.456	18.100	6,2%	9,8%
1976	213.431	15.887	19.595	7,4%	9,2%
1977	231.979	19.574	21.852	8,4%	9,4%
1978	247.040	22.831	23.344	9,2%	9,4%
1979	265.552	26.817	25.661	10,1%	9,7%
1980	278.045	30.509	27.192	11,0%	9,8%
1981	285.988	33.913	30.137	11,9%	10,5%
1982	311.089	38.370	31.243	12,3%	10,0%
1983	318.515	40.068	31.249	12,6%	9,8%
1984	333.816	44.822	32.055	13,4%	9,6%
1985	348.394	48.331	33.594	13,9%	9,6%
1986	359.377	50.543	37.188	14,1%	10,3%
1987	375.367	53.625	39.661	14,3%	10,6%
1988	395.812	63.293	40.334	16,0%	10,2%
1989	423.790	71.634	42.875	16,9%	10,1%
1990	438.355	77.678	45.059	17,7%	10,3%

Source: National Statistics Service of Greece; Greek National Tourism Organisation; Tzanelli and Koutoulas (2021).

civilisational hierarchy: whereas it is fine for an illiterate working-class man to instruct an English tourist, a female working-class woman can only be 'put in her place' by them (Skeggs, 2004). A gender order (women are inferior to men – Connell, 1987, 1995) was superimposed on the heterosexual matrix of Greek society (women are supposed to behave in particular ways to be accepted as 'decent').

Again, we notice how place assumes anthropomorphic gendered qualities that feed into its network capital in rather complicated patterns. Equally important is the fact that Ilya represents a lateral connection to Greece's disreputable cultural heritage: an embodied habitual narrative of music-dance directly descending from Asia Minor refugee lowlifes that populated the Athenian centre after the massive population exchange between Greece and Turkey in the 1920s. Ilya's *zeibékiko* habitus, drinking and chain-smoking were associated with Greece's crypto-Islamic habitus, as this was acquired during centuries of contact between Ottoman Turks and Greek Asia Minor communities (Tzanelli, 2011). Ilya's whole being is nothing short of a fall from the grace of Europe, a symbolic return to ethnic nature in need of sculpting by an educated English tourist.

Although, inversely, in *Boy on a Dolphin*, the *feminine mystique* is romanticised as the eventual guardian of ancient Greek culture, its association with prostitution persists. The heroine of the movie, Phaedra (Sophia Loren), a poor Greek sponge diver on the island of Hydra, and her boyfriend, Rhif (Jorge Mistral), an immigrant from Albania, on whose boat she works, are still representative of Greek identity's abject margins: female, ethnic, migrant and working class. Phaedra's initial decision to flog to the antiquities market an ancient statue she fishes out of the deep sea suggests vulgarity and lack of loyalty to the Greek spirit – something resolved by the eventual homecoming of the finding to the island community at the end of the film. The arc suggests that an unscrupulous outsider, who tours the Greek island interior (Victor Parmalee [Clifton Webb], who is an aesthete dealing in historic artefacts) is ready to plunder Greek heritage à la Elgin. Significantly, this heritage involves not only antiquities but also sponge-diving (an embodied craft destined to join the tourist souvenir trade mostly associated with men, rather than women), the atmospheric background of the sea (that would transform into a symbol of bodily freedom, unrestrained sociality and sexual experimentation for foreigners) and an artistic parable of nature-as-culture (a boy and a dolphin) (Tzanelli, 2018a). Where Mercouri sang the high-impact *Ta paidiá tou Peiraiá* ('The children of Piraeus') that tourists loved, Loren dubbed *Ti'nai aftó pou to léne agápi* ('What is this thing they call love') in an underwater sequence as an ode to her love for an ancient Greek treasure to the same end.

The shared arcplot across the three films is more evident now: it involves the atmospheric element of Greek identity, which is phenomenologically associated with its marine environments and allegedly unmediated relationship between them and their human inhabitants. The latter feature as the embodiment of this heritage – or we may say instead that they are the carriers of an axiological form of inheritance of Greekness (Tzanelli, 2013a). Sea, sun and coastal landscape become parts of a particular experience of the Greek-Cretan aura, which is mediated to tourists through the embodied rituals of Zorba, Phaedra and Ilya. Endowed with an 'attitude of expectation', this auratic/atmospheric transfer makes joy/heritage not just an interpersonal event (Rauch, 2018, p. 71) but also a possibility to connect human subjects (tourists) to native environments in a meaningful way. I return to this issue in the fourth phase of *ZG* tourism design. Needless to add, that where such possibilities open up the gaze of tourists to visited destinations, markets see opportunities and natives may see threat and risks. The subplot of Greek heritage/inheritance's somatic spoliation by deceitful foreigners in tourism was yet to take shape in the following stage of film-tourism development on Crete. That these three films would change the place of Greece in international civilisational recognition, transforming it into an essentialised agent in tourism business, is the least controversial part of the development. The phantom of embodied heritage would insert an emotional element of gendered adventure/risk in this political complexity, with far-reaching consequences.

Phase 2: Lovemaking as Placemaking

Heritage, inheritance and property would go hand in hand in the second phase of Cretan tourism development. Their complicity with capitalist expansion is well documented in sociologically informed economic theory, which suggests that those with access to land always secure a head start in development and a cushion in difficult times (Piketty, 2014). Thus, cinematically recorded elements of Cretan-Greek memory entered a complex web of capitalist transactions that translated them into landscape, and then land-as-property: literally, a plot to buy or rent. Regardless of their hostility towards the film, the Cretans were the main beneficiaries of the film's tourism impact. What used to be land unsuitable for agriculture became very expensive and highly sought-after plots for building seaside hotels and restaurants. Many farmers became workers in the tourism sector or opened their own businesses such as souvenir shops, holiday apartments, bars and tavernas. The money spent by millions of tourists on Crete each year brought prosperity to the island, making it one of the country's wealthiest regions. *ZG* remained popular for many years, establishing Crete as a fashionable destination for generation after generation of tourists.

It may be argued that the film did not really succeed in selling topographic particularity to tourists, in that even its famous dance routine was never physically placed on the map by tourist industries. Usually, filmed locations (Stavrós in Akrotíri in *ZG's* case) are widely advertised by the tourist industry to attract film fans (Croy, 2010). Nobody in the industry expected from *ZG* to project anything accurate about Cretan culture and people; what mattered was that it succeeded in authorising tourist agencies to treat the island more like an empty supra-modern entity: a non-place. 'Non-places' are vestiges of capitalism, because their normative and semiotic core remains pliable to the needs of customer demand (Augé, 2008). It can be argued that non-places develop a life parallel to real places, and often become parasitic upon them, because they borrow from, and shuffle their more durable characteristics and inheritances (Hollinshead, 1998a). This observation connects to my original reference to placemaking as an exercise in assemblage, but focusses on the problematic aspects of such development, if it prioritises capitalist accumulation instead of local well-being.

Because the first phase of tourism development was anchored on the development of the film's central character, location was superseded by the atmospheric characteristics that the film represented. Otherwise put, when Zorba's character became the primary atmospheric locus for tourist industries, location (*tópos*) was replaced with the ways human nature moves in particular directions: it transformed into *trópos* (attitude and intentional movement) (Tzanelli, 2018a). Where topological analysis adheres to a spatial logic, tropological considerations adopt a temporal one, which vies to assert how the arrow of time (progression towards Western European modernity) affects the practice of heritage-based tourism (Kirschenblatt-Gimblett, 1997). This deviation exposes the alleged ethnic style of experience a visitor can have as a potentially marketable product in consumption domains, such as those of film and tourism ('selling native style off to the higher bidder' while hiding the ignominy the native seller experiences – Tzanelli, 2018a,

p. 11). Marx would have approached this as the stripping of the aura from the subject's being in the world: the seller stands naked in front of bidders that appropriate his/her existence (Berman, 2010, pp. 105–107, pp. 115–116).

The dancing Zorba offered an alternative route to affective atmospheres through what Malbon (1999) calls 'ecstasy', an extension of land to the human subject's embodied externality and psychic internality. Malbon's study attributed to the dancing body that attunes to the qualities of association: listening to music and performing rhythmical movement reproduces a special sensation that is unconsciously shared while experienced. Down the line of reflective engagement, rhythmical movement's extensive qualities usually act as community-building mechanisms (Malbon, 1999, pp. 73–74). The idea of studying embodied capital so as to incorporate the other's exotic 'essence' is a quintessential component of atmospheric consumption when sexual attributes and ethnic characteristics can cater for the same experience. Not only is embodied sensuality valuable as an oriental fantasy but it also endows the Western tourist/apprentice's unlimited desire with 'deep generative energies' (Said, 1978, p. 188). Enter tourist modernity, thanks to the depiction of a local 'Jack of all trades' by a Mexican actor: Quinn's entirely fictional cinematic interpretation of a generic Greek lust for life would just enable the stylisation of Cretan memory in souvenir ways over several decades (Eisner, 1991). Especially female tourists started visiting the unexplored Greek islands in search of this 'commodity', hoping for a spiritual escape or just a brief affair with a Zorbaesque character. Unsurprisingly, many Greek men willing to engage in paid or unpaid casual sex were quick to respond to this trend by offering what these women were looking for (Swarbrooke et al., 2003).

The Zorbaesque character's transgressive attitude would shape and be shaped by the female tourist's desire to experience the 'edge' in emotional (*Kéfi*) and physical styles (picking an ideal lover for her holiday – Ryan and Hall, 2001, p. 60). As the era of sexual liberation, the 1960s saw women stepping out of the household and being authorised (by the tourist industry and the hosting nation state) to access roles previously monopolised by men. In Greek tourist settings, this newly acquired female agency generated new contexts of hospitality supply involving the emergence of a particular type of sexualised host known as *kamáki* (literally 'harpoon'). It has been well-documented (Zinovieff, 1991) that female European travellers started visiting Greece for enjoying brief sexual encounters during their summer holidays by liaising with these kamákia. These 'Greek lovers' have been a mainstay of Greek tourism for most of the 1970s and 1980s, also leading to a significant number of mixed marriages and the settling of European women in Greek tourist areas. Gendered hierarchies were replaced with ethnic and class inequalities, which would eventually feed back to global social hierarchies. In the case of Zorba-led consumption, notions of Greek landscape as a tourist commodity became tightly intertwined with the Greek male body that was available for sexual objectification (Veijola & Valtonen, 2007). The three-minute dance scene at the end of the film is still perceived by millions of people around the world as the quintessence of Greece, embodying the wild beauty of the Greek islands, the spirit of the people living on them and their zest for life.

Known as *sirtáki* (diminutive of *sirtós*, or 'dragged'), the Zorba dance evolved into an odourless staged authenticity for tourists, which would be performed in the tavernas that began to bourgeon in Crete and elsewhere, as well as during Greek nights in hotels organised for tourists. Though this decade marks the turning point in the image-based atmospheric genesis of touristified Greece (Papadimitriou, 2000), the ritual has survived into the twenty-first century (Banio & Malchrowicz-Mósko, 2019; Dawe, 2008, pp. 18, 231). Zorba's instantly recognisable earworm tune triggered these stereotypical perceptions – even in the minds of people who haven't seen the film – wherever and whenever the melody would be played. With an estimated 50 million record sales and innumerable recordings by artists from around the world, 'Zorba's Dance' has itself become a tourism ambassador for Greece (Koutoulas, 1998).

As a traditional form of Greek dance associated with Greek island heritage stretching back to antiquity, *sirtós* originally featured a spatial segregation of gendered performance, with men and women dancing in rows. The Zorba-inspired variant produced a different form of community-bonding, suitable for participants in the tourist *communitas*, who looked for 'peak experiences' (Graburn, 1983a, pp. 13–14). Dancing the Zorba *sirtós* supported fewer rigid flows of movement, which both referred to Cretan habit-memory and transformed it into a souvenir accessible to women. Indeed, in tourist settings, the Zorba *sirtáki* would often be performed under conditions of alcohol-induced stupor that countered traditional spatialised gender orders, encouraging the mingling of sexes and flirting. Foreign female tourists were visiting Greece to experience a sensual and emotional edge, involving sexual collaboration with a selected partner for as long as they pleased (Newmahr, 2011). What had first led in the context of *ZG* tourismification to a topological eradication (Crete would be replaced by Greece) would further devolve into a tropological 'undoing' of Greek unwritten laws in gender performance – a change to which the *kamákia* willingly contributed.

Refracting this nexus of tourism/hospitality through sexual agency placed *kamákia* in a very ambivalent position: as fully employed as sex workers, it threatened their share in perceptions of dominant masculinity, which continued to define tropes of Greek identity. This ambivalence has been observed in other national contexts of sexualised hospitality provision, in which men, customarily regarded as superior to women, were placed in the position of carers for female strangers looking for sexual gratification (Bowman, 1996, p. 3; Cohen, 1986, p. 126; Simoni, 2016). If *kamákia* were men engaging in casual sex, therefore still potentially dominant Alpha-males, the reality of women's sexual liberation in more developed countries still challenged their position in the gender order: they could claim sexual prowess but were still part of a 'backward society' willingly objectifying itself for tourists. In such interstitial spaces, citizenship claims cannot be made on the basis of disempowerment: to admit subordinance is equivalent to public humiliation. The traditional role of women in these host societies, which are structured on overlaps between sexist and nationalist values, is supposed to be inferior to men.

It is significant that Greek *kamákia* were men of low social standing: their low status in Greek society matched their internationally recognised role as paid or unpaid sex providers (Tzanelli, 2011, pp. 134–135). Research highlighting the need to support women's participation 'in broader community relations outside those of the extended family household and into tourism sectors has a clear place in debates on fair distribution of opportunities and the critique of commodity fetishism' (Mowforth & Munt, 2016, pp. 66–67; Ateljevic & Doorne in Jamal, 2019, p. 78). However, the ambivalent agential role in sex trade – as oft-voluntary contributors to market exploitation – together with the symbolic threat they posited to traditional family mores turns them into a sui generis precarious category. With these complexities of status in mind, one can only conclude that their intersectional interpellation does not apply only to Greek social trans-formations in the long twentieth century: it is the outcome of a universalised hierarchy of valuing and knowing (Porter et al., 2021), initially connected to embodied performances of masculinity in Greece (Cowan, 1990) and elsewhere (Knox & Hannam, 2007) but progressively to regimes of cinematic and digital representation in most international tourist destinations. Lack of recognition as hospitality labour cuts across hierarchies of work where tourismification happens rapidly and with little planning or care for those carrying it emotional burn, Córdoba Azcárate (2020) attests in her case study on the thoughtlessness of tourism design in Cancún, the Yucatan Peninsula in Mexico. But how does the plight for presence and advocacy really meet the right to fair representation (Jamal, 2019, pp. 84–86)? Above all, what does this really mean in practice?

Siegfried Schmidt's integrated media thesis reminds us that particular semantic effects, which are hard to 'measure' across and with particular forms of media are structured at the 'technological level' (Schmidt, 2011). The latter refers to the availability of technology, whereas the former warns us that even when certain populations may be able to interpret their semiotic potential (they possess digital literacy – Pangrazio et al., 2020), they remain powerless. The Greek *kamákia's* basic cinematic literacy was a skill and a curse, as the actual hospitality contexts of their embodied labour structured them as objects/signs. Their cinematically determined labour interpellated them as a liminal sexual category in an imaginary gender order of transnational mobilities, in ways that echoed gendered orders in other world polities that had not escaped the double standards of crypto-colonisation (Herzfeld, 2002). For example, there is ample evidence that in international markets, Sri Lankan hierarchies of cultural value structure gendered agency in relation to technology as a form of skilled education. Female travel writers who are (self-)employed in the private sector of digital journalism, trade their Sri-Lankan identity in the private sphere of the family for an ethics of individualism, which trades a fine line between conformism and normative rebellion. This brand of individualism appeals to Western understandings of professional conduct in the public spheres of cross-cultural exchange without 'betraying' family loyalties (Tzanelli & Jayathilaka, 2021). Unlike the Greek *kamákia*, whose working-class positioning excluded them from the publicness of Greek 'high culture', such Sri Lankan female professionals turn their techno-logical craft into a mark of civility by schematising narratives of their country's heritage in tourism mobilities (Jayathilaka, 2020).

Approached from such a comparative perspective, gender and sexuality acquire in *ZG's* tourism worldmaking the qualities of a cosmetic cosmopolitan manifesto (Nederveen Pieterse, 2006) in which the desire to be heard and seen as a 'citizen of the world' connects in crypto-colonial contexts to technologies of glamour. It helps to reiterate that the actual source of such technologies of glamour and fascination are a metropolitan project (see Introduction). Despite (or perhaps because of) their political commitment to a leftist imaginary of society, neither Cacoyannis nor Theodorakis ever asserted an autobiographical solidarity with rural identities in their creative projects – these served mainly the sources of romantic sublimation we identify in Zorbas' know-how agency. Working either from the Athenian centre or from European metropolitan outposts, such as Paris, both creative agents sustained a proto-geodesic poetics of presence for Crete, so that Greekness, rather than Cretan-ness 'travels the world' and invites foreigners to its hearth. In this respect, we may see in the *ZG* cinematic tourism mobilities an example of a cluster of projects. These projects manage the public face of provincial 'exopolitanisms', such as the one generated by Cretan tourism outposts.

We are talking about economies of worth then (Sayer, 2011, p. 173, 235) – or, rather, the effects their schematisation in new media landscapes has on those striving to be recognised as worthy of public attention (Honneth, 2007). By this I refer to the realist outcome that the construction of mediation ended up having on the ways sex labour responded to the calls to act as a collective civil agent with no real power (for, is this practically possible?). *Kamákia's* lack of real agency in what we may call 'primary intermediality' (i.e., their inability to change the social effects of cinematic products such as *ZG*) manifested in the interrelation between the film's stereotypical aesthetic forms (the uncouth but sexually arousing Zorba) and the ad hoc encounters of sex workers with tourists. This 'secondary intermediality' (Neumann & Zierold, 2010, p. 106) triggered a new techno-Anthropomorphic cycle, in which the disempowered *kamákia* granted themselves with a voice and agency in the private sphere of sexual intimacy in which they were trapped in rather problematic styles. Hence, quite often, the Greek *kamákia* would express their frustration towards the superiority of European civilisation, as this was reflected in female tourism mobilities, by deceiving their casual lovers or treating them roughly (Moore, 1995; Zinovieff, 1991), thus extracting symbolic vengeance 'as members both of an underprivileged social and economic class and a subordinate European country' (Tsartas and Galani-Moutafi, 2009, p. 309).

The demand for Zorba's rough and direct style helped local men to negotiate a sliver of empowerment in the 1970s context of tourist mobilities at home. Trading primary intermedial structures for their body, which could exert violence on foreigners (copulation), allowed for a modification of *ZG's* secondary intermedial effects in the private sphere of friendship and labour camaraderie. Indeed, the erotic seems to be a ubiquitous strategy in the generation of agency, where national and international systems divest people of their civic presence. Sheller's (2012) work on post-slavery Jamaica, post-independence Haiti and the wider Caribbean reveals a similar interplay between the state, the body, race and sexuality. 'Citizenships from below' are formed in these alternative spaces of alleged indecency in transgressive styles, allowing the significatory power of the body to rectify a crisis of presence with a game of representation. As informal 'hosts', the Greek *kamákia* freely drew on *ZG's* 'script-come-imaginary of Cretan-ness' to craft their own performances of intimacy, which simultaneously protected their own experience of place as a secondary intermedial space of carnal and sensual interaction. By turn, this allowed them to interpret this space as the domain of self-serving commodification through their embodied acts of sex-making (Trauer & Ryan, 2005, p. 482). However, the new 1980s health scare would remove this cushion, positing new challenges for Greek tourism and the Greek *kamákia*.

Phase 3: Small Worldmaking and the (Bio)Politics of Care

Tourist consumptions of place as memory are often assembled around conceptions of care (Bærenholdt et al., 2017, pp. 32–35). In humanist geography, Tuan (1996, p. 455) discussed the tourist's emotional investment in experiencing destinations by stressing the importance of time. Hollinshead and Suleman's (2018) 'worldmaking instillations' suggest that such investment is achieved in tourism with not only the development of nets of human relations but also the instillation – and phantasmagoric *installation* by tourist and other cultural industries (Böhme, 2017; Jansson, 2002; Rojek, 1998) – of symbols generating emotional fields. Such investments bring to the fore the importance of temporal stretches: seldom do we invest in shallow experience for long, if at all. I will reverse Tuan's thesis to examine how the host's investment in Crete's Zorba-inspired place image ended up producing a more reflexive discourse on self-care. Drawing on tropes of risk aversion that actually masked nationalist tropes of moral pollution and danger (Canguilhem, 1991), the Greek *kamákia* began to set their own physical welfare against the sexual demands and desires of international female guests. The third phase of Zorba-inspired tourism in Crete and elsewhere in Greece saw significant overlaps between the affective dimensions of hospitality and biomedical risks stemming from the emergence of a new global threat to sexual liberation: AIDS.

For decades, sex and love have been booming sectors in tourism, with all sexes and genders looking for suitable destinations to enjoy erotic adventures (Dicken & Laustsen, 2004). Where Thailand, for example, catered for middle-aged male tourists by providing young female brides (Cohen, 2003), countries such as Cuba and Greece developed a thriving business for men selling romance and sex to female tourists (Simoni, 2012, 2016). Drawing a line between these two affective domains is a minefield, mainly because ludic and romantic motivations in tourism mobilities can, on occasion, overlap, depending on the sociocultural profile of the traveller and other circumstances that we cannot measure or know. Importantly in our case, love does not just connect to a bundle of romantic experiences during one's travel, it defines travel: making love in novel environments, free from the inhibitions of familiar contexts, writes Fussell (1980, p. 113), *acts as a motivation to travel*. Generally speaking, romance and excess are a privilege for tourists in tourist destinations, not locals and workers, as labour needs to put up a good act and be watchful hosts for all eventualities (Singh, 2019, pp. 93–94).

Greece was a very conservative society in the 1960s, so to accept that it is fine for Greek men to have brief affairs with foreign female tourists as long as they marry and create families with Greek women later in their life was not uncommon. If this marriage involved the female guest, it socially *normalised* their strangerhood, by turning them into wives and mothers. At the same time, there was money to be made from foreign female tourists with sexual appetites. During this period, Crete and other Greek islands established themselves as places of tolerance and sexual liberation for holidaymakers, a development frequently depicted in popular culture as in the case of the American film *Summer Lovers* from 1982 and the British production of *Shirley Valentine* from 1989 (Wickens, 2002). Nudism and topless bathing were a widespread – and mostly non-sexualised – practice throughout the Greek islands, whereas Mykonos became a haven for gay holidaymakers at a time when homosexuality was still widely considered a deviating lifestyle in Europe and the United States of America.

Regardless, catering for love on Crete necessitated infrastructural support: airy suites, comfortable beds, swimming pools and bars to serve as flirting venues and so forth. All interviewed tourism industry veterans stressed that besides Zorba's tourism-inducing impact, the European tour operators facilitated Crete's tourist boom of the 1970s and 1980s. Tour operators provided the required airlift capacity on their charter flights with millions of seats for connecting the island with numerous European cities. They even financed the construction of hotels on the island due to an acute shortage in room capacity especially in the early 1970s. However, they soon gained enormous market influence and forced an oligopsony on Cretan tourist businesses (Koutoulas, 2006), with one interviewee (Zacharias) commenting that tour operators had a 'colonial attitude' towards Cretan businesses that enforced low prices on accommodation and other tourist services. This intervention of European tour operators starting during the early 1970s launched a period of rapid growth for the Cretan hotel sector, with hotel room capacity doubling every 5 years. The island's tourist accommodations developed at a much faster pace than on Rhodes and in the rest of the country, also thanks to the boost provided by *ZG*. From controlling only 1.9% of the total Greek hotel room capacity back in 1964, Cretan hotels came to command 17.7% of the country's capacity with a room count of 77,678 in 1990, thus dramatically outperforming both the Greek mainland and Rhodes (compare Table 1 with Table 3).

Once the increased hotel bed capacity was in place, tourism traffic to Crete took off, also in conjunction with the introduction of direct charter flights from European cities. Thousands of sun-seeking North and West Europeans swarmed the island in search of Zorba, golden beaches and Crete's fascinating history. In 1970, 732,646 overnight stays were registered at the island's hotels, and by the early 1990s, these would surpass the 10-million mark (*see* Table 2 *and* Table 5). Crete overtook Rhodes in 1982 and established itself as the country's most frequented destination, accounting for one in five hotel stays made in Greece since 1990. These figures can be considered as evidence of how *ZG* contributed to catapult Crete to the top of Greek tourist destinations. The high consumer awareness of Crete globally and the desire of many people to follow in the footsteps of Zorba made the film a catalyst for the island's success. Unfortunately, no further secondary data are available from these decades. However, it would be quite safe to assume that several millions among the holidaymakers visiting Greece during the 1960s, 1970s and 1980s were inspired to make this trip after watching the movie.

The previously mentioned interviews conducted between 2011 and 2014 with veteran hotel owners and managers in Crete show a rising trend in family and couple visits after the late 1980s and the AIDS scare. The island's hedonistically oriented tourist clientele – mostly female visitors from Nordic countries – was gradually substituted by more mainstream 'sea 'n' sun' travellers from the same origin countries. To use a well-worn cliché, Crete, once known as a popular 4S destination (with the 4S standing for 'sun, sand, sea and sex' – Marques, 2016) has mostly dropped the last 'S' since the 1990s.

This qualitative change in visitor profile merits explanation: in the second phase of Zorba-inspired tourism development, I examined how the projection of Greek *kamákia's* resentful agency ensured that, what was lost on the macro-social level (lack of symbolic power over their more civilised sexual partner leading to symbolic 'loss' of masculinity) would be gained on the micro-social level. Often, *kamákia* could exchange spicy stories about their sexual exploits and belittle their lovers to peers. The onset of incurable viral mobilities associated with sexually transmitted diseases in tourist settings would replace such patterns of imaginary revenge with solid political action. The growing number of infections by the HIV virus and several AIDS-related deaths of Greek celebrities in 1987 quickly created awareness of this threat in Greek society. The sudden realisation that casual sex can kill resulted in the withdrawal of the *kamákia* from the 'game' and brought this phenomenon to an abrupt end. Another development limiting nudism and especially topless bathing during the early 1990s was the health scare associated with skin cancer caused by long exposure to the sun (Hobson & Dietrich, 1995).

The shift to couple and family-centred tourism overlaid sex-orientated consumption of Cretan/Greek place identity with a different form of intimacy based on consanguinity or kinship. The Cretan backdrop was now used to reinforce personal inter-relationships, side-lining the otherness of the host, in favour of memories which were family-made or produced by more enduring couple relationships during holiday time (Trauer & Ryan, 2005, p. 483). Therefore, the third phase of Zorba tourism development was dominated by a double interpretation of biopolitical progress, which steered the arrow of time in ways compatible with established Greek *habitude*/heritage. On the one hand, by 'biopolitics' I refer to the management of human life and social identity by centres of power, which, in the case of tourism splits between the nation-state (Hollinshead's (2009a) conception of 'tourism authority') and market networks that operate in non-centrally controlled ways (Bærenholdt's (2013) 'governmobilities' and Lapointe and Coulter's (2020) 'labour (im) mobilities'). This sort of biopolitics did disservice to *kamákia*, by ignoring their welfare needs, where the provision of sex services was their livelihood rather than a 'sport'. The second version of biopolitics sought to rectify this inconsistency in problematic ways, because it did not eliminate the gendered script (and thus tourism imaginary) from its strategic development. The intrinsic knowledge of class-based injustice was suppressed in these demands, even though professional and casual *kamákia* were aware of the fact that in an increasingly bourgeoisified society, catering for international tourists affected their social opportunities (see Sheller, 2009 on a similar case of tourismification versus human rights).

The withdrawal of hospitableness in the form of romantic love or sex made space for the development of new fields of sex care. Tropes and practices of self-identity (Giddens, 1991) introduced a new dynamic in placemaking, which fostered new conflicts between the *ZG*-inspired travelling partnerships of *kamákia* and their prospective lovers as outsiders to Greek national decency on the one hand, and the overarching discourse of family travel networks and the symbolic Greek nation-family on the other (Trauer & Ryan, 2005, p. 490). And to return to the centrality of affect in the consolidation of the new spirit of hospitality, one may have to concede that all atmospheres are dynamic interpersonal configurations that can be harnessed to serve new, collective in our case objectives (Sumartojo & Pink, 2018, pp. 3–4). Lack of nourishment transforms fields of care into minefields of conflict.

However, collective affective labour produces its own alternative imaginaries 'that do not attach agency to unidirectional and straightforward processes alone' (Kolehmainen & Mäkinen, 2021, p. 450). Indeed, as affective agency circulates between technologies of glamour, such as those of moviemaking, and biopolitical technologies harnessed by central institutions, such as the nation-state, its micro-social, interpersonal qualities begin to mediate the grand projects of post-modernity (Harvey, 1989). There are good reasons Iris Marion Young ([1990] 2011) situated injustice between the sites of oppression and domination, as both sites overlap with the relationships established between and among nations and states. To be clearer here, the *kamákia's* response to the risks born by their material conditions never challenged the national centre's policies: instead, it directed the hatred to female tourists. By blending physical biomedical risks (AIDS infection) with the 'parasitological' discourse of national purity (on guests as parasites, and hence outsiders, see Veijola et al., 2014, p. 43), the *kamákia* did not challenge the post-Fordist ethos that dominates contexts of tourismification around the world – something that enhances status and labour insecurity.

Directing affective action against the tourist reinforced the sexist ethos of Greek national identity, which uses tropes of masculine empowerment to achieve recognition in international spheres of political engagement (Tzanelli, 2006, 2008). This ethos hides a process of deep intersectional layering of identity-building, whereby Greece as a country and a culture are institutionally reduced to an abstracted agent willing to do anything to transcend their historical-material conditions. Historically interpellated as a de-civilised culture, subjected to successive forms of foreign control (Ottoman and European) and subsequently economically disenfranchised, the Greek nation-state would do anything to be regarded as a successful tourist state in Europe and beyond. There is a structural isomorphism between the *kamákia's* response to risk and the Greek nation-state's response to the danger of being demoted to a pollutant of European purity of affective nature, which brings to mind Minca's (2007, pp. 82–83) reading of Agamben as a spatial ontologist. As the original sphere of sovereignty, the bare life/body of humans desiring to be constituted as citizens becomes the first surface of inscription for their political communities, which lack international validation by an imaginary authority/community (Europe, the West).

Kamákia's affective action resembles retrogressive forms of collective action we find in repertoires of organised social movements (Touraine, 1995). When placed in the grand scheme of modernity, such movements begin to communicate with nationalist action (Delanty & O'Mahony, 2002) as well as other funda-mentalist renditions of identity (Eisenstadt, 1998, 1999). Consolidated on ideas of heritage and ownership, such action also bears all the characteristics of what Herzfeld (2019) called 'subversive archaism'. This is a repertoire of performative acts that challenge the moral authority of modern Western variations of bureaucratic power. Not only are they connected both to the workings of the state and tourism markets but they also remain closely related to the ways the latter construct and circulate normative discourses on middle-class orderliness and style as homological to the systemic ethos of capitalism (Harvey, 2006). Ultimately, the *kamákia's* affective labour began to inflect the grand projects of a post-crypto-colonisation, masqueraded as social stratification through artistic refinement, regimes of self-care and a general maintenance of bodily health (Giddens, 1990; Herzfeld, 2005).

Overall, the *kamákia's* affective labour would partake in non-planned, on-site *and* digital capitalisations on 'Greek exoticism'. We can trace Crete's Zorbaesque '*exopolis*' in their affective labour, rather than directly attribute it to the creative middle classes that work today in this sector. Presumed to be freely chosen even back in the 1970s, this participation in technological representation would later transform *kamákia's* affective labour into property not belonging to them alone (Clough et al., 2007). Circulating now in a new techno-Anthropocenic field, it would allow markets to suggest that collective artistic representations (filtered through a film) can counter the crisis of *Greek presence* in international relations and global middle-class markets.

Phase 4: Cinematic Tourism as Structural Technomorphism

When *ZG* tourism enters the 'film-induced' phase, it does not endorse 'place-making' as some tourism scholars may rush to argue, but a dissolution of spatial configurations as the *modus vivendi* of heritage. In addition, not only does such 'blueprint utopianism' (Bauman, 2007) suppress the endemic social conflicts that it generates in the public spheres but it also leads to a homogenisation of citi-zenship as a form of 'utopian subjectivity' (Sorkin, 1992, p. 231): visitors to filmed places are promoted to premium guests, whereas hosts/residents are either homogenised as consumers of their own home or second-class caterers for tourists.

In the fourth stage of *ZG* tourism design, the Greek island's heritage becomes a rapidly fading heritage text – something that enables tourism systems to feign Zorba signs as heritage (see also Lash & Urry, 1994). In the 2020s, in addition to any hotel expansion, which is not connected to the film, various local and international independent tour operators run tours to *ZG* locations. Feigning Crete's micro-geographical specificity, they cater for generic flânerie, sprinkled with religious heritage locations that featured in the film (e.g., the Byzantine Monastery of Agia Triada). Notably, the latter are symbolically ingested in a programme of culinary tourism (consumption of local produce). Alma de Creta's (Alma de Creta 2, 2022) tour to the monastery, Stavrós in Akrotíri and other locations featuring in *ZG* are notable examples. This time, however, there is a twist, which did not exist in the era of *kamákia* mobilities: the digital enterprise's discourse of labour is embedded in the biographies of its founders and operators, which comprise a hybrid group of lifestyle travellers (some born and raised in Crete, one in Athens and two abroad) in love with the island (see 'About Us', Alma de Creta, 2022). Analytically, the enterprise exemplifies the cultural entanglements and economic complexities of lifestyle mobilities. On the cultural front, it tells us several stories not only about self-identity choices, blends of travel, tourism and migration (Benson, 2010) but also the hybrid spaces of belonging younger generations of creative workers enter today (Cohen et al., 2013). It is only when such ventures enter global capitalist networks that they cease to project situated subjectivities and enter neoliberal processes which are not just about marketing or advertising film tourism.

We enter an unexplored post-phenomenological sphere, which we must tread softly. However, it may be incorrect to 'judge' such lifestyle choices out of context; in any case, my target is not what the new digital creative classes do individually, but how (a) their personal visions become integrated in a post-industrial economic landscape and by turn, (b) their visions are used by global markets to interpellate filmed lifeworlds as aspects of a uniform Cretan *nature*. Before I discuss the systemic effects of the new spirit of hospitality, here are some other variations of the *ZG* tour in the early 2020s: based on Heraklion, Cretetravel.com (2022) offers a similar culinary-cinematic tour, which is suitable for families and children, thus mirroring the third phase of the *ZG* tourism design – but not quite. This is so, because as much as they claim difference, all these tours follow the same niche pathway as post-Fordist copies of the same. Take, for example, the tour organised by Suffolk-based The TravelPorter (2022), which invites prospective film tourists to 'live like Zorba for a day' but delivers a blend of film-site visitation and culinary tourism. We should not miss the fact that TheTravelPorter is managed by a group of educated female entrepreneurs, some born in the Greek metropolis and some of dual Greek-foreign cultural citizenship. Their short biographies match those of the Cretetravel.com's principal operators, as they emphasise a loose form of cosmopolitan identity.

In blended post-industrial ventures such as that of *ZG* tourism, this sort of creative labour has become auxiliary to a proliferation in modes of organisation. I am not interested in the creative classes' hybridity itself, but their role in recent changes in what Nederveen Pieterse (2008, pp. 662–664) originally called 'structural hybridisation'. For me, the fourth phase of *ZG* tourism is emblematic of structural technomorphism, an ad hoc and progressive change in place identity within and thanks to new technological networks. Drawing on post-phenomenological theory (Rosenberger & Verbeek, 2015), I regard structural technomorphism as the transformation of collective, rather than individual identity via technology. Such changes commenced in *ZG* tourism with the *subjective* male experience of hospitality (catering for foreign women), but now seem to favour the institution of an *objective* and disembodied reality of who the *ZG* tourist is or can be. And there is more: the manifestos of post-identity and cosmopolitan belonging that new cinematic tourism digital markets allegedly uphold (on post-identity see also Hollinshead & Vellah, 2020) do not always cancel the tourism mythomoteur's regressive identarian projects (e.g., Hollinshead, 1998b, 2009a). Instead, they may consolidate the categorical segmentation of populations in leisure peripheries to conflate state and market biopolitics with pro-environmental, nature-based or agro-tourism mobilities (Urry, 2014, pp. 24–25). Minca (2010) has aptly noted that although islands may function as haptic contact zones in the production of the tourist experience, where habitus, gender, sexuality and class are negotiated (the first and second phases of *ZG* tourism design), they never cease to be the theatre of new capitalist structuration (Skeggs, 2004, p. 49). This theatre turns (tourist and labouring) bodies into categories (of production and consumption), thus de-hypostasising them. The very mythical hero of the movie-novel (*Zorba the poor but exotic Cretan labourer*) set the pace of this structural process (of representation) decades ago.

The mitigation of structuration through a disease (HIV/AIDS) in the third phase of *ZG* tourism design strangely harmonised the sex workers' affective action (their withdrawal of labour) with the fourth phase's digital re-naturalisation (or, rather, artificial naturalisation): the preservation of utopias of pristine land and sea amidst rising numbers of tourism incomers on the island. Like other Greek islands, Crete struggles with the effects of overtourism and bad guest behaviour, which affect its localities' well-being (Vourdoubas, 2020). On the one hand, the grand biopolitical projects of our times are based on technomorphing such labour bodies as those of *kamákia* into signs or bytes. Their non-body-ness allows them to circulate across regimes of tourism easier, because they forgo the stage of risky exchanges of bodily fluids and affects. However, this sterilisation is more-than-digital: it hands *ZG* leisure to film fans, eco-friendly visitors and the respectable middle-class families. Simpson and Sheller (2022, p. 2) suggest that such developments may 'create a new geography of exploitation that undermines sovereign territories and currencies, empowers cyber-kinetic elites, and exclud[e] and marginaliz[e] existing island communities and natural ecosystems'.

In new digital markets, Zorba the uncouth and revolutionary character is smartened in every sense: save his implication in some rather over-processed rituals (music, dancing) for the tourist gaze, his cultural presence is mostly based on his *tacit absence* from technological narratives of the actual tours. Instead, prospective tourists are literally introduced to landscapes – the basis of pseudo-dark tourism (see also Urry, 2004). If indeed landscapes have the power to

symbolise the modernity of those who traverse them or who act as their custodians (Minca, 2013, pp. 49–50), the landscaping of *ZG* is an attempt to remove
the disorderly and abject aspects of the native culture that nourished them
(Sandywell, 2006) – nothing better than a good cleaning of one's personal garden
from 'weeds' and 'pests' (see Bauman's (1992) metaphor of the 'gardening state').
The paradox of this transformation is hard to miss: a notional project previously
used to resist Western civil codes becomes outsourced for the encrypted design of
hybrid hypermobile spaces (McGrath, 2021) – a collection of tourist playscapes
(Sheller & Urry, 2004).

   Thus, I would argue that key to the development of new encrypted geographies
of cinematic tourism is the structural transformation of fictional characters into
semantic nodes. I return to this point in Chapter 2, which sheds new light on
fiction as a marketing strategy. This strategy does more than what has been
argued in film tourism scholarship: that is, the enhancement of identity, heritage
prestige and so forth. Like money symbols, fictional characters have always been
in a position to re-code *in absentia* more-than-economic flows (Simmel, 1991).
However, in the new encrypted geographies of capitalism, they function both as
symbolic cultural capital, where ethno-cultural values used to stand, and *network
capital*, objects in larger-than-tourism or film knowledge economies, enabling the
host's global networking (Germann Molz, 2006b, 2014; Urry, 2007, p. 223). Let
me apply this to Crete: where, according to Simpson and Sheller (2022), such
encrypted geographies are supposed to act as 'exit routes' from state control and
politics, allowing leisure in our case communities to build bonds on shared
interests (Thiel, 2009), they may modify instead the semantics of internal
(national) and external borders. It is old news that digital technologies serve in
islandic outposts as networking infrastructures across different activities,
including trade, migration and asylum seeking (Loyd & Mountz, 2014). However,
their implication in digital crypto-secessionist planning via tourism is another
matter. Here, we must have recourse to local historical knowledge to consider the
effects such new markets have on Greece and Crete in particular in terms of
sovereignty.

   As an island, Crete has always demonstrated a strong local identity politics,
here feeding into nationalist pride (e.g., during the Axis Occupation), there
standing against internal enemies (e.g., the island's 'clans' supported the country's
leftist politics, which from the late 1980s would don a peculiar blend of
pro-socialist and pro-market principles (Herzfeld, 1985, 2005)). Anyone who can
still not comprehend the connection of these histories to contemporary *ZG*
tourism playscapes may have to consider how their affective atmospherics (pride,
collective effervescence and even the spirit of life/*kéfi*) survived in contemporary
ZG travel design. As explained in the Introduction, the tourist is a real and ideal
type suffering from a particular lack of moral legitimation in the social sciences,
which its performative subjects and scholars alike often draw from discourses of
'serious leisure'. The most common way to achieve this moral legitimation
involves a shift of the activity of touring itself the highly politicised domain of
volunteering, which turns leisure into both the display of special skills and the
cumulation of earnest experience (Stebbins, 1992, p. 3). Otherwise put: if Zorba

enters thematic activities such as justice activism, his uncouthness (and by extension the tourist activities stemming from his atmospheric essence – of *kéfi*) become detached from working-class imaginaries of leisure with no purpose and enter the moral sphere of middle-class civility, which is purposeful and potentially utilitarian (Stebbins, 1996).

The project of serious leisure needs Zorba-the-peasant, as both its antithetical pole and the focus of its civilised mission. On this one may consider the rationale of changing imaginaries of tourism in Greece in the context of the global economic crisis that affected European and world economies from 2008. A radical change in the 'picture' of the country began to be circulated in global media conduits (YouTube, Facebook, official press websites and personal blogs). This change corresponds to a radical imaginary of growth through labour, which adheres to justice and draws on the origins of civilised modernity in rural cultures. These origins connect to past media representations of Greece as an idyllic peasant and working-class site, which we find in movies, such as *ZG*. One can detect the presence of such transformations in contemporary justice activism led by public personalities both in the world of art and academia in Greek islands that now serve as refugee camps. The transformations are exploited by the new spirit of commercialised hospitality in tourism mobilities, which promotes a hybridisation of the gaze of giving with the tourist gaze. Two such examples treading a fine line because of their widespread broadcasting by media channels are: Ai Weiwei's activist art on Lesbos (Tzanelli, 2018b) and a petition to nominate the island's residents for the Nobel Peace Prize because of their philanthropic interventions in the Moria camp (countersigned by renowned social scientists from the Anglophone and Francophone academia and supported by two Nobel Laureates, Archbishop Emeritus Desmond Tutu and the Economist Sir Christopher Pissaridis). In such interventions, the vitalist energy of characters, such as Zorbas, is channelled into a different imaginary of mobility – that of a plodding worker (Arendt's (1958) *Homo Faber*), who is set to rectify an axiological (ethical) damage inflicted upon post-industrial societies by war, genocide and migration/ rootlessness. This working human should be gazed upon and scrutinised in global media spheres, if (s)he is to make a real difference to their social world (see also MacCannell, 2011 on the ethics of the gaze). And yet, this is precisely how dark/ slum tourism commenced: so, not only is the change in imaginaries of islandic Greekness informed by the European histories of art, slum and dark tourism, focusing on middle-class refinement and philanthropy but it also bears the potential to promote Greece as a cultural tourist destination in global value hierarchies in controversial ways (Tzanelli & Korstanje, 2016, p. 15).

Rose (2003) warns us, after Fyfe and Law (1988), to consider depictions of geographical places not just as 'illustrations' but also sites for constructing and depicting difference. Unlike the introspective sensibilities of regionalism and ethno-nationalism, the new *ZG* spirit of hospitality seems to be using activist attempts to salvage a 'decent' version of this local identity to empower global markets. Therefore, digital transformations in *ZG* tourism did not allow just for the embeddedness of regressive historic characters into new leisure regimes. They also consolidated the de-semantisation of those embodied labour mobilities that helped to institute *ZG* tourism in the first place. Stigmatised by a version of indecency, today, these erstwhile international love heroes are nowhere to be found in digital advertising or *ZG*-inspired tourist resorts. Emphatically standing for the twin anti-Western ethos of modern Greek identity, they have been morphed into anodyne beauty in the Techno-Anthropocene: natural destinations, worthy of scientific conservation and digital cosmeticism echoing the romantic ethos of an equally ghosted cinematic hero. It is debatable whether Cacoyannis and Theodorakis – the two left-wing avant-garde artists who experienced both political persecution and international recognition around the time that *ZG* was travelling the world – would have endorsed such technomorphic design. As figments of an old-fashioned creative class, both of them are also interpellated as romantic creators of what ended up being a polysemic 'product-thing' in domains of tourist fascination (Urry, 2011b).

Conclusion

It is time to consider the results of my truth and reality tests in the design of *ZG* tourism. In my assessment, I highlighted the role of design as part of large processes of identity-making for the tourist state-host, distinguished artistic, common sex and other hospitality labour on Crete. From all these actors and their actions in the field of *ZG* tourism design, I endeavoured to explore in more detail the affective agencies of sex workers to uncover the less organised aspects of the overall venture. My viewing position became constitutive of the ways the geographically localised ethics of cultural mobility became contingently entwined in macro-political designs of belonging. The production of a 'truth' about Greece and Greek progress in tourism was based on processes of taste adjustment in tourism design; although these appeared to be class-based, they were actually ethno-racial and gendered in nature. 'Truth' was manipulated through both digital (film) and embodied (hospitality labour) styles of action and performance to conceal the realities of intersectional inequality. Played out both domestically in realist styles and internationally in symbolic codes of presentation and absence alike, the reality test uncovered the sinister workings of capitalist structuration. The profitable abstraction of tourism design based on a movie erased the needs of certain groups, 'specifically those who are intersectionally disadvantaged' or excessively burdened by prejudice 'under white supremacist heteropatriarchy, capitalism, and...colonialism' (Costanza-Chock, 2020, p. 23, 37).

In *Discipline and Punish*, Foucault (1979) reminds us that a 'genealogy of morals' helps us to uncover the mundane but complex genesis of social phenomena. He places particular emphasis on the role of contingency in the genesis and development of social, political and economic structures with a view to unearthing causality in transitions from one way of thinking, behaviour or mode of policymaking to another. Although causality certainly features in my analysis, because such transitions could not have been foreseen or pre-empted, I am more interested here in the 'how', rather than the 'why' as such: the ways contingencies modified human behaviour or strengthened reaction to social change. In my examination of particular Greek and Cretan human actors and institutions as drivers of tourism development after the release of *ZG*, I highlighted the endurance of particular gendered discourses of belonging. Existing independently from these actors and institutions, such discourses masked the consolidation of new social inequalities in modern tourism mobilities, which were based on class (labour identities in the *ZG* hospitality) and race/ethnicity (being Greek, civilised and European) (on affective labour and intersectionality see McRobbie, 2010; Skeggs, 2010). The extent to which different players in this field of development aligned with dominant patterns of belonging was affected by their relative personal power in it. We are still in the domain of the 'why' (*see also* Table 4).

It has already been noted that capitalism works these days through a concerted expropriation of common wealth in the form of affective labour (Oksala, 2016; Tzanelli, 2018a). Thus, the 'how' begins to feature when we consider that the *kamákia's* limited power in the social field ensured that their agency was more directed towards practical action and self-preservation. Although economically detrimental, such action rectifies the inauthentic feel of an atmosphere of romance, which intensified the sense of exclusion and non-belonging (Carlson & Stewart, 2014). As atmospheres are also about normative judgements, the display of bad taste in a field of international tourist traffic, however profitable, amounts to social suicide. Cultural and social stratification began to butt heads in a duel to death, in which sex workers merely acted as disposable specimen. In other words, to attribute the impediment of tourism's peace-building potentialities to a group of frustrated men provides a poor conclusion to the causes, consequences and constrictions involved in the development of Cretan tourism. Far more accurate would be to consider the increasingly less regulated capitalist expansion in the

Table 4.   Growth of Hotel Bed Capacity on Crete and Rhodes and in Greece Over the Period 1970–1990 Compared to the Base Year of 1964 (Base Year Value = 100).

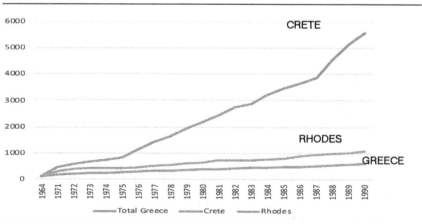

Source: Tzanelli and Koutoulas (2021).

tourist trade and its satellite mobilities (such as sex tourism) across Europe and beyond. I attempted to examine such macropolitical and macroeconomic developments through first-hand testimonies of hoteliers, who experienced such developments, as well as hard data on tourism expansion and infrastructural development in Crete and secondary research.

This allowed me to bridge the micropolitics of affect with the macropolitics of mobilities and globalisation. Macropolitically, I note that *ZG*-related tourism had

Table 5. Growth of Overnight Hotel Stays on Crete and Rhodes and in Greece Over the Period 1970–1990 Compared to the Base Year of 1970.

	Total Greece	Crete	Rhodes	Share of Crete	Share of Rhodes
1970	17.514.450	732.646	1.725.189	4,18%	9,85%
1972	23.962.800	1.267.700	3.535.086	5,29%	14,75%
1973	25.351.740	1.551.565	3.727.427	6,12%	14,70%
1974	19.013.326	1.209.647	1.965.399	6,36%	10,34%
1975	25.016.580	1.982.119	3.114.542	7,92%	12,45%
1976	31.306.502	2.878.791	4.432.228	9,20%	14,16%
1977	30.929.881	3.041.768	3.769.884	9,83%	12,19%
1978	34.923.050	3.873.201	4.586.943	11,09%	13,13%
1979	39.802.114	4.915.827	5.420.712	12,35%	13,62%
1980	40.354.154	5.453.785	5.775.221	13,51%	14,31%
1981	41.032.029	6.042.583	6.059.690	14,73%	14,77%
1982	40.522.036	5.947.654	5.931.387	14,68%	14,64%
1983	37.438.013	5.806.713	5.198.739	15,51%	13,89%
1984	43.838.880	7.421.691	6.535.660	16,93%	14,91%
1985	47.017.186	8.092.260	7.333.099	17,21%	15,60%
1986	46.067.822	7.996.592	7.694.150	17,36%	16,70%
1987	46.102.747	7.724.520	7.380.878	16,76%	16,01%
1988	46.034.045	8.355.950	7.334.164	18,15%	15,93%
1989	46.477.627	8.637.111	7.691.073	18,58%	16,55%
1990	48.887.583	9.709.937	8.083.794	19,86%	16,54%
1991	42.639.811	8.320.031	7.385.042	19,51%	17,32%
1992	49.973.111	9.954.904	8.952.234	19,92%	17,91%
1993	49.592.246	10.096.172	8.550.124	20,36%	17,24%
1994	53.435.111	10.771.918	9.646.298	20,16%	18,05%
1995	50.636.292	10.110.597	8.937.691	19,97%	17,65%
1996	48.662.379	10.096.819	8.018.603	20,75%	16,48%

Source: National Statistics Service of Greece; Greek National Tourism Organisation; Tzanelli and Koutoulas (2021).

less to do with the moving image and more with the politics of representation – an observation I unpack below as part and parcel of the 'how'. Tourism expansion's primary discursive drivers involved a strategic admission of 'foreign' identities in understandings of modern Greekness, so that it becomes a property that moves in global markets.

Practically, this involved the incorporation of marginal and uncouth versions of the Greek margin as an object that responds to tourism demand (the Zorba-like Cretan type of masculinity, which enabled tourism mobilities) and the 'outside' that enunciates such demands (female tourists/guests, who, from the 1980s, would also become carriers of a real threat to native life due to the global spread of HIV and AIDS mobilities). Micropolitically, the objectified host (men often flirting with foreigners to accrue symbolic capital at home) saw their status inconsistency (turning into pleasure caterers) even more threatened, when viral death entered this game. Where originally their investment in ethno-nationalist sexism accommodated their symbolic domination over their casual female foreign partners, now it necessitated complete withdrawal from the game.

It is significant that, as the *kamákia* began to disappear from the mechanisms of hospitality supply, family tourism became more prevalent on the island. This change aligned the pragmatic 'why' of discursive change (viral threat) with the symbolic 'how' of Greek ethno-nationalism (the nation as a family not to be penetrated or polluted from the 'outside', unless this willingly becomes acculturated into its principles – see Diagram 1). Ultimately, disempowered actors, international and local tourism business agents and the state came to a silent agreement on how to worldmake tourism through *ZG* (on such paradoxes of mobility see Korstanje, 2018b).

To conclude then, I should stress that the design of tourism through the moving image is never bound exclusively to a film or a network of media. When one examines the phases of development, 'film-induced tourism' or 'film tourism' tends to be reduced to the causal structures of one or two phases of the overall tourism development of a destination. A mobilities approach highlights this limitation of the model while also stressing that the 'worldmaking' thesis needs to be extended so as to consider the ways capitalism works in the development of new hospitality systems. My phased design development model, which amends the objectives and structure of Butler's (2006, 2011) 'life-cycle' thesis, better exposes how the contingent workings of capitalist expansion in tourism interfere in the biopolitical organisation of the host country, its labour force and identity. In a global system of tourism services, the *kamákia* featured as even more disempowered actors, and the same applied to the Greek nation state, which was demoted to one of the many partners/agents in the management of Zorba-inspired tourism mobilities.

The onset of neoliberal structuration in world economies in the last three decades shrank *ZG's* Crete to a spot in a vast traffic of 'Sun n' Sea' and beach tourism services. The result of this downgrading has been the development of a reactionary 'how': an identity narrative drawing on habit memory that stressed integration on perceived civilised codes in an increasingly fragmented world. In this theatre of political violence, a fictional character, who had started his life as a

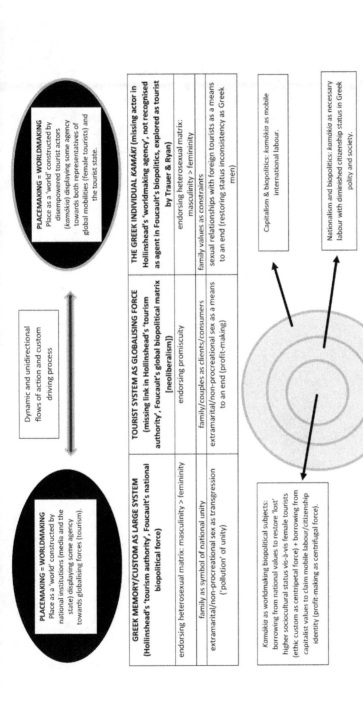

Diagram 1.   A Map of Conceptual Connections and Process-Driven Placemaking as Worldmaking. *Source:* Tzanelli and Koutoulas (2021).

gendered ode to the Greek good life and cinematically represented an internal ethnic working-class margin, ended up being a means to symbolically command the respect of foreign guests and international tourist markets likewise. As such, the theatre of violence runs full cycle when its technomorphic tools and digital travelling styles are not handed over to the new creative classes, but those constituencies in market politics that forge international Cretan presence as a *heteronormative character*: never gay or lesbian, but even at its lowermost sex trade phase, commanding a masculine worldmaking project of tourism mobilities.

Chapter 3

From *Borat* Post-tourism to Market Post-truth: Kazakhstan's New Spirit of (In)Hospitality

Film Tourism, Art and the New Spirit of Hospitality

In Chapter 2, I explored the ways in which the cinematic design of marginal ethnic masculinity produced new worlds of tourism on Crete and new inhospitable situations for particular forms of unregulated labour. To be more precise, the movie *ZG* set in motion a chain of unpredictable post-industrial installations on the island, which bifurcated hospitality into formal (package tours, virtual consumptions of Greekness) and informal networks of labour supply (sex tourism). This chain bore the twin characteristics of popcultural mobility and strategic geopolitical alignment with markets that manipulate truths about styles of (social) exclusion and (environmental) destruction with planetary consequences. Buried under piles of Greek cultural-political intentions to join civilised tourism networks for refined clientele, we find the affective action of sex workers and the dreams of the film's creators, who, also subjected to market imperatives.

Chapter 3 shifts emphasis to the fates of such creative agents to interrogate their role in the production of post-truths, where these films lead to tourism designing. Again, cinematic performance and tourism design do not inform a linear scale of development, nor do they convey the intentionality of cinematic art. Again, we deal with the capricious workings of the supersystem under which different creative industries converge in the production of tourism: the capitalist, rather than the tourist or cinematic system (Lash & Urry, 1987). Be as it may, such networks of 'reflexive accumulation' facilitate unreflexively created messages about what can be consumed by the post-modern tourist, who is a middle-class globetrotter: the more media and tourism networks de-differentiate (Lash & Urry, 1994) and promote the global dissemination of lifestyle signs (Jenkins et al., 2013; van Dijck & Poell, 2013), the more social and cultural difference is subjected to 'adiaphorisation' or systemic indifference (Bauman & Lyon, 2013, p. 8). In such contexts, the playful behaviour of distinguished creative labour can have a trickle-down effect, at times damaging the life opportunities of those who are already socially marginalised or disadvantaged.

The New Spirit of Hospitality, 73–99
Copyright © 2023 Rodanthi Tzanelli
Published under exclusive licence by Emerald Publishing Limited
doi:10.1108/978-1-83753-160-820231004

As explained in the Introduction, when we connect environmental change to social categories such as class, the challenges of the Anthropocene generate different types of responses and problems that call for a localisation of vulnerability and precariousness (Lövbrand et al., 2015, p. 115). The fates of vulnerable groups of humans, who are poor or experiencing inequalities (i.e., ethnic minorities and female professionals in cultural industries) are of some importance in this chapter in the ways the new spirit of hospitality produces post-truths about cinematic tourist destinations. The two categories cannot be merged – poverty and inequality are eidetically different and methodologically merit different tools to research in a consideration of systems of engendering through atmospheric analysis. I enact an examination of the socio-political complexities involved in the representational repertoires of the notorious *Borat: Cultural Learnings of America for Make Benefit Glorious Nation of Kazakhstan* (dir. L. Charles, 2006 – henceforward: *Borat 1*) and its recently released sequel, *Borat Subsequent Moviefilm: Delivery of Prodigious Bribe to American Regime for Make Benefit Once Glorious Nation of Kazakhstan* (dir. J. Woliner, 2020 – henceforward: *Borat 2*). In line with Chapter 2's analysis of structural technomorphism in cinematic tourism, I examine why the 'Borat tourism effect' side-lined the widely renounced narrative core of the films, which involved representing human characters as landscape specimen or objects available for light consumption. At the level of representation, a slide from social category to cultural style takes place, with consequences across different ecologies: media, social but also environmental (see also Guattari, [1989] 2014).

On this particular point, my differentiation between 'film-induced tourism' and 'cinematic tourism' is pivotal. 'Cinematic tourism' is etymologically and ideologically loaded with variations of artistic and political movement: on the one hand, the word *kinēma* as cinema commonly refers to a technological complex orchestrating sound, image-based and imaginative movement (Rose, 2012); on the other, it metaphorically refers to ecologically delineated social movements, which may support or oppose tourism mobilities (Guattari, [1989] 2014, pp. 19–21). In other studies, I focused on film auteurs' and actors' pilgrimages-as-political movements in filmed locations (Tzanelli, 2013a, pp. 3–6, 2018, p. 52), but here I dig deeper into the cultural politics of movement in global spheres of capitalist exchange by key drivers in tourism development. 'Cinematic tourism' is a process of inscription of movement on a surface or ideational body (*kinēmatográphos*: the inscription of movement – Tzanelli, 2013a, 2018). The 'body' is not that of art, but of national heritage. I observe how subjecting artwork to the political and economic priorities of national memory side-lines systems of endangering, which favour addressing human and environmental vulnerabilities (Clark & Szerszynski, 2021, Chapter 2). It helps to stress that the technological-representational hypermobilities of cinematic tourism affected both the nature and speed with which vulnerability began to be governed in Kazakhstan: the 'slow violence' inflicted on natural resources and vulnerable groups (Nixon, 2011) was accelerated, facilitating a seamless blend of their properties as objects of tourist fascination.

In this process, the 'humourous activism' of Jewish British actor Sacha Baron Cohen was grossly misplaced, ultimately endorsing an array of structures of inequality. I will briefly discuss the value of 'camp' and 'kitsch' in the production of 'Borat humour' and stress that 'in-group affinity' ensures that jokes may offend people in such successful films as *Borat 1* and *2*, because they enter global dissemination. 'Cosmopolitan irony' as a commitment to postidentity or reflexive self-critique (Turner, 2002) of this type has its limitations. Parenthetically, I also find the suggestion that all media messages are adopted and acted upon uncritically equally problematic. And yet, the argument that it is fine for creative industries and their distinguished labour to endorse hate speech or denigrate difference, just because the 'message' can be interpreted in different ways by different audiences is equally disturbing. Baron Cohen's performance of the slapstick Borat persona was never politically innocent or a piece of fun 'art for art's sake'. As a clear statement on the ways satire markets cast political journalism as post-tourism, it was set from the outset to 'move' audiences. As it turned out, due to the misogynistic and racist repertoires on which it repeatedly and stubbornly drew, the caustic style of its left-wing satire enabled other cultural political agents in the making of tourism mobilities to endorse an authoritarian agenda.

We are in the domain of hospitality and the functionalisation of revolutionary styles. Luc Boltanski and Eve Chiapello (2018) suggest that in the mid-1970s, Western capitalism replaced the hierarchical Fordist structure of work with a new network-based form of organisation founded on employee initiative and autonomy in the workplace. The new organisational style used the emergent libertarian and romantic currents of the period (its revolutionary 'spirit') to ensure that innovation would be placed at the top of the desired employee skills. Not only did this generate a new and more pernicious form of exploitation but also amplified the creative labour's material and psychological insecurity. Art became subjected to the idea of originality in contexts of extreme competition, which was elevated to a value. I import this argument into the field of cinematically-induced tourism, to interrogate what such creative industrial connections between freedom in initiative and profit-driven capitalist control over the employers' creative work actually do, as well as some unpalatable and unintended in *Borat 1 & 2's* case consequences. My exploration of this 'doing' focuses on the pragmatic basis on which solidarities are forged or modified in tourism markets (see Tzanelli, 2018a, 2020 on all phases of such design). How do host communities end up *functioning* and behaving in such competitive environments, in other words? If we want to establish a solid chain between *engendering* earthly systems and *endangering* multispecies ecologies, we may have to take one more time the route of affect: how this slide is performed to mobilise audiences of all kinds, including those of the cinema, tourism and nationalist propaganda.

The tourism industries' strategic repression of the stereotypical repertoires employed in *Borat 1 & 2* exemplifies the new spirit of hospitality: the tourism sector refuses to address the normalisation of sexism and racism in any explicit style, by relocating the ethical slide in the manufacturing of new forms of cultural tourism for *respectable* consumers. In this respect, the Kazakh nation-state's direct involvement in the airbrushing of the two films' stylistic subversiveness matches *ZG* tourism's movement away from social-come-cultural marginality (Zorba the illiterate Cretan hero as the metonymical modern Greek heroic character) and towards technomorphic design. To facilitate this connection, I stress that both *Borat* films are humourous in ambivalent terms: you cannot always tell when their extreme cheap humour ('kitsch') consciously crosses the line to communicate the irony of a learnt cosmopolitan subject ('camp'). The outrage that used to surround 'kitsch' and 'camp' has subsided in most Western societies, but the recognition of 'camp' as a middle-class pursuit persists (Holliday & Potts, 2012). However, the implication of both in the pragmatics of image management and 'public decency' continues to matter, because it guides the politics of mobility even in Western worlds (Cresswell, 2006).

To explore *Borat 1 & 2*'s entanglements in regimes of representation and presence, I consider how deconstructing technomorphic styles of capitalist worldmaking facilitates the adjustment of 'reality glances' or perspectives on culture (Ateljevic et al., 2009; Hollinshead, 2009a; Hollinshead & Suleman, 2018; Lynch et al., 2011, p. 14). On the one hand, the 'Borat effect' enables a link between systemic tourist production and exploitation of place and culture and their impact on conceptions of identity (Sheller & Urry, 2004). On the other, the recent suggestion that in post-colonial contexts tourism development can generate possibilities of becoming retains an ambivalence that does not address the workings of capitalism – lest we conflate this with the post-colonial condition, which Hollinshead and Vellah (2020) do not (see also Tzanelli, 2020b on problematic links between capitalism, travel, tourism and post-colonial becoming). To this end, we must ascertain how the *Borat* tourism industry was based on the generative potential of the symbolic capital accrued by lead artists across a global cultural field, modulated by and shared between nation-state and markets.

Deciding how the 'what' (ideas) and the 'who' (human categories) are modulated in contexts of cultural-industrial de-differentiation highlights what is truly objectified in the enterprise. Part of the problem is detected in the ways the system of 'art' in the form of film currently operates, with another part being the workings of tourism mobilities and how the two feed into each other to repeat the same mistakes (Büscher & Fletcher, 2017; Cresswell, 2010). Both systems are overlaid by the flattening of local/ethnic experiences in contexts of rapid globalisation (Habermas, 1989; Tuan, 2001). On this, it is worth noting that even the 'transmodern' manifesto of critical tourism studies takes for granted the reality of tourism as a system, within which justice is supposed to be delivered (e.g. Ateljevic, 2008). Diversity often requires considering developmental formulas beyond tourism, to see how some populations are affected by the mandate of tourism business, which endorses the pragmatics of Western mobility.

My reading of the *Borat* case focuses on how the cinematic inscription of stereotyping endorsed biopolitical experimentation in tourism mobilities that became enhanced by its global cybernetic distribution as an anodyne form of digitised landscape for tourism consumption. I use 'landscape' as an ecological plane subjected to the politics of nationalist valorisation. This epistemological scaffolding informs my data collection, which are digital as all press releases, the digital advertising of Kazakhstan and the three films I use are forms and products of our digital age. Designing mobilities, argues Jensen (2014), involves a great deal of montage and perspectivism. His thesis encompasses ideas of 'staging' subject and cause-directed movement, which cut across architecture and film-making, with particular emphasis on movement through built urban environments, 'and the vistas and sights ... that emerge as one, for example, turns a corner to find new sights and impressions' (Jensen, 2014, p. 32). Jensen's analysis, which borrows from European filmmaking techniques, discusses perspectives but not phases in design. The 'phasing' (from *fáskō*: to agree) of movement and its corresponding mobilities of ideas, objects, technologies and humans have a strong phenomenological character (*fáskō* from *phaínomai*: to appear, become apparent), which stems from discourse, hence is associated with the ways knowledge is wedded to authorial scripts (power) (Foucault, 1980). The architect's or the filmmaker's camera will never simply present reality, they will direct attention through technology, thus representing versions of it in agreement (*fáskō*) with pre-set intentions. The design of *Borat 1 & 2* tourism mobilities produced not a static, but evolving reality about the fictional character's alleged homeland, Kazakhstan. However, the evolution (or 'phasing') conformed to the contingent calls of the new spirit of capitalism, fostering a problematic 'post-truth'. This truth embraced innovation in flux, to address contemporaneous economic needs and statist political ambitions.

The following section sets this blended ecological scene by exploring the damaged post-political (see Ek, 2011 in Introduction) landscapes of the post-Soviet Kazakh nation. This historical regression is part and parcel of my methodology of 'live sociology' in the Anthropocene (see Sheller, 2014 in Chapter 1). Kazakhstan's implication in the dark histories of nuclear disaster is replaced in the *Borat 1 & 2* design of tourism with softer approaches to power, which 'translate' dark tourism into ecotourism. The following section explains how, in its first, cinematic phase, *Borat 1* created a satirical post-tourist hero, who establishes global networks of blame and shame in these Kazakh histories, involving approaches to human corruption. Unfortunately, the *Borat* creative teams' strategy would be mobilised by other agents in the field of global mobilities, to shift attention from controversial discourses on other-hate to the design of tourism. In the third section, I examine how in the second phase of design, Kazakhstan's tourism industry repressed the stereotypical repertoires both films employed. This is an example of the new spirit of hospitality, which prioritises smooth production rather than the engendering of terrestrial life. I follow the development of the design of Kazakh tourism policy and advertising between 2006, the year *Borat 1* was released, and late October 2020, when *Borat 2* hit the TV screens amidst the COVID-19 pandemic. I conclude with observations on the ways the new spirit of hospitality contributes to the standardisation and serialisation of what it means to be the perfect and imperfect human in contemporary image-based markets, with a particular emphasis on tourism.

Hyperobjects of the Anthropocene: Cold War and Hot Zones of Kazakh Extinction

Overall, the ethics and aesthetics of phasing and staging Borat-related tourism were conditioned by convergences and divergences between cinematic and tourist representations of Kazakhstan as a blended human (the 'Kazakh ethnic character') and post-human (environment) ecology. But what exactly does this entail? Sometimes, we want to talk about phenomena that stretch across periods, centuries or millennia, exposing the limitations of our comprehension. At other times, we wish to narrate our experience of briefer events that affected whole communities or post-human ecosystems, but the feelings such narratives bring to the fore are too overwhelming to complete the task. Crises such as climate change and war generate silences about what is unprecedented (Arendt, 1958) or 'Hyperobjective' (Morton, 2013). Arendt's term spatialises our lack of knowledge, whereas Morton's temporalises it: we want to grasp what transcends the objective conditions of our life and enshrouds in its totality what no world history can present (Morton, 2013; Tzanelli, 2021a). All we can do is have recourse to representational snapshots of this gigantic whole – a technique cutting across different domains of human creativity, including art, as well as the human and social sciences.

Naturalist scientism does not accept such haphazard games of second or third-order discourse – at least not past the Popperian analogue of individualism. On the other hand, subversive art reflects upon human disempowerment in the face of Hyperobjective changes, by being 'unserious' or what Obadare (2009) calls 'infrapolitical'. Whereas on-stage subversive performance is the style of the elites, infrapolitical performance and discourse are the weapons of the disenfranchised or oppressed masses, who have to find ways to psychologically survive their dire material conditions (Tzanelli, 2016b). Responses to the Hyperobjective can also subvert the neat narratives of planetary discourse, which deals both with multiple ecologies and several natural environments, therefore, different representational contexts that may correspond to different apparatuses. When we disambiguate these, we get two competing social-scientific programmes: one acknowledging modernity as the psychomotor of planetary biographies and another focusing on systems of engendering earthly life (Latour, 1993, 2018). This section scopes Kazakhstan's place in these two programmes to facilitate a better understanding of the ways the Kazakh nation-state governs the content of Borat moving images and their tourism mobilities.

That Kazakhstan stands in the social-scientific programme of modernity as one of the post-Soviet political formations and as an amalgamation of ethno-religious communities is only part of its memory archives. The 'Kazakh nation's' recognition and self-recognition as an autonomous polity in the twentieth century was haunted by the cultural scripts drafted by the two political poles of the Cold War, the Soviet and the American. Centuries before this polarisation, Kazakh ethnic groups were subjugated to the whims of the Russian Empire, which wanted to control Central Asia in the so-called 'Great Game' for dominance. In this game, the British Empire stood as the main competitor of Kazakhstani ambitions (Zabortseva, 2012). From the eighteenth century, the tsar colonisers imposed their own administrative system and introduced the Russian language in schools in the regions now belonging to Kazakhstan, thus *endangering* the Kazakh tribes' cultures and livelihood. As members of the so-called 'Great Powers of Europe', both empires sought to extend their influence in Asian dominions, establishing trade routes and securing the extraction of natural resources from colonised regions. Resource extraction provides the first opportunity to transition this section's biopic to the social-scientific programme of engendering-come-endangering, which is non-linear, if not a-historical. The Kazakhstani ethnic formations' implication in Russian imperialist planning was inevitable because what most of them came to recognise as their geopolitical cradle (a transcontinental zone stretching between Central Asia and Eastern Europe) includes some of the richer in minerals and oils areas in Asia.

The Soviet state did not alter these conditions of oppression, only added to them with a plan to weaken Kazakhstani cultural structures. More specifically, to the concerted oppression of indigenous natural, economic and cultural lifeworlds, the early twentieth century imposition of Soviet collectivisation and organised in-migrations of 400,000 Russians and about one million Slavs, Germans, Jews in Kazakhstani regions generated secessionist resentment. Such soft and hard forms of cleansing led in 1936 to revolts and the autonomation of the Kazakh Soviet Socialist Republic, one of the seven republics of the Union of Soviet Socialist Republics (USSR). Still, this proved far from a complete emancipation from the Soviet political and economic agenda. Although the Republic continued to have an agricultural economy well into the 1950s, the Soviet-German War (1941–1945) introduced in its grounds practices that conformed to the scripts of the Anthropocene: industrialisation and mineral extraction.

The Republic's strategic position in Central Asia (bordering Russia to the north and west, China to the east, Kyrgyzstan to the southeast, Uzbekistan to the south, and Turkmenistan to the southwest and having a coastline along the Caspian Sea), and its spatial vastness made its empty grounds good candidates in the Soviet politics of nuclear domination. In 1947, the Soviets introduced in the Republic their atomic bomb project, by founding the first test site near the north-eastern town of Semipalatinsk, where they tested the first Soviet nuclear bomb in 1949. This was one of many nuclear tests conducted in the region until the dissolution of the USSR, which adversely affected local ecosystems and Kazakh populations. It would not be injudicious to argue that the emergence of a Kazakh anti-nuclear movement in the 1980s and the continuous anti-Soviet resistance of the Kazakh people well into the beginning of the 1990s, when Kazakhstan declared its independence from the Soviet rule (1991), further conflated different ecological priorities in cultural politics, as well as the two aforementioned social scientific systems/programmes. As much as this conflation was assisted by the fact that Kazakhstan is a Muslim country that lived under the influence of an Orthodox Christian ruler for centuries, its abundance in mineral and fossil fuel resources (petroleum, natural gas – it has one of the largest uranium, chromium, lead, manganese and zinc reserves in the world) consolidated its nation-state's entanglement in self-made now ecocidal projects (Fatima & Zafar, 2014).

This background is constitutive of the authorial forces of the Kazakh tourist state, as well as its haphazard collaboration with independent tourism markets. The country's feigned 'democratic', 'secular', and 'constitutional' public face hides the wrongs of an 'intimate cultural self' (Herzfeld, 2005), best represented by its authoritarian President Kassym-Jomart Tokayev. In an extraordinary breach of democratic conduct, following public unrest in 2022 during a spike in fuel prices, Tokayev kicked out of office his predecessor Nursultan Nazarbayev and took control of the powerful Security Council (Pachucki-Włosek, 2022). Not only has the scandalous authoritarian self in Kazakh politics not forsaken Soviet-style governance, but it has also extended its styles to American market ideologies, which seek the consolidation of 'network capital' in cultural affairs at all costs (Larsen & Urry, 2008). Taming its intimate Muslim past through 'McWorld infotainment' channels (Barber, 2003), the new authoritarian governance of its big urban centres, such as Almaty, allows for the state's acculturation into Western norms of production and consumption.

Meanwhile, the faults of *endangering* terrestrial life are strategically streamlined into a cost-efficient anti-Soviet/Russian diplomacy – note, for example, that Kazakhstan supported economically the Ukrainian people after the Russian invasion but did little to support its own affected by the Soviet era's regions of nuclear experimentation, which maimed and killed. The still environmentally *endangered* and uncompensated residents of the now decommissioned nuclear test site in Semipalatinsk have to welcome international dark tourists who want to 'experience' the thrill of visiting sites of death (THE POLYGON, Dark-tourism.com, n.d.). The market card is played across two different fields: of native civic betterment and of international tourist satisfaction, both allegedly 'safe' to promote. In 2016, a review of Kazakhstan's infrastructure for a nuclear power programme was released at the Kazakh government's request by the International Atomic Energy Agency, an intergovernmental organisation that seeks to promote the peaceful use of nuclear energy. The report supported Kazakhstan's continued involvement in 'developing its civilian nuclear program' (IAEA, 8 November 2016). This further accelerated plant construction with the contribution of Japanese, American, Korean, Chinese and Russian suppliers (Collins & Bekenova, 2017).

The launching of a 'Green Economy Plan' in 2013 promised to secure half of Kazakhstan's energy needs from alternative and renewable sources by 2050, while also increasing its GDP by 3% and generating 5,000,000 new jobs (Uyzbayeva et al., 2015). Interestingly, to enhance a sense of national pride and solidarity in the face of disaster, the former nuclear testing sites of eastern Kazakhstan (the so-called 'Nuclear Polygon') are rhetorically presented in public discourse as victims of the Soviet project. However, the uneven development of the oil economy and the geographical peripherality of such sites of disaster hardly address the realities of perforation of their localities by environmental degradation and post-Soviet capitalism alike (Wheeler, 2021, p. 16, 225). The government of Kazakhstan recognises that the three provinces of Eastern Kazakhstan, Qaraghandy and Pavlodar have been affected most by the nuclear tests: miscarriages, stillbirths, physical and neurological defects are high among their younger populations. It has been estimated that radiation, 'which can be transmitted down through five generations' continues to affect some 100,000 people in the Polygon (Genova & Hatcher-Moore, 2017). However, complains that 'benefits are mostly provided to people who have obtained an official certificate proving their status as a radiation victim' match widespread accusations that more than 50% of the affected suffer without welfare support (Najibullah & Akaeva, 2019). As is the case with other regions affected by nuclear disasters, such as the one in Fukushima/Daichi in Japan (Kohso, 2020), the emergence of novel biological subjectivities in the affected regions fostered alternative narratives of non-belonging and hostility within the nation (Alexander, 2020; Stawkowski, 2016).

At this stage, I forgo the comfortable linearities of 'modernity', to suggest that the abandonment of the victims of the nuclear crisis produced a massive crate in the Kazakh Anthropocenic memory. Morton (2013, p. 52) uses the concept of the 'geotrauma' to articulate the ways collective memory marks physical sites of loss. The transformation of Kazakhstan's Anthropocenic geotraumas into commer-cialised dark tourist sites (Stone, 2013; Stone & Sharpley, 2008) attempts to fit rhizomes of living assemblages into old-fashioned modernity theories. This is because it can appeal to the extremophilic tendencies of those guests/visitors, who are interested in 'evidence' that life survives the most inhospitable environments. As 'guilty landscapes' of the Cold War, the sites and their living assemblages are sieved through the colander of serious entertainment for those who are there to watch, photograph and peregrinate, but be gone tomorrow (Reijnders, 2009).

Crucially, the demarcation of such physical sites as possibilities of multispecies survival in the future releases them from topicalised concerns. Minca (2007) suggests that national biopolitics finds its expression in camp-like sites, which can stand as symbols of 'caesurae in the body of the nation' (p. 78), thus allowing the state to treat them as mere spatial concepts. However, it seems that those dwelling Kazakhstan's nuclear sites in the now-time lose their presence in planetary dis-courses regardless of their enunciation as local, regional, national or global sentient lifeforms. There is no geography (of modernity, the Anthropocene or otherwise) in which they can claim homeliness, as even in collective narratives of national trauma their voices are not heard (Alexander et al., 2004; Nora, 1989; for comparison see Isaac et al., 2016, Chapter 17). Qualified as 'non-places' (as per Augé, 2008), they enter mediatised techniques of the twin systems of production and *endangering*. These systems endorse extinction as an *atmospheric technique*: ghosts break your heart in moving pictures and staged exhibitions alike, but you cannot engage with them on a materialist and realist basis.

Indeed, a careful reading of *Borat 2* unveils the presence of not just more-than muted communal voices but also the unsettling complexity of Baron Cohen's performance as a diasporic subject who remembers collective violence in styles not everybody can understand or accept. I will be problematising established arguments on volunteering to disturb the comforts of 'touring history' (Žižek, 2002), by 'thinking through' politically correct renditions of the 'volunteer tourist gaze' in the moving image. The cinematic tourist volunteer gaze emerges not in as clear-cut domain of shaming and blaming as the ones suggested by Žižek. Such binaries of good and evil disregard the complexities of living with the stigmas of privilege and inequality associated with class, gender, ethnicity and network identity, as a well the invisible worlds of affective commitment to different projects. Even Baron Cohen and other creative artists involved in the Borat controversies of designing mobilities enter non-places not always as powerful agents of capitalism, but enunciators of what Everingham and Motta (2022) call 'critical intimacies': invisible non-places in which they can feel and relay their own and other sympathetic subjects' vulnerabilities in controversial ways.

Thus, the chapter's study is situated in the mayhem generated by the polar opposites of accelerated but cruel development and thoughtful but sabotaged flourishing. In fact, the *Borat 1 & 2's* implication in development invites for the topicalisation (see Introduction and Chapter 1) of more than one 'dark crates' across different phase/blocks in the design of Kazakh tourism mobilities. More specifically, the design of such mobilities commences with a variety of controversies over xenophobias entrenched in Kazakh, American and Jewish diasporic memory. These are supposed to address the natural inclinations of the fictional Borat as an uncouth form of otherness inviting disgust and ridicule by international civilised film spectators. However, as human faults, such inclinations expose the civilised spectators'/actors' entrenched prejudices (Herzfeld, 2005, 2019). In the latter phases of design, I consider the attempts of the Kazakh 'tourist state' (Hollinshead, 2009a) to purify the cinematic human specimen of Borat (an alleged sample of 'agrarian folk culture') from its ignominious habitus with the help of refined styles of tourism marketing, addressed to a Western middle-class (post-)tourist gaze.

On Phasing the New Spirit of (In)Hospitality in Kazakhstan

Jensen (2022) suggests that the subjectivities and identities of homeless people are materially interpellated as 'undesired' with the help of design that amplifies 'atmospheres of rejection'. Public places are organised in such ways that the 'undesired' simply cannot visit or dwell them. Likewise, Ahmed (2007) argues that the visible aspects of race facilitate the production of 'geographies of whiteness': materialised as 'no-go' places by virtue of their dense white mobilities and dwellings, such geographies prompt Black subjectivities to even self-exclude in anticipation of encountering hostility in them. Based on the previous section's analysis, Borat's new spirit of hospitality was based on the ideas of inhospitableness: practices of *schematic* exclusion of identities from the design of image, digit-based and tourism mobilities.

Sacha Baron Cohen starred in *Borat 1* as the fictitious Kazakh journalist Borat Sandiyev. Borat is asked by the Kazakh Ministry of Information to visit the 'US of A', the 'Greatest Country in the World', to produce a documentary on its culture and society. Standing between a mockumentary and a travelogue, the film features real-life interactions with Americans, some of which led to lawsuits after the release of the movie. The film produced several controversies, not least because among its participants, who were unaware that they participated in a satire, there were gay pride groups, African American youth and politicians. The fictional journalist's speech is characterised by excessively strong antisemitism, sexism and antiziganism. In Israel, a proposed poster featuring Borat in a sling bikini was rejected in favour of one in which the anti-hero was fully suited (Anderman & Haaretz Staff, 2006). The film was banned in almost the whole of the Arab world, whereas the government of Kazakhstan denounced it. The Foreign Ministry threatened to sue Baron Cohen and the film's Kazakh-based website www.borat.kz was taken down (Wolf, 2007). In the last three instances, accusations of racism were used to modulate perceptions of decency in public in the form of a discourse on shame/shaming.

Widely circulating in the Eastern World but also in traditional enclaves of the Mediterranean societies, the call to avert 'shame' is the responsibility of women, in opposition to 'honour', which is the quality of hegemonic masculinity (Herzfeld, 2006a). Repressing a shameful representation of Kazakhstan in the film made sense in these terms in 2006. If anything, the Kazakh state's advertising via a 'Heart of Eurasia' campaign privileged a masculinised merger of the tourist and the national gaze to endorse heritage/nature tourism (Pritchard & Morgan, 2000). However, about a decade after the film's release and several mostly failed lawsuits on the production company and *Borat 1's* protagonist, the film was recognised by Kazakh Public Relations guru Yerlan Askarbekov as the product of a misread genius. According to Askarbekov, the film was designed 'to get an outsider's view of the US and reveal the prejudices of the Americans who Borat interacts with', making him the '21st century Alexis de Tocqueville' (Askarbekov, 2016). Askarbekov also suggested that those who felt the most unease about the film were Kazakh students studying abroad, because 'their fellow students were sure that the movie showed the real Kazakhstan' (Askarbekov, 2016). Again, behind such comments one may discern the fear of resurgence in racist stereotyping, rather than the conventional Public Relations offence, but such concerns were dismissed. Some Kazakh press, especially tabloids, had even applauded the film for being not only 'cruelly anti-American', but also 'sad at the same time' (*Guardian Film News*, 2006).

Internationally, the celebration of *Borat 1's* anti-Americanism was also endorsed by the BBC, a channel notorious for its sexist treatment of female professionals, whom it underpays vis-à-vis its male presenters. This makes the jubilant tone of the comments twice as problematic. Such uncritical acceptance of the genre discarded how Baron Cohen's public appearances on shows connected to the public defamation of several female professionals: WAPT news producer Dharma Arthur resigned after Baron Cohen, whom she booked for an interview, caused havoc during the show in which he was invited. After the episode, her boss reportedly 'lost his confidence in her abilities' and started 'second-guessing everything she did thereafter', an attitude that led to her depression and worse (Friedman, 2006). The fact that Borat's unruly behaviour exposed the sexist prejudices of Arthur's boss did little to improve his ex-employee's wellbeing and ended her career, leaving her in debt. Pamela Anderson, who starred in *Borat 1*, also filed a divorce from her husband Kid Rock, who called her a 'whore' and a 'slut' for her involvement in the film (Bonawitz, 2006). This time, tabloid gossip finished the job of the pseudo-Kazakh clown, by preying on the actress' personal life. Many celebrated the fictional character's on-stage 'camp' performance, which yielded millions, while indirectly affecting female professionals, who ended up becoming the target of negative public judgement.

One may rightly argue that Baron Cohen's performance as such did not enable the design of tourism mobilities. However, the (anti)aesthetic overlaying of his ethics of representation with cultures of mirth stands at the heart of debates on the emergence of post-tourism mobilities as markers of status and class. Baron Cohen's personal life and artistic biography are bound to further baffle socially and culturally sensitive audiences. Born in the Hammersmith area of London into a devout Jewish family, and graduating from Cambridge with a degree in history, he turned to acting detestable characters with homophobic, sexist, racist and antisemitic inclinations. His satirical extremism often targeted celebrities from the world of politics and entertainment with the aim to expose their entrenched prejudices (Encyclopaedia Britannica, n.d.). At the same, there is evidence that the actor takes his Jewish heritage very seriously: his lifetime partner, Australian comedian Isla Fisher, with whom he parents two children, converted to Judaism before their marriage, and the couple value their privacy – a contentious issue for an actor, who exposes other celebrities' dirty laundry with serious consequences. There is little space here to debate Baron Cohen's biography; however, a note must be made to the ways his subversive style was recruited in as dissimilar to Borat genres as that of *The Trial of the Chicago 7* (dir. Aaron Sorkin, 2020). Released online at the start of the pandemic, this is a documentary-style biopic of the trial of seven political activists accused of orchestrating anti-war campaigns during the 1968 Democratic National Convention. Playing Abby Hoffman, one of the earliest forms of media influencer, activist and founder of the Youth International Party (Yippies), Baron Cohen demonstrated a troubling, if remarkable adaptability from clownish to serious critiques of American politics.

All this seems to be irrelevant to tourism analysis, if one ignores that the character of Borat represents the incompetent and socially illiterate end of the 'post-tourist subject'. As an ideal type in tourism analysis, the post-tourist received attacks from both left and right ends of the scholarly spectrum: for critics of the McDonaldisation of society, their emergence as mobile subjects is the effect of indifference towards engaging with cultural authenticity (Ritzer & Liska, 1997; Wood, 2005). For those who question the sincerity and motivations of those who seek authenticity by means of volunteer tourism in the poor areas of the world, responsible eco-tourism or alternative urban tourism in heritage spots, the post-tourists' thirst for adventure and risk-taking conceals their narcissistic tendencies under a discourse of self-liberation from the pressures of contemporary life (Jansson, 2018). Post-tourists are also increasingly found among individuals with occupations in the media industry, such as reporters, travel journalists, home sellers and even chefs, because the exotic backgrounds they visit provide the best way to frame their professional activities (Fürsich & Kavoori, 2001). Indeed, Feifer's (1985) original definition of the post-tourist stressed that all post-tourist performances respond to visually coded renditions of place and culture that shape our search for authentic places and experiences.

Hence, at the heart of the post-tourist's birth, lies a battle for symbolic legit-imation of skills and knowledge, which foretells recent formations of class and status (see Savage et al., 2015). This battle's role in future transformations of elite tourist categories was predicted early on, in Urry's first edition of *The Tourist Gaze* (1990, p. 11), and Corrigan's (1997) and Calhoun's (2002) elaborations on the power of travel-activity to produce class-informed realities. The post-tourist subject's activities, which accept the presence of inauthenticity and simulation in the provision of tourism, are also debated as the effects of immaterial and reflexive capitalist accumulation of signs (Lash & Urry, 1994). The ideal type of post-tourist had its own phased design: it commenced its life in de-differentiated zones of leisure for the less affluent who, until the introduction of package holi-days, could only consume simulations of tourism on the TV and the big screen (Franklin, 2009). Such forms of leisure extended to visitations in themed locations designed as simulations of authentic heritage locales (e.g., Disneyland). They also informed contemporary digital nomadism for the affluent workers of the digital sector, who relocate to beautiful island locales, where they enjoy sun and sea while working (Campbell, 2005; Dervin & Jacobson, 2021; Uriely, 2015). The original collapse of tourism into accessible leisure patterns challenged the boundaries of class, prompting the middle classes to define new ways to demonstrate their social difference from the working classes via techniques of post-tourism playfulness or knowledge and refinement of inauthenticity involved in post-tourist engagement. It may actually be more correct to argue that, as post-Fordism increasingly dis-solves tourism into a design agenda for 'lifestyle mobilities', the new middle classes become associated with different ethics, aesthetics and ecologies amenable to post-tourist performances (Cresswell & Merriman, 2011, pp. 6–7).

Placed in these intersections of becoming, Borat and Baron Cohen's identities formed a highly questionable synecdoche between the stereotypes of the unci-vilised Islamic peasant of the Kazakh hinterlands and the versatile, two-faced networked Jew, who speaks the conservative revolutionists' language of social corporatism (Žižek, 1993; Žižek & Dolar, 2002). The atmospheric re-emplacement of such banal racist styles in blended human-non-human fields of captivation, in which objects and environments become part of the same con-sumption deal, cannot be dismissed (Tzanelli, 2022b, pp. 78–79). Arguably, one can conclude that the devastating trading of one field of social performance (ethnicity and gender) for another (class and/or status) is lost on Baron Cohen. In neoconservative countries, 'poking fun' is authorised for socially recognised male agents, such as Baron Cohen, whose performances can inspire other mobilities, such as tourism. But then neoconservatism demands that what is moved is decent heritage, rather than the two Borat movies' original script of ethnic ridicule.

An obvious focus becomes how *Borat 1* valorised the Kazakh nation-state's tourist brand, prompting its policymakers to manipulate the 'Borat effect' to its economic and political benefit. In fact, the film's success triggered a proliferation of stakeholders in the global and local cultural fields (Heitmann, 2010), including media conglomerates, the Kazakh tourism organisation, independent tourist business and localities filmed as 'colourful landscapes'. As we will see below, the state's official tourism handle and independent tourism designers from

Kazakhstan and the United States would eventually form a Destination Marketing Organisation (DMO) group based on constellations of signs to promote key Kazakh biomedical and international cybernetic interests. The filmed places' ecological integrity and their communities' wellbeing were subjected to these interests (in contradistinction see Japan, where even rural communities are actively involved in tourism development of this kind – Thelen et al., 2020, pp. 294–295).

This is where the national poetics of phased design give way to the international politics of mobility: award-winning *Joker* (2019) director Todd Phillips, who had made a career on successful comedies, resigned from his post as Borat director in early 2005, citing 'creative differences'. Contemporaneous events suggest that his withdrawal had more to do with a filmed Virginia rodeo event, in which Baron Cohen jokingly told spectators in his Borat alter-ego that 'US President George W. Bush should drink the blood of Iraqi civilians he kills' (World Entertainment News Network, 2005). Such comments would not appeal to American markets so close to the 9/11 tragedy; in addition, the antisemitism and sexism of both films certainly had an active role to play in thinning Borat tourism traffic (Thelen et al., 2020, p. 300). However, the Kazakh poetics of design return us to controversies over the ways distinguished creative labour may also knowingly and simultaneously enter non-places of vulnerability: in Kazakhstan, the film made Baron Cohen a moving target, because re-building the country's image would urge investment in a new tourism campaign that steered international visitors' interest away from the film's unpalatable aspects. Adopting a comparative cross-cultural (Kazakh and American) perspective, I argue that the poetics of cinematic-come-tourist design merged with the politics of national (im) mobility: intimate glances into ethnic culture, involving antisemitism and sexism, as well as terrorism and unbearable multiculturalism, had to be silenced. It helps to bear in mind that in most international relations contexts, the politics of nationalism are based on a representational script, which is constantly repeated. The script endorses the policing of the domestic hearth, which is feminised (Cresswell, 2015, p. 40), and casts women as carers or whores and men as warriors and leaders of the nation (Walby, 2006). This authorial script also informs cultures of hospitality, which are heavily feminised in most international labour contexts (Paolucci, 1998). All in all, market pressures in the fields of tourism and hospitality may reinforce nasty stereotypes entrenched in given social roles and conservative identity narratives (Lugosi, 2014).

Thus, we must examine the ways a putative network of mobilities was organised so as to ensure not just 'recovery' from the ridicule but also complete alignment with the rules of hospitality in cinematic tourism. The filmic component would not survive the design of tourism mobilities, which were progressively more aligned with standard notions of tradition, landscape heritage and history. As Osman et al. (2013, p. 244) aptly suggested in the context of McDonald's food consumption, the very premises of the business often end up becoming integrated into the ways visitors experience place – and thus, an 'authentic' version of it. The 'tourist state' had to work hard to harmonise ('author', in Hollinshead's (2009a) terms) the flow of production within and across individual market chains: from design/designer to product/producer, audience/tourist and, of course, industry/ tourism/film. To do so, one does not exclude such a 'black sheep' or 'intruder' as Baron Cohen, a British-born Jew who topographically and ethnically had little to do with Kazakh identity, they use their skills and assets in productive ways, often at the expense of those who are not deemed to be as immediately 'useful'. Let me outline how this happened in two distinctive phases, earmarking the nation-state's change of attitude towards the Borat effect from the first to the second film.

Phase 1: Borat 1

The first phase of the rebound did not focus on Baron Cohen's performative antics at all. It was organised around a multi-million dollar 'Heart of Eurasia' campaign, involving the production of feature films on the country's mythic past, to counter the *Borat 1* effect. Heritage, not insulting popular culture, had to win the day and the tourist markets. The turn to memory repositories that produce a coherent public image focussed on landscapes reflecting Kazakh ethnic essence. Otherwise put, Borat prompted a modulation of Kazakhstan's heritage/land into tourist landscape in styles endorsing environmental aesthetics as dark tourism (Urry, 2004). The gaze was 'darkened' to suggest seriousness – a strategy of normalisation that bestows upon the nation the honour it deserves. However, then Baron Cohen became even more provocative. After the Kazakh *Borat 1* website was removed, he denounced the Kazakh campaign at an in-character press conference in front of the White House (President Bush refused to accept him) as the propaganda of the 'evil nitwits of Uzbekistan'. 'I would like to make a comment on the recent advertisements on television and in media about my nation of Kazakhstan saying that women are treated equally and that all religions are tolerated. These are disgusting fabrications', he added (Inskeep, 2006). We should not ignore the core of Baron Cohen's counter-attack, which used the denigration of women to discredit the Kazakh campaign: his satirical obstruction of tourism mobilities was built on stereotypical female immobilities, but his comments angered this time Uzbekistan and Kazakhstan for their insolence, making him a target. Unravelling the Kazakh government's design was based on a disruption in the chain of production between the meanings of the film, the performances of its key actor/character and the touristic representations these yielded.

Satire has been the weapon of the weak since time immemorial. However, we must be able to discern when profit displaces the content of the message to such an extent that violence is not inflicted upon the sources of power (the nation-state), but specific categories of citizenry, which are already vulnerable. The Borat sexist jokes' unfortunate effect involved an increasing corroboration between popular feminist stereotypes of the confident new woman and popular misogyny, thus endorsing audience prejudices, instead of crafting a critical gaze on the ways women are discriminated against even via satire (Banet-Weiser, 2018; McRobbie, 2009). From the professional demise of Arthur to the Kazakh tourist state's endorsement of crypto-fascistic authorial scenarios that present native environments as the heart and soul of the nation, Baron Cohen's sexist jokes produced nexuses of prejudice between neoliberal individualism, profiteering at all costs, and a post-feminist aesthetic of ridicule that truly harms (Gill, 2007). Indeed, as I explain in the second phase of *Borat (2)* design, if we push the envelope of tourism authorship under the door not of intersectional prejudice, but its uses in International Relations, 'network capital' (Larsen & Urry, 2008) and the 'tourist gaze 3.0' (Urry & Larsen, 2011) continue to do the digital business of nation-building for Kazakhstan in unjust ways. Any futural 'tourist gaze 4.0' scenarios of recovery from crises, such as those of climate catastrophe and the coronavirus pandemic (e.g. Larsen, 2023) call for international coordination in the design of just tourism and not more business as usual (Jamal, 2019).

Baron Cohen himself is a highly mobile subject of the global now artistic elite. Such elites are certainly faced with obstacles in their personal developmental projects (Favell et al., 2007), but their privileged positionality in global cosmopolitan hierarchies is indisputable. There is an obvious clash between universalist principles and access to resources or implementing democratic justice in context, which guide liberal pretentions to equality (Cresswell, 2006, p. 14; Cresswell, 2010, p. 21; Seiler cited in Adey, 2017, pp. 107–108; Sayer, 2013, p. 252; Tzanelli, 2013a, Chapter 1). Though not exactly part of the 'kinetic elite' when the film was released, Baron Cohen would soon become both affluent and highly mobile in media networks. Post-phenomenologically, his Borat impersonation crafted problematic continuities between extreme habitus performance and the usual wealth display characterising the lifestyles of the kinetic elites ((Birtchnell & Caletrio, 2014, p. 9). Below I explain how such conceptual mutations of excess would land the Borat enterprise of allegedly critical mirth at the doorstep of mobility injustices in the age of extremes (Sheller, 2018b).

As explained above, the Kazakh government realised that the *Borat 1* effect could be beneficial for the country. Especially young audiences became excited about the prospect of visiting the country – so much so, that the UK Kazakh Embassy recorded a rise in visa applications for British tourists. It is unsurprising that by 2012, the country's Foreign Ministry had associated this change in tourism influx with the film. Visit Kazakhstan's established non-*Borat 1* branding was based more on nature-based activities associated with its mountains, such as trekking and winter sports, visits to lakes, water sports or health resorts. In fact, even independent tours that bothered to juxtapose this branding to *Borat 1*-based perceptions of the country seemed to favour the cultural, recreational/sport and eco-friendly end of activities. New blended genres of tourism, which facilitate mobilities of active relaxation and self-care (Hexhagen et al., 2022), were placed at the service of a blended business-state economy. These would include visits to cosmopolitan city centres, such as Almaty, tours to ancient sites, engagement with local people and activities, food tourism, such as tasting local produce, as well as shopping flâneries in traditional bazaars, craft workshops and fashion boutiques (Pratt, 2015, p. 282).

Pratt (2015, pp. 185–286) suggests that we need to take a closer look at the factors contributing to this tourist influx after 2005–2006, which may not always have to do with *Borat 1*, as the Kazakh Government's commercial campaigns never really focused on the film (Macionis, 2004). More importantly, the overall increase of tourism over the 6-year period seemed to have an adverse impact on other public sectors, such as that of welfare provision: drawing resources from other areas to support tourism led to a neglect of other priorities, including of course the welfare of those areas affected by nuclear testing. A 6.4% increase in tourist expenditure because of the film, in which we can include the 'Heart of Eurasia' campaign, decreased the GDP by US$2.78 million, producing a net loss of US$1.43 million over the same period (Pratt, 2015, p. 290). Lack of detailed data may never help us to determine the true impact the film had on Kazakh tourism. However, we can still interrogate the core narratives informing the design of Kazakh tourism, which, in terms of visitor attraction, adopts an overwhelmingly customer-orientated and heritage-conservation 'utilitarian' approach (Schiavone et al., 2022, p. 1111). Nevertheless, note that the reference to utilitarianism conceals a cultural-economic approach to tourism, whereby the common good is undercut by capitalist growth, especially where heritage placemaking is concerned (Douglas, 2014).

As explained in the introduction, phased design participates in the production of an image of the tourist destination (Agarwal & Shaw, 2017), which projects place authenticity as an unequivocal reality or 'truth' (Hollinshead, 1999a, Hollinshead, 2008). It is apposite to talk about regimes of truth at this stage to ascertain not the accuracy, but processual production of reality in markets that rely on representation (Hollinshead, 1998a; Hollinshead & Vellah, 2020; Tzanelli, 2011). Truth regimes are pliable to contingency, and the design of tourism can work wonders on the ways the content of a message is manipulated. By 2012, *Borat 1's* toxic content had been normalised, to potentially allow Kazakhstan to reap the benefits of the tourism it induced. Regardless of the actual results, we need to examine something that received little, if any, attention in scholarship: Kazakhstan's landscapes never featured in *Borat 1*. The movie was filmed in the Romanian village of Glod. Situated 85 miles from the Romanian capital, Bucharest, Glod was at the time of filming a place of some 1,400 inhabitants, mostly Roma and definitely poor. Featuring as Borat's native town, Glod's cinematic design is constitutive of those economies of snobbery that craft the middle-class gaze (Urry, 1990, p. 11): literally meaning 'mud', the village's inhabitants ring to affluent ears as a dirt alarm, so the place itself must conform to such stereotyping. Indeed, *Borat 1's* Glod is visualised against a pseudo-folkish soundtrack as a predominantly muddy environment, full of dirty carts and cows, which cohabit houses with their human masters. Such seemingly unhygienic conditions clash with the beautiful setting of the real Glod, which could easily have featured in a fairy tale (*see* Fig. 3). It is of course questionable what the film's makers truly wanted to achieve through such depictions. I would not rush to exclude from the cinematic script and its artistic staging and performance an attempt to expose the geographies of the moral sentiments on which class identity is sustained, as a battle between public demonstrations of egalitarianism and private snobbery (Jarness & Friedmann, 2017). Beyond the social fields of tourist identity, we can find the cultural-political fields of geopolitical

Fig. 3.   Glod Is a Roma Village in the Commune of Moroeni, Dâmbovița County, Romania. *Source:* Andrei Stroe, CC BY-SA 4.0 <https://creativecommons.org/licenses/by-sa/4.0> via Wikimedia Commons.

strategising, where it is not disingenuous to argue that Glod supplants *Borat 1* with a double *exopolitan* asset: as a 'freeported' cinematic non-place, which is unwanted in the national dominion it belongs (on which see the following paragraph), it allows for the portability of imaginaries of snobbery with impunity, because its Borat version remains disconnected from Romanian identity. However, as a fresh generic signifier of 'ethnic trash', in a show of aesthetic hegemony, it 'nucleates' the real geographies of modernity on which it was based (contra Minca, 2007).

Clearly, I am not talking about cinematic texts. The release of the film enraged village inhabitants, many of whom had featured in it as paid extras for what even external observers found a demeaning depiction of a community living in an arid, forgotten area without much welfare support (Hasan, 2008). The remunerated Glodian extras were left to believe that they participate in a documentary exposure of the hardships of poverty. It is small wonder that anger led some of them to filing a lawsuit for the representational context of the film. The lawsuit mentioned the lack of linguistic communication with the English-made film crews, something that clearly posits questions of exploitation compound with aesthetic marginalisation. Now we can address bigotry in all its glory: Croy et al. (2019, pp. 399–400) sharply critique the marginalisation or erasure of certain stakeholders from DMO strategies, pointing a finger to film industries' indifference in the effects of their presence in localities. In the first *Borat* development phase, an 'image dissonance' (p. 398) or representational conflict emerges between cinematic industrial and community interests: note that neither Bucharest, nor Glod, nor the Romanian nation-state tried to reap any benefits from associations with the film. Kazakhstan's tourism campaigns erased this 'backward' rural element from their script too, which mostly conformed to imaginaries of hospitality inextricably connected to slow tourism (Germann Molz, 2006a; Milbourne & Kitchen, 2014). Poignantly, the village featured only 3 years later in *Carmen Meets Borat* (2009), a film directed by Dutch Mercedes Stalenhoef. Far from being a disinvested travelogue, the film documented local life before and after the *Borat 1* crew visited Glod, with particular emphasis on the impact this had on its small society. The film/documentary narrates through the eyes of a 17-year-old woman trying to escape this life how after *Borat 1's* release, lawyers seeking to capitalise on its controversies, incited anger among locals and promised huge compensations to them if they sued Twentieth Century Fox. The actual lawsuit (filed for US$38 million in damages on account of the thin reimbursements of locals for participating in scenes, as well as libellous depictions of local life as incestuous and ignorant) was dismissed by US District Judge Paska in early December 2006. Its result was the production of local jealousy, anger and further global humiliation (Cecchine, 2009). Refilling the complaint was also dismissed on account of insufficient evidence (Cecchine, 2009) – something provoking further questions regarding the prevalence of racist prejudice in international justice.

Here it helps to compare notes: Baron Cohen's camp depiction of Borat as the comic figure of the yokel, whose predictable humour is based on backwardness, was perceived as a reflexive performance of racist Nazi propaganda that could highlight, equally reflexively, the 'foreignness' of multiculturalism and cosmopolitan irony (Bornstein, 2008). The reactions of the Roma of Glod were never regarded on a par with this: after being positioned as illiterate kitsch objects within the film's narrative, their angry reactions confirmed their cosmopolitical immobility, discrediting their legal claims to compensation. The rules of belonging to an aesthetic cosmopolitan elite fed back into the Kazakh and Romanian nation-states' biopolitical interests to erase them altogether. However, all this translated into tourism mobilities: although national(-ist) valorisation trumped the film's sexist and racist subtext, elsewhere in the world, the content of human rights objections to *Borat 1's* sexist and antisemitic representations did not change. I therefore re-iterate that the 'truthfulness' of what *Borat 1* is and does was verified contingently, in particular (national and international) contexts by particular institutions, which either safeguard specific political interests (e.g. Kazakhstan's reputation in the world) or global economic mobilities (film and tourism markets).

However, even this truth-making pathway disregards how the Kazakh tourist state decided to manipulate *two travelogues based on Borat 1*. Incidentally, 'travelogue' here stands not for mere audio-visual storytelling. All types of travel writing, Holland & Huggan (2000, p. 12) explain, refuse to give up their claims to documentary veracity but also rhetorical excess and even mockery. The general genre's claims to transgression are also as ubiquitous, as their writer's 'flirting' with veracity, which is always in the eye of the beholder during one's encounter with alien environments. Nevertheless, when placed in the hands of tourism governance centres, the genre's inherent malleability can also facilitate trans-formations of emancipatory codes into a technomorphic apparatus of fixed representations. Bulkens et al. (2015) have already explained that quite often, spatial planners attempt to justify their ideals for landscape development on normative stories that allegedly encapsulate local knowledge and views. The Kazakh state's technomorphic design of 'Heart of Eurasia' certainly favoured such normative storytelling, whose digital versions are discussed in the following section. However, unlike *ZG's* technomorphism, this design would repress both dominant travelogue genres associated with *Borat 1*. The first such genre was explored in detail: it emerged from Baron Cohen's/Borat's 'faux' recorded ethnography of Glod/Kazakhstan and based on slippages from refined travelling art to the disreputable gaffes of trippers with no money or manners that we find in working-class and ethnic comedies. We could view this travelogue as part of the so-called 'geographies of snobbery' (Morgan, 2019, pp. 64–66), which attach low values to particular places populated by the wrong 'type of people' (for example: working class, poor or immigrant populations).

In short, Baron Cohen's Glod/Kazakhstan capitalised on joking associated with variations of 'lack' – one of the most favoured terms in the production of discourses of authenticity (Moore et al., 2021). As a travelogue, *Borat 1* stands between the class geographies of snobbery and the crypto-colonial geographies of political, cultural and economic dependency still plaguing post-Soviet national landscapes (Zakharov et al., 2017). Such geographies form palimpsests of storytelling that can only claim decency, if they suppress ethno-racial, gendered and classed differences. The satirical stint of Baron Cohen/Borat's performance structures the first travelogue on precisely these speech-contested 'variables', thus accentuating the incoherence of Kazakh national identity (see discussion of Riessman's 'structural narrative analysis' in Bulkens et al., 2015, p. 2311).

Where Baron Cohen's travelogue facilitates a snobbery of status/position, which targets Kazakhstan's public culture (as per Hollinshead, 1999b), Stalenhoef's produces what I may dub 'geographies of intimacy'. The term recalls a body of research on intimate citizenships and the cosmopolitan condition that dominates the programme of modernity (e.g. Benhabib, 1992; Lister, 1997); however, such debates alone may not best address the complexities of cinematic tourism mobilities in the era of terrestrial endangerment. Stalhoef's geographies of intimacy are mostly based on a particular form of agential realism: far from deferring what is experienced as landscape to a second frame, it calls to life an environmental reality as it records it. More akin to the 'revealing' experiences of committed voluntourists, who immerse themselves not just in cultural but also the visceral environmental contexts that they visit (Hannam & Diekmann, 2016; Tzanelli, 2015), Stalhoef's para-travelogue crafts its stylistic itinerary 'non-representationally', at the most basic level of everyday practice and affective performance (Lorimer, 2005; Thrift, 2008). As such, it promotes emotion to a force that is constitutive of tourism worlds, 'lead[ing] down a somewhat different theoretical path than the impulse to measure, market, and manage tourists' emotional experiences' (German Molz & Buda, 2022, p. 189).

It is important that both travelogues built their powers of persuasion on social categories of being. However, even more significant for this book is how the techniques on which they were based would eventually be co-opted by cinematic tourist markets for structural-technomorphic ends. Because geographies of intimacy debate and represent the ways mobilities and inequalities operate at an *evenemential* level, they may expose processes that stem from lifeworld practices, rather than the workings of capitalism. Also, if treated within the discursive limitations of a travelogue (with an excessive emphasis on motivation, the masculine gaze of the Western tourist or the dynamic gaze of female spatial interactions – Fullagar, 2002; Wearing et al., 2010), such (agential) real(-ist) entanglements of lifeworld, system and environment may easily facilitate regressions to problematic pedagogies of the marketplace. This may happen because even a critical cinematic travelogue has to reduce experience to frames of action – the first phase in the design of mediatised forms of tourism, and therefore the design of palatable tourist sensibilities (Dunn, 2015). Otherwise put, what markets do with artistic creativity is often disconnected from what artists wish to convey. The exposition of critical darkness in Stalhoef's work or satirical critique in Baron Cohen's mockumentaries is structurally modified into new types of dark design that concretise already existing injustices or produce new ones if this suits the tourist state or the powerful international tourist markets. If we modify Jensen's (2019, pp. 128–119) reflections on Young's thesis (1998, 2005, 2011), the end result is not experienced just at a micro-social and *evenemential* level of redistributive justice. Such dark representational apparatuses tend to fortify relationships of domination at the level of transnational mobilities, techniques of bordering and scapal economic planning (Sheller, 2018b).

Phase 2: Borat 2

If the first phase of Kazakh tourism image-building involved the complete suppression of 'everything Borat' in the country's international advertising, the second phase engineered a volte-face conforming to the new spirit of hospitality at a materialist level. Otherwise put, in the second phase of tourism design, all spatio-cultural imaginaries of Kazakhstan were subjected to an intensive governmental programme of non-human mobilities. Landscapes took over the space of cross-cultural exchange, and their erstwhile cinematic *exopoles* of Glod vanquished.

Let me commence the analysis by browsing through some hard data on international tourism mobilities in Kazakhstan between 2008 and 2018: taking on board the 2008 global recession, which slowed down tourism in the region, the numbers of visitors to Kazakhstan between 2008 and 2011 were mostly not from the two international target Borat audience pools, the United States and Europe, especially the United Kingdom, but regional, from other Asian countries (World Data Info, 2018). In 2018, the country recorded a total of nine million tourists, ranking 45th in the world in absolute terms and first in Central Asia. Notably, World Bank data on inbound tourists projecting tourism mobilities up to 2021 without the coronavirus pandemic in the horizon referred to the number of arrivals, not to the number of people travelling, which means that anyone entering the same country more than once is counted each time as a new arrival (Trading

Economics, 2021). When in 2017 the Government of the Republic of Kazakhstan approved the concept and official design of 'Tourism Industry Development of the Republic of Kazakhstan until 2023' (Ministry of Justice of the Republic of Kazakhstan, 2017) and 'Film and Literary Tourism: Analysis and Strategy' (Tourism in Kazakhstan, 2017) was published, *Borat 1* featured nowhere in the statement. The rise in tourism mobilities after 2012 prompts us to reconsider the production of post-truths and how these fit into the more recent *Borat 2*, which is used by the Kazakh tourism discourse.

We deal with two separate controversies in phase 2 of Borat tourism mobilities: the first connects to the film *Borat 2* and the fact that it displays a clear political orientation that its 'prequel' lacked. Again, the story's fictional journalist depicts his homeland as misogynistic, homophobic and anti-Semitic, but the film's narrative arc 'turns the horns' specifically on the US political establishment. The appearance of personal attorney to Donald Trump and former mayor of New York city Rudy Giuliani in the film, who is putting his hands in his trousers, while reclining on a bed in the presence of Maria Bakalova (the actor playing Borat's daughter and posing as a TV journalist), is a direct attack on the Trump administration (Shoard, 2020). This is conventional political satire, and it is unsurprising that Mike Pence and Rudy Giuliani complained that they appeared in the film without their consent. In an out-of-character interview in *Good Morning America*, Baron Cohen renewed his joking about Giuliani by using Trump's catchphrase 'It is what it is. He did what he did' (Blackwelder, 2020) – something that infuriated the then campaigning American President and led to further satirical exchanges (Associated Press, 2020).

More important here is how *Borat 2* incorporated an invisible movement-travel to a non-existing homeland, which was not as obvious in *Borat 1's* arc. The heirs of late Holocaust survivor Judith Dim, who appears in the film, sued *Borat 2* creators alleging that she did not consent to commercial uses of her likeness (Ghermezian, 2020). However, Baron Cohen dedicated *Borat 2* to Dim's memory and claimed that he even broke character to reveal to her that its script was designed to dispel her concerns that the antisemitic jokes were real (Fleming, 2020). All the same, the film's misogynistic and antisemitic content provoked reactions once more, this time from the Kazakh American Association, in which even *Borat 2* distributor Amazon Prime was dragged (Welk, 2020). The dis-organised nature of new capitalism prompts us to treat actions independently, conceding that in this instance the one who 'worldmakes' is Baron Cohen, not the markets. The ambiguity of his actions is dispelled only if we accept that he engages in self-subversion, by adopting an ironic stance towards his own heritage (Turner, 2002). It is not injudicious to argue that, although Kazakhstan features as the putative 'destination' of the cinematic tourist gaze, *Borat 2's* performative design refracts transformations of an imaginary homeland (Israel) into essentialised spirituality.

Joking about the Holocaust produces a memory-souvenir (see also section 1 of chapter 2), which is controversially deconstructed through Baron Cohen's anti-semitic performance (Powers, 2017; Ricoeur, 2004, p. 24; Tzanelli, 2011, pp. 95, 143). For tourism studies scholars, *Borat 2* can be a shock reading of spiritual travel, intentionally defiling both the activity through its sexist joking, and the destination of this putative pilgrimage through Borat's satirical Holocaust denial. This is a cinematic travelogue writ large as a mockumentary (Holland & Huggan, 2000, p. 16), in which post-truth does not conform to the transgressive logic of the absurd, but above all an atmospheric rendition of autobiographical vulnerability.

However, this section promised to transition from the poetics of redistributive justice in tourism to those of market domination, so other questions also need to be asked: What did such cinematic authorship yield for Kazakhstan's tourism authority? The current phase of touristic image-building in Kazakhstan is instructive of the ways the new spirit of hospitality colonises the moral sphere, endorsing complete destabilisation of meaning, so as to adjust political narratives to the circumstances (I see in the construction of these circumstances 'biopolitical interests' that sanction the politics of mobility – Fuller, 2011). In an unprecedented convergence of international cybernetic and national interests, *Borat 2's* rather unflattering depiction of Kazakh culture was not erased (as was the case with the response to *Borat 1*) but *airbrushed*: cosmetically modified with the help of digital/new media platformisation. The cosmetic dimensions of this enterprise borrow from the old scripts of post-colonial desire to join the coveted world of Western civility and progress but interpret them in aesthetic terms that reduce process to appearances (Nederveen Pieterse, 2006). The adoption of platform-based development is not consigned to mere business strategy but reflects a reading of de-differentiation between tourism and other social realms, including that of 'home-making': otherwise put, the 'Heart of Eurasia' gets to travel without travelling at all. In terms of marketing strategy, the Kazakh tourist state's and the tourist markets' selection of media platforms is based on their high spreadability (Jenkins et al., 2013), so what is prepared for such post-travels is visual constructions of real environments.

The overall modification was based on two technomorphic techniques, the first of which involved the displacement of human *characters* from tourist discourse in favour of post-tourism *activities*. Characters are 'the masks worn by moral philosophies' to place moral constraints to those personalities that get to wear them in the form of expectations and, importantly, occupational roles, argue Boltanski and Thévenot (2000, p. 221). As factors in measuring economies of worth, they clash with playful tourist and post-tourist mobilities. Although Kazakhstan's original and modified 'Heart of Eurasia' campaigns drew heavily on national landscape characterisations as a synecdoche of occupational excellence in tourism design, they adopted a more blended approach in the production of ideal tourists/ guest types, ranging from functional to playfully ironic. The advertising strategy incorporated pictorial and audio-visual transitions from Kazakh environmental authenticity (ancient mountainous areas steeped in awe and unique floral biotopes) to ubiquitous 'placeless' consumption and inauthentic performances in the country's major cities (Boorstin, 1961; Gottdiener, 2001; Meyrowitz, 1986; Relph, 1976). Overall, the advertising campaign's ideal type of post-tourist both deliberately dislocated guests from Kazakh histories and selectively conflated environments with national identity.

Unlike the design of types of mobile human, the ideal (post-)tourist *activities* suggested by the campaigns attempted to bridge the gap between character and inauthentic performance. The attempted convergence drew on the qualities of an educated flânerie, which is supposed to be 'the art of producing the now' in refined styles (Wood, 2005, p. 318; Thrift, 1996). More gender-inclusive than its industrial predecessor but also Baron-Cohen's satirical projection of ethnic masculinity (Buck-Morss, 1986; Wolff, 1985), this convergence drew on educated middle-class encounters with adventure, risk and the environment. Hiking, climbing, ecotourism and agrotourism are amongst the top risky post-tourist activities advertised by Kazakhstan Travel (2020), with cultural/heritage and dark tourism (Edensor, 2005a) lagging behind in this particular campaign's representational portfolio. Again, the selection conveys an intelligent reading of 'non-touristic tourism' as a sign of distinction: social for the prospective middle-class visitors, but cultural for the Kazakh tourist host. The individualistic ethos of post-tourism that allows the middle-classes to differentiate their post-tourist activities from those of the masses, is translated in the Kazakh campaign into a project of emancipation from the crassness of Borat-related ethnic simulations. Offering 'specialised tourism' to visitors that addresses environmental and social concerns, or involves intellectual activities, such as getting to know indigenous cultures sets both the guest and the host apart from ordinary tourism and hosting (for an analysis of post-tourism see Munt, 1994). Hence, it is not that the campaign rejects the construction of Kazakhstan as a montage of post-tourist activities; the trick is to present those as a highly refined and unique narrative of dwelling-with-travelling – a 'conjunctural' style of travel that can never be copied by the uneducated masses (Campbell, 2005, pp. 209–210).

The second technomorphic technique was based on a selective discursive montage of 'Boratisms' that fit such established touristic imaginaries of the country in advertising as the aforementioned blends of post-tourist activities (on imaginaries see Salazar & Graburn, 2016). Here, the post-tourist shed some pretentions to serious leisure to join a modified world of Borats. This aspect of the national facelift focussed on things 'nice', to borrow Borat's repeated catchphrase: aesthetically pleasing, if morally wanting statements. Kairat Sadvakassov, the Deputy Chairman of Kazakh Tourism, said in a statement to the *Huffington Post* that adopting Borat's catchphrase 'very nice' offers 'The perfect description of Kazakhstan's vast tourism potential in a short, memorable way' (Sullivan, 2020). This strategic alignment featured in a promotional video, depicting tourists who hike the mounts of Kazakhstan with a selfie stick, exclaiming 'Very nice!'; drink fermented horse milk after Kazakh tradition saying 'Mm, that's actually very nice!'; marvel at Kazakh architecture ('Wow, very nice!') and pose for a photograph with Kazakhs in their traditional costumes ('That's very nice!') (Kazakhstan Travel, 2020).

'Very nice' is a phrase that belongs to some of Borat's most indecorous cinematic moments that I will not mention here. Significantly, this time the campaign was designed by Stanford-educated American Dennis Keen, who had first travelled to the country on a high school exchange. Keen now lives in Almaty, where he gives walking tours to visitors, so he is part of the hospitality industry without the nationalist investment of a native Kazakh. His collaborator in the design of the campaign, Kazakh Yermek Utemissov, is not concerned about adverse reactions to the film, stressing that younger generations 'get it': 'They've got Twitter, they've got Instagram, they've got Reddit, they know English, they know memes...They're inside the media world. We're looking at the same comedians, the same Kimmel show. Kazakhstan is globalized' (Stein, 2020). On the one hand, his statement highlights that cosmopolitan irony and the capacity to 'worldmake' from below has a strong generational element, with younger citizens keener to explore alternative worldviews through self-subversive forms of identification or engagement (Germann Molz, 2006a; Salazar, 2017; Swain, 2009). However, it is fair to stress that as designers, Utemissov and Keen belong to the highly mobile middle classes, and it is very likely that most of the young Kazakh audiences with access to technology are of the same class profile (Nederveen Pieterse, 2019). Hence, on the other hand, the campaign's airbrushing brings to the fore the role of media systems in marketable manipulations of memory (Tzanelli, 2007b, p. 255).

Of course, it is one thing that it took an outsider to enable this airbrushing, another to consider how his design was embraced by the Kazakh Tourism Board. In the latest phase of the design of Kazakh tourism, the Borat image was turned into a discursive tabula rasa, a sign ready to be re-encoded in cosmetically plausible ways. This time, the new spirit of hospitality embraced the innovative take of an outsider to the Kazakh nation, for his ability to remove unpleasant gendered and racialised scripts from *Borat 2's* superscript (Huyssen, 2000). At this stage, Baron Cohen was reduced to a marketable catchphrase for the tourist state of Kazakhstan. Practically, neither he nor Keen were promoted to Kazakhstan's distinguished kinetic labour, but their symbolic presence in tourism marketing campaigns is at least tolerated. Kazakhstan's Tourism Board Deputy Chairman, Kairat Sadvakassov revealed that the decision to let the *Borat 2* controversy 'die its natural death and not respond' was planned (Stein, 2020). The discourse of honour gave way to the acknowledgement that cosmopolitan irony controls late modernity's most powerful steering medium, money (Habermas, 1989, pp. 118–119). The model of Humanity 2.0 promoted in the Kazakh tourist imaginary conformed this time to an even more advanced conflation of ecology, biology and cybernetics (Fuller, 2011, p. 130), which enmeshed elements of Borat's ignominious craft into noble Kazakh heritage.

In both phases of tourism development, we deal with a strategy of biopolitical 'sorting', whereby tourism design draws on ideas of the national body as a text, coded in genomic keys, which may be violated and destroyed by the outside, if the nation's 'immune system' is not careful. Successful immunisation borrows from haphazard strategies of exposure to 'a bit' of the 'other' (Esposito, 2011, pp. 148–150), who in our case can only be the cosmopolitan ironist, the tourist designer or anyone from the global kinetic or distinguished creative labour classes. Granting access to such cosmopolitan subjects, who can enhance the nation's immune apparatus (e.g. valorise national image despite their strangerhood and all the tensions it introduces), contrasts to the rejection of anything that is not strong enough to support its flourishing. Despite their differential status, both professional women and the ethnic poor do not fit into this agenda. As a result, their fortunes were simply silenced in the design of tourism mobilities – a new unethical habit that also endorses conflations of different sociocultural categories with its complete (ironically equitable) disregard for their wellbeing.

Conclusion

In this study, I amend the implicit in film-tourism studies suggestion that, when films generate tourism, scholars can deal in research with a self-contained form of economic development. Borrowing and further adjusting arguments from mobilities design and critical tourism analysis, I shed light on the discursive potential of phased design when a film is connected to tourism. Specifically, I highlight the traps of such discursive evolution in a world dominated by the capitalist organisation of lifeworlds, from localities all the way to the nation and its official handle, the nation state. In analytical terms, I explained (contra Hollinshead et al., 2009) that in film tourism, the authorial powers of development are free-flowing in global realms but socially distributed in contingent ways across the nation state and global markets (Urry, 2007). As a result, what develops as a tourist destination (or bundle of destinations) out of popular cinematic texts can endorse mobilities of ethnic, racial and gendered character in both beneficial and highly problematic ways. What in the case of Borat tourism is problematic, may be beneficial in a different context. All the same, luck and contingent interests seem to inform such 'good luck', positing questions concerning the moral coding guiding market mobilities.

My example of film tourism development, *Borat 1 & 2*, errs on the latter case due to the films' virulent sexist and antisemitic focus, which caused social harm, regardless of their transgressive satirical pretensions. The harm was amplified due to the indifference harboured by tourism authorities, the markets and the Kazakh nation state, in an attempt to maximise profit. I examined how indifference was crafted across different phases of tourism design. The first phase of designing tourism associated with *Borat 1* redirected attention away from the ignominious fictional character of the film to the noble romantic features of Kazakh landscape and modern culture. It replaced the admittedly contentious popular-cultural element of the film with the folk, techno-cultural or natural elements of Kazakh identity. The second phase completed this process, by accepting the racist and sexist elements of *Borat 2*, while appropriating two outsiders' creative labour (Baron Cohen and Keen) to cosmopolitanise Kazakh identity in the tourist trade.

We should not lose sight of the fact that tourism design communicated with the projection of a particular version of 'human': technologically advanced, masculine and ruthless. To return to Fuller's (2011) apt analysis of 'Humanity 2.0', the Kazakh design of tourism conformed national identity to a blueprint of what it means to be modern, progressive and civilised. Ticking the cybernetic (technology, architecture), biomedical (a nation facelifted as a valorised/manly specimen) and ecological boxes (beautiful landscapes to visit), produced an 'acceptable', 'decent' brand. To achieve this, the brand did not simply appeal to a purified version of art/heritage, which is not polluted by vulgar 'pop' elements. In addition, it adopted the Western middle-class ethos of post-tourism as a new form of status differentiation from what is demoted in global hierarchies of cultural value. Thus, Kazakhstan's tourist branding consolidated the nation's cybernetic, biomedical and ecological interests via processes of artistic axiology that we associate with successful/aesthetically pleasing design. From now on, what would 'move around' the world would be a noble version of host identity, compliant with a model of modern Western development. This compliance erased the modal calls of all those terrestrial, natural and post-human pluriverses on the back of which film audiences tour what they cannot know from within.

Chapter 4

Spirited Edgeworks: *Breaking Bad's* (In)Hospitable Worlds of Soft Crime

Legacies of Endangering, Futures of Reviving

The suggestion that tourist consumption is organised from a single industry is as established as conceptions of a 'tourist system', the coordination of which may remain dependent on its plural industrial poles – of airports, hotels, amusement venues and more (Jafari, 1987). Tourism theory has explored the rationale of 'consuming places': indeed, due to its identification as a source of authenticity, place is always incorporated into global knowledge economies that package and market it in intelligible formats (Sheller, 2003; Urry, 1995). As already explained, of particular importance in organisations of knowledge about tourist destinations has been the production of groups of 'signs' that brand and circulate images and narratives of place, creating 'imaginative geographies' (Urry & Larsen, 2011, p. 116). In hybrid industries that thrive on a convergence of interests such as those of cinematic tourism or film-induced tourism, the arrangement of signs is necessary for placemaking and marketing as a tourist destination (Beeton, 2005; Edensor, 2005b; Iwashita, 2008; Tzanelli, 2007a, p. 18). Regardless of declining cinema attendance and corresponding increases in TV viewing (Page & Connell, 2010), increasingly more sophisticated joint initiatives between DMOs and filmmakers systematise hospitality in filmed locations for crews and provide tax-relief incentives for media industries (Christopherson & Rightor, 2010). Not only do such synergies promote organised tours to filmed locations, making some places popular but also may change the demand for tourist activities or even promote infrastructural development for new tourist performances in new film-tourism destinations (Buchmann, 2006; Reijnders, 2011). Such marketed activities attain the nature of pilgrimage, which, in the case of televised drama, constantly draws viewers back to the original filmed sites and creates long-lasting cultural and economic legacies (Beeton, 2005; Couldry, 2000).

More recently, planetary theory began to explore what goes amiss in this frenzy of post-industrial renewal. At its most radical end, the critical planetary argument interrogates the adventurous educational pursuits of tourists, who are treated as earth's 'neo-colonisers' due to resource extraction, extravagant amusement park development and extreme urbanisation (Sheller, 2021; Stinson et al., 2020). Another

The New Spirit of Hospitality, 101–131
Copyright © 2023 Rodanthi Tzanelli
Published under exclusive licence by Emerald Publishing Limited
doi:10.1108/978-1-83753-160-820231005

version of this thesis focuses on the way the atmospheric residue of placemaking participates in any place's global biomediation (Thacker, 2004): how, in other words, the place's residual environmental and cultural properties become strategically implicated in the advancement of techniques of moving image production and digital advertising to dazzle audiences (Sheller, 2009; Thrift, 2010). Both such political-economic and cultural-political approaches debate the colonisation of imagination through the commercialisation of environments and belong to what Latour (2018, pp. 79–80) dubbed the 'Critical Zone': a group of competing debates regarding the relationship between artifice, imagination and nature. At stake is not only what we may think of as a set of relationships of cinematic tourist production (the 'sign industries' argument – Tzanelli, 2007a) but also a different type of worldmaking based on relationships of engendering human and non-human life on earth.

This chapter emphasises not only the civic-democratic limitations but also aesthetic uniqueness of new forms of pilgrimage in sites damaged by human biopolitical engineering. I examine convergences between film and tourism in the globally popular TV series *Breaking Bad* (2008–2013, dirs. multiple – henceforward: *BB*). The case presents tourist and consumption studies with an interesting twist due to the series' focus on drug crime – a theme that would normally condemn filmed locales to criticism and oblivion. On the one hand, tourism theory stresses that place is recreated through the cinematic story rather than the objective features of landscape imagery (Frost, 2010). On the other, film genre theory focusing on crime attests that there is ample business opportunity in crime and violence (Tudor, 1989; Tzanelli, 2013a, Chapter 3). From both perspectives, one's task would be to explain how this fascination links the *BB* series to tourism, and then to techniques of endangering or engendering human and non-human life in the filming and touring grounds of Albuquerque. The key objective would not provide an empirical study of tourist experiences and performances of the series, but an alternative conceptual and theoretical discourse on the ways the rationale of its tourist industry (Connell, 2012, p. 1008; Månsson et al., 2020) supplants systems of structural violence and regeneration in different ways.

Often an either-or verdict in the Critical Zone seeks to suppress a rather uncomfortable admission that regeneration and violence do not really occupy separate moral universes in the age of speed. There is no smooth way to break the news: the good and the bad coexist on this messy planet, making discourses of the virtuous look utopian at best. Even by slightly shifting our perspectival study of mobility justice in terms of what is created, nourished and how, we may have to concede that terrestrial engendering is a property of post-truthful making-and-breaking of the rules of development. And although the observation still draws on Young's ([1990] 2011) politics of difference, it does not contain them to racial recognitive or distributive rights. Competing fields of domination treat such arguments on a par with extra-variables of (gendered, racial or non-human) presence in which the disenfranchised collectivity is overridden by urban systems. It is an open secret that these systems of mobility are conditioned and defined by the aesthetic and economic imperatives of production and consumption. Some may agree that it is both exuberant and frightening to treat a system of mobility as a vitalist model for our collective futures.

One may claim that film and tourism do not connect to such observations. I object to such hasty claims, arguing for a particular contextualisation of the role of film tourism within cultural and media studies, suggesting that tourism theory alone cannot do the job of other fields such as those of popular culture or the sociology of deviance and crime (Ryan et al., 2009), nor can it promote cross-disciplinary (Beeton, 2010, p. 5), or indeed needy *transdisciplinary* methodological fertilisation without having recourse to the poetics of race, gender and class. In planetary terms, even such *problématiques* come short of a reasonable expectation to accommodate such poetics within entangled natural, social, cultural and political ecologies, where all recognitive battles take place these days, after all. Admittedly, to address such big themes through a cinematic tourism thematic, one needs to coordinate regional biographies (the *BB* city of Albuquerque) with the emergence of cultural practices (of consuming risk) that both amplify and problematise localised justice deficits (or, as is this chapter's case, support a policy of selective flourishing).

And here we are, again, pulling out of the large social-scientific cabinet some well-worn ideal types of (im)mobility: Simmel's 'flâneur', whom feminist theorists rebut as the masculinist sham of a failed Western modernity (Wolff, 1985); the 'sandwichman' and the 'whore', who are condemned to cater for the needs of some-bodies loaded with cash (Buck-Morss, 1986) or the awkwardly articulated 'choraster' (Wearing et al., 2010, p. 10), who claims space as the domain of lived experience vis-à-vis that of the 'tourist for a day' (Fussell, 1980). Let me be clear on the last case: a *chora* is not the 'motherland' of political theory; it is a place that addresses personal needs to belong and the certainty of an intimate knowledge that cannot be attained by a fleeting tour to a resort, or its portable tourist imaginaries that feature in advertising (Grosz, 1994). Because of its intimate nature, its behind-the-scenes existence, a *chora* is also the domain where structural violence, camaraderie and love make worlds of neglect and/or care. *Choras* are the key subject matter of the Critical Zone.

To these ideal types, I will add those of the 'nomad', who will feature prominently in the following sections, as well as the 'digital tourist', the 'adventurer' and the 'edgeworker'. This cluster of ideal types transcends the conceptual constraints of metaphors because each one of them communicates with real social conditions, roles and social statuses. In this chapter, their invisible counterpart (what is hauntingly absent from the spaces of tourist enjoyment) is not only the 'vagabond' but also the racial other and the 'new poor subject'. Their invisibility is partly the effect of a necessary structural technomorphism that allows the cinematic city of Albuquerque to align conceptions of cosmopolitan citizenry with life-projects 'built around consumer choice rather than work, professional skills, or jobs' (Bauman, 1998, p. 1). But whilst this model of citizenship is linked to the profiles of ephemeral cinematic tourist visitors, and professional attainment to the middle-class Albuquerquean hosts, the migrant subjects of the Mexican-American border and the city's poor populations feature nowhere.

It is impossible to build a chapter about tourist performance exclusively on absences, so my strategy is to amplify the presence of those who feel entitled to the chorastic endeavours of the cinematic tourist. My intention is not one-sided: on the one hand, the more the cinematic tourists' *faux* daredevil activities feature in the performative spaces of the city, the more readers may wonder what is going on in Albuquerque's real crime underbelly (and on this, some notes are provided along the way). On the other hand, to dismiss such consumption rituals as trivial is *bad* social analysis: not only do they tell us meaningful stories about new designs of leisure but they also expose how these deal with anxieties about crime, risk and the decline of subjective wellbeing at any and every social status bracketing.

I begin by acknowledging that televisual fan communities can be 'staged' with the help of new media technologies (Tzanelli, 2007a, p. 17) before or after their independent development through performances of media texts (Hills, 2002, p. 144). There are intersections and disjunctions between televisual and tourist imaginaries that I explore as discursive tropes – or rather, the ways such discourses are interpreted and marketed by various agents virtually and terrestrially (D'Andrea, 2006, pp. 114–115). The internet as a medium absorbs and recreates itself through hyperlinked content, breaking this up into 'searchable chunks' while also surrounding itself 'with various other media it has absorbed' (Adams, 2006, p. 33; Anastasiou and Schäler, 2010; Carr, 2010, p. 91). Considering that web texts have an intertextual and hyperlinked nature (Mitra & Cohen, 1999), I focus on the ways *BB's* anti-heroes produce anodyne consumer and tourist rituals in filmed sites and through 'bad' souvenirs addressed to tourist senses (candies or bath salts). As an internet tourist myself, I acknowledge the potency of gender stereotyping in consumption rituals and cinematic tourist pilgrimages. Though not focusing on gendered representations, I note that the series' arc constructs a masculine gaze which is nevertheless feminised though shopping rituals and tourist pilgrimages in Albuquerque and on the web (Friedberg, 1995; Mulvey, 2006). This gendered play of (dis-)embodied mobilities matches the global criticism of *BB* consumption as 'socially risky', irresponsible and shameful – tropes that remain traditionally gendered and correspond to Walter's move from disempowerment to illicit control and high status in criminal networks.

With these controversies in mind, in the following section, I unpack the atmospheric capital of the series through the design of its three key characters, Walter White, Jesse Pinkman and Gustavo Fring, as well as the latter's Latino network of drug mobilities. I view this character's cine-cosmos as the first phase of *BB* tourism worldmaking, which turns dreams (or, rather nightmares) into the subject matter of a controlled, *themed* environment (of *BB* tours and units of consumption – see Hollinshead, 2009c, pp. 273–274; Urry & Larsen, 2011, p. 127). In fact, Albuquerque's natural environment and the region's geomorphological profile also become cinematic characters. Their role is to relay geographies of crime and guilt as pleasure in the second phase of *BB* tourism design. Hence, in phase 2, I explore the tourist performances of *BB's* social nightmares as anodyne adventures and safe edgework that never breaks health and safety regulations or the law. The analysis, which spans embodied and virtual stagings of *BB* consumption and tourism, is extended to explorations of what may truly be endangered in the *BB* industry's current advanced phase (3).

Phase 1: Consuming Social (Extra-)ordinariness: Real Crime and Cinematic Tourist Anomie

Originally a sleeper hit, the series attained an ever-growing pool of global fans, as it went on to attain record-breaking ratings (Hibberd, 2013). Launched on January 2008 in the United States and Canada on the cable network AMC, by the end of the final season, it had won various awards, including ten Primetime Emmy Awards, three consecutive wins for Best Actor for Bryan Cranston (playing its principal character), two wins for Best Supporting Actor for Paul Aaron (his collaborator in crime, Jesse Pinkman) and a Best Supporting Actress win for Anna Gunn (featuring in the series as Cranston's wife). In addition, it was nominated for a Golden Globe Award for Best Television Series – Drama. Cranston was nominated three times for Best Actor and four times for a Screen Actors Guild Award for Best Actor, winning once at the 19th Screen Actors Guild Awards. In 2013, the Writers Guild of America named *BB* the 13th best-written TV series of all time (Deadline Hollywood, n.d.).

In order to grasp the attraction of *BB* for tourist consumers, I must briefly review the plot, crime content and characterisation of the show. The show focuses upon the travails of Walter White (Cranston), a high school chemistry teacher living with his family in Albuquerque, New Mexico. At the start of the narrative, a frustrated Walter dutifully performs his job in the face of indifferent students, while the family struggles financially on his modest income, supplemented by his wife Skyler's (Gunn) earnings as a part-time bookkeeper. The responsibility for looking after their teenage son Walter Junior (R.J. Mitte), who has cerebral palsy, is intensified when Skyler finds she is pregnant. At this point, Walter is diagnosed with inoperable and apparently terminal lung cancer and faces a terrible dilemma: paying for cancer treatment will bankrupt the family and leave them in penury – yet foregoing treatment will destroy any chance of surviving the disease. In desperate straits, Walt uses his expertise in chemistry to enter a new line of business – the production of methamphetamine or 'crystal meth'. He teams up with his former student Jesse Pinkman (Paul Aaron), who is now a low-level drug dealer and user, living an aimless and dissolute life. Between Walt's brilliance as a chemist, and Jesse's contacts amongst drug users, they launch a successful enterprise. Soon, their product ('blue meth', named after its distinctive colour) is being hailed as the best and purest 'product' ever seen. Over the course of the show's span, we see Walt forced to go ever deeper into criminal activity (including multiple murders, arson and poisoning a child) in order to protect his business, his freedom, his family and the sometimes-hapless Jesse. Under the alias of 'Heisenberg', he becomes a ruthless and powerful force in the international drug trade, working alongside drug impresario Gustavo Fring (Giancarlo Esposito), who runs a cross-border distribution empire from behind the front of a fast-food chicken franchise, *Los Pollos Hermanos* ('The Chicken Brothers'). Meanwhile, Walt's family remain oblivious to his double life (including his brother-in-law Hank (Dean Norris), a Drugs Enforcement Agency officer, who himself becomes increasingly obsessive in his pursuit of the mysterious 'Heisenberg').

The confluence of the crime (producing and dealing in 'crystal meth') and the protagonist (a respectable, middle-class family man-turned-master criminal) furnish the basis of audience fascination, and consequently the tourist industry that has emerged around the show in post-phenomenological and psychogeographic styles. The post-phenomenal engagement with the plot is designed in harsh audio-visual aesthetic styles, which produce a post-tourist journey to a second order reality: the more the frames of crime are deferred in a spectacular background, the more the organisations later involved in the construction of themed *BB* locations can claim participation in the rhetoric of community-orientated planning (Hollinshead, 2009c, p. 274). The gap between the 'needs' and 'wants' of those communities inhabiting the said design ecology (Papanek, 1991, pp. 219–221) is usually exposed long after form takes over content and utility. This formalist move, which is essential in cinematic-tourist design, will irrevocably shift attention to virtual and embodied psychogeographies of *consuming* place (Urry, 1995, pp. 134–135). The cinematic tourist design's emergent choraster will also take over the space of place performance, making their 'wants' a priority. A Marxist may suggest that post-phenomenologies of filmed places should stress how tourist outsiders split chorastic activities into two separate worlds, directing mediated publicness (world 1) away from the intimate everyday rituals of dwellers (world 2) – their 'place-ballet' (Seamon cited in Cresswell, 2015, pp. 63–64). However, I find that it is more accurate to see in this shift not an erasure of place-ballets, but a particular formatting of their meaning and function as aspects of a cinematic drama from which different interest groups may benefit or not (on hospitality and performance see Bell, 2007, p. 40; Osman et al., 2013).

The show's focus upon the production and distribution of 'crystal meth' draws upon the cultural notoriety that the drug has acquired over recent years. The major attraction of *BB* resides, I suggest, in its portrayal of white middle-class masculinity in contemporary America during the global economic recession. Because this is consistently juxtaposed with an abject form of Black Latino stratification by criminal means (Gustavo Fring is an as elegant and polite public figure in Albuquerque's business community, as he is cruel in his exchanges with cross-border drug lords in his secret business networks and a-sexual in his private life), audiences become accustomed to read the *BB* plot as a racial geography of privilege and inequality early on. It is precisely this sexually and emotionally crippled version of Fring's blaxploitation positioning as a middle-class 'fake' that will pave the ground for the design of an essentially *white psychogeographic pilgrimage* to the filmed *BB* sites. Fring allows viewers to abort the baby of critical thinking, by erasing all traces of both white settler and post-tourist responsibility from the cinematic and then terrestrial map of *BB* consumption rituals (Stinson et al., 2021).

Or it seems so. To determine what actually happens, I can now pay attention to these whitewashed *BB* psychogeographies, which, after closer inspection, seem to overlay racial privilege with class and status anxieties, ultimately settling for the latter. D'Andrea's (2004) argument that mobility and marginality provide ideal conditions for transgressive experiences might work in this instance at the fantastic level, as a libidinal economy for *BB* audiences, once affluent social groups who can at least experience adverse lifestyle changes as simulations. This regression from the harsh reality of recession to an unreal plot allows for the production of white irrealist pilgrimages (Tzanelli, 2020a), whose meaning can constantly mutate to address status inconsistency and fear of being left behind in the highly competitive American society. Walter serves as the archetype of this identity, and his travails appeal to audiences because of the way they articulate experiences of unfairness, marginalisation and frustration. Unlike the cruel and conniving Fring, who slowly climbs up the social scale, Walter is painted as the hard-working, responsible, law-abiding American, who finds his contribution to society ignored, and when he needs support and recognition the most, he finds himself forgotten in a country that seems to place little value on men like him (the issue of ill-health is especially resonant, as medical bills are held to be the most frequent cause of bankruptcies in the United States – reaching some two million in 2013 alone, when the *BB* series came to an end – Mangan, 2013).

The notion of a white middle-class masculinity 'pushed to breaking point' by sociocultural change has featured repeatedly in American popular culture – for example, the 1993 film *Falling Down* (dir. J. Schumacher) depicts a middle-aged unemployed engineer who 'cracks' under the pressure of his frustrations and goes on a violent rampage across Los Angeles (Prince, 2000). Likewise, Walter White offers a point of identification for the audience's resentments at 'the system', and his growing resume of violent crimes is contextualised through an appeal to values such as family, responsibility, loyalty and above all 'getting what's due' to a 'model citizen' (the evocation of familial loyalty as a motivation and justification for crime recuperates popular themes in the representation of the Italian-American Mafioso, apparent in films such as the *Godfather* series (1972, 1974 & 1991 dir. F. Ford Copolla; Hess, 1975). In sociological terms, Walter is the 'innovator' who responds to anomie by turning to crime – his attempts to live the 'American Dream' by playing fair have been sabotaged so, much like Gustavo Fring, he turns instead to crime, but unlike him, he does so to secure a 'good life' for his family (Merton, 1938). This depiction makes Walter available as an 'anti-hero' for whom audiences can 'root', rather than the conventionally villainous 'drug lord' of Hollywood – typically represented as either a Black inner city 'gangsta' or a Latin American cartel boss (Boyd, 2002). The consumption and enjoyment of *BB* is inextricably tied to the possibilities that Walter White offers for middle-class white America to vicariously release its frustrations – one famous Albuquerque newspaper (the *Albuquerque Journal*) even went so far as to publish an 'obituary' for the fictional Walter, concluding with the words 'he will be greatly missed' (*Huffpost*, 2013).

To capitulate, *BB*'s budding cultural industry capitalised on the series' *ethographic* exposition of some ordinary human characters. More specifically, the centrality of Walter's moral 'fall' associates the series with both criminological and tourist understandings of anomie in terms of the human subject's relocation outside acceptable boundaries and norms that define everyday life. I should briefly reflect here upon the seeming perversity of consumption experiences that find pleasure in crime, death and murder as these frame *BB*'s hybrid sign industry. Far from being a fetish consigned to the morbid few, the very popularity of crime in its various cultural incarnations points to a widespread (if not universal) appeal of such experiences. Of course, myriad psychological, psychoanalytic and socio-logical explanations might be mobilised to account for such interests. From a sociologically informed standpoint, I should note two strands of thinking that bear centrally on this question. Firstly, following classical Durkheimian theory, it can be suggested that the 'spectacle' of crime serves a valuable social function in that its confrontation and condemnation activates conventional norms and moral sentiments and in doing so helps sustain the 'collective consciousness' of the social group (Durkheim, 1982, pp. 99–101). In a society where the incidence of murder and violent crime has followed a long-term historical trend of decline (Elias, 2000; Spierenburg, 2008), we might view the public fascination instead with the cultural representation, simulation and staging of such offences as an *ersatz* opportunity for the activation of moral norms in the terms set out by Durkheim.

However, such explanations are not entirely adequate in the face of the pop-ular enjoyment of crime, precisely because so much of the pleasure taken in it is oriented not to condemnation but to celebration of offenders (spanning the kinds of serial killer enthusiasts and 'murderbilia' collectors explored by Jarvis (2007), to the public appetite for autobiographies of 'celebrated criminals' examined by Penfold-Mounce (2010)). Additionally, the *BB* tourist fascination does not pre-sent the first instance whereby crime and adventure facilitate the emergence of tourist consumption tied to performances of an imagined masculinity: as Reijnders' (2010) ethnography of James Bond tourism has shown, cinematic tourists enter the world of Bond through visits to filmed locales because they are afforded the opportunity to perform an imagined masculinity. And although Bond is on the right side of law, his methods are no less criminal and violent. Consequently, one must acknowledge the complex and ambivalent character of our cultural responses to crime: the offender is both an object of vilification and the subject of identification for an audience that takes vicarious pleasure in what Katz (1988) calls 'seductions of crime', the joy and existential thrill of trans-gression and rule-breaking. I suggest that the pleasure afforded by the touristic consumption of *BB* is closely tied to how the show represents both the crimes (primarily those associated with the production of 'crystal meth') and crucially the criminal (Walter White).

As offshoot of individual status enhancement, tourist mobility is mostly based on authorised transgression (Dann, 1977), which clashes with ego-enhancing profit-making by illicit means. However, *BB* successfully bridges this polar opposition to explain Walter's moral descent on the basis of a constantly denied social (and economic) recognition of his worth. Watching on screen, and now immersing themselves into Walter's shady business via visits to his work and family environs allows fans to be publicly accredited tourists, safe and legally protected 'witnesses' of a life hidden behind conspiracy and crime. Cohen (1996), who suggested a phenomenological typology of tourist experiences rooted in the concept of the 'centre', the cosmological point at which heaven, earth and hell meet, nicely sketches both the experimental properties of contemporary risk-free *BB* tourism and fan consumption, and the infernal character of its criminal protagonists. *BB's* 'experimental' mode of tourism suggests the presence of alternative hedonist consumptions that transcend neat classifications between 'good' and 'evil' – not just because they are harmless as mere simulations of a TV story but also because the story's characters are easily identified as struggling Everymen.

I mentioned the *BB* fans' willing immersion in Walter White's business and private life as a gateway to a far larger world of tourist mobilities in what we may dub Albuquerque's '*exoscapes*'. In media tourism analysis, the concept of 'play-scapes' is understood as an urban interface, in which aesthetic performances and technical infrastructures converge to produce new styles of and physical stages for tourist play (Junemo cited in Jang & Kim, 2022, unpaginated; Sheller & Urry, 2004, p. 4). Specifically in the *BB* industry, an exoscape is a contiguous development of televised crime narratives, real geographies of marginality and hyperreal design of themed (by the cinematic story) environments. Exoscapes are the imagined counterparts of cinematic *exopoles*; their role is to facilitate a smoother rhizomatic movement of façades, behind which money and prestige can flow in combinations of secrecy, privacy and safety. But this is not exactly Urry's (2014, pp. 48–50) approach to 'façades', which focusses on tax evasion and off-shoring. Unlike tax evasion in offshoring strategies, exoscapal evasion occurs whenever the material and immaterial (i.e., representational and stereotypical) conditions of urban life may actually hinder just creative policies of development. Heretofore, I explore discourses of inhospitality through practices of taming ecological anomies and hostilities into a novel technomorphic design as part of a localised civilising project. In this design, creative decriminalisation comes closer to policies of soft power (Nye, 2004). It helps to note that, unlike the case of *ZG* mobilities, Albuquerque's soft power is exercised in a decentralised network of growth, which is endowed by the American constitutional system: as early as in 1917, Albuquerque became a 'charter city'. This means that home rule is exercised locally and since the mid-1970s through a mayor-council system (City of Albuquerque, charter, n.d.).

The *BB* story unfolds in one of the most populous cities of the American state of New Mexico and a historic melting pot for European and Native American cultures. The 2020 census listed 564,559 residents, making Albuquerque one of the largest **urban formations** in the Southwest (Albuquerque city, New Mexico, 2020), whereas its metropolitan area exceeds the 1,000,000 permanent dwellers (Combined statistical areas – 2020 census, 2020). Official resources also account for the presence of growing technological hubs and media companies in its heart, a 'Smart City' and 'Information and Technology' plan of development stretching back to the first decade of the twenty-first century (City of Albuquerque, Technology and innovation, n.d.), as well as a strong heritage and art culture (City of Albuquerque, Planning, n.d.). It takes a cultural webnographer a while to realise that Albuquerque's official websites are an exercise in digitised painterly narratives: in every page, sunset panoramas and red soil, fauna and a blasting sunlight frame the city's policy statement. A first note on the softness of the city's power is that it is mediated atmospherically through aesthetic styles that appeal to artistic registers of the picturesque.

Let us explore the wider frame in geographical and environmental terms: the city's elevated place in the Albuquerque Basin's ecoregion is framed by the Rio Grande and its Bosque forest in the centre, the Sandia-Manzano Mountains in the east and the West Mesa on the west, making its geomorphological profile uniquely 'picturesque'. This picturesqueness borrows from German idealism's definition of the term in relation to the affective and emotional movement of baroque that is 'painterly' and affective in a Bergsonian style (Macarthur, 2007, pp. 246–247, 256). However, associations of soft power with the affective poetics of landscape, which would recall *ZG's* playscapes, are not enough. Here, the picturesque is preliminarily defined by an atmospheric indeterminacy, which is based on fusions of arid semi-desert, plain steppe ecoregions and juniper/pine forests. One may also concede that cultural landscapes are ideological products (Minca, 2013, p. 58), but they must still find ways to discern how their atmospheric unity is approached by cultural experts (i.e., how an *atmosphere* which unifies a situation is defined), from the presence of *plural atmospheres* which are directed to specific senses through the uses of specific environmental/aesthetic stimuli (Rauch, 2018, p. 93). The dissolution of the boundaries between recording and sensing/perceiving atmospheres defines the urban projects of sociologists, such as Thibaud (2011), who assure us that, as much as physical and architectural landscapes are the products of ideologies, those who traverse them can also reshape their meanings to some extent. The latter features prominently in the *BB* cinematic project, but the former merits further exploration.

Officially classified as cold, semi-arid, semi-desert temperate climate, Albuquerque's atmospheric blueprint communicates not only harshness and inhospitability but also serenity and diversity. The city itself is also anything but socially and geographically uniform, featuring four dissimilar 'quadrants': in the north-eastern part, the most affluent neighbourhoods sit just outside the city limits; the north-western quadrant features the historic eighteenth-century Old Town, the Indian Pueblo Cultural Centre, several museums and galleries, a blend of high- and low-income commercial areas, as well as all the media hubs that contribute to the city's global iconic presence (e.g. Netflix Studios); the south-eastern quadrant, which is a mix of agricultural and suburban neighbourhoods, includes the most ancient communities of the region, and some rapidly growing areas, such as the Barelas, the South Valley of New Mexico and the west side. Especially the north-western quadrant's development into a digital and audio-visual node facilitated the emergence of a twin cybernetic and biopolitical formation: an *endopolis* of capitalist mobilities and spectacular consumption, and an *exopolis* of racial poverty, on which *BB's* representational capital of crime would be based. It is an open secret, for example, that downtown stratification has affected the once diverse racial profile of the quadrant's Latino neighbourhoods, paving the path for social mobility and racial marginality in equal measure (Patterson, 2020). According to urban modelling projections, the north-western quadrant is set to experience slow growth in the next few decades, due to lack of sustainable water supply. Also, other areas outside the city borders have been earmarked as better candidates for urban growth, due to their lack of housing and the presence of empty grounds (Bajracharya et al., 2020, p. 188).

To cut the story short, for Old Town, the *BB* industry is a good alternative to a plan of urban growth, which may never be supported by the city. Its zombie capitalist nature assures the biopolitical longevity of Albuquerque as a phantasmagorical city that feeds on imagined crime. Place and cultural narrative are closely connected, after all (Bulkens et al., 2015). Several scholars have explained that both individuals and social groups connect (auto-)biographical storytelling to landscapes so as to consolidate sociocultural identities. Uses of landscape are significant in analyses of cinematic or film-induced tourism (Connell, 2012; van Es & Reijnders, 2018). As instant identifiers or promoters of cultural specificity, landscapes may crystallise the essence of televisual narratives. We may indeed talk about cultural 'topophilia' (Tuan, 1974) or love of place in its various narrative forms. Topophilic rites promoting rural innocence reach their digital apogee in the enclaves of post-modernity: global cities (Sassen, 2001). In contemporary televisual tourist contexts, the city acts as repository of phantasmagorical images, readily available to global flâneurs and tourist visitors for inspection, consumption and reinvention in personal narratives. By the same token, however, cinematic urbanism provides ample opportunities to bring together different forms of capital and social stratification strategies that are not readily available in the fields of realist design (AlSayyad, 2006; Hanquinet, 2017).

The explosion of tourism-inducing urban filmographies is closely connected to post-modern adulations of contemporary 'speed cultures' including those of the specialised (televisual) tour (Savelli, 2009, p. 151). Albuquerque's media staging as a city that is both intimidatingly grand and comfortably communal, 'where small towns find themselves neighbouring seas of desert and the looming shadows of the mountainous teeth' (Kelly, 2013), participates in *BB's* topophilic marketing. Originally scripted for California, the series' relocation to Albuquerque's desert landscape convinced its creator Vince Gilligan that the place would develop into a character in a show resembling a modern-day Western (Albuquerque Convention & Visitor's Bureau, 2013). 'All the wonderful topographical and geographical elements, we put to good use', he explained, stressing the significance of the dramatic clouds, 'which you don't see in the blank blue skies of Southern California'. The interview advertised the city's 'stealth charm' and stark beauty, with the Sandias, the mountains to the east, as a centrepiece (Brennan, 2013).

When one places Albuquerque's diaphanous evolving social biography on top of a maquette of the region's environmental-geomorphological blueprint, two atmospheric qualities appear to act as qualitative post-phenomenological constants: indeterminacy and bordering. The amazingly long Rio Grande and the Sandia-Manzano Mountains physically segment the region, whereas uneven transitions from forests to deserts and steppes produce unevenness and physical inhospitality. When viscerally confronted with such abrupt, if magical transitions, viewers are asked to translate their vagueness on their own terms. But this is also the job that *BB's* creators did so elegantly, transforming mountainous backgrounds, clouds and reptiles into entities that 'while being fundamental under the anthropic and perceptive profile', may be positioned as 'superfluous under the predictive-scientific one' (Mark-Smith cited in Griffero, 2014, p. 61).

Nevertheless, there is a difference between a tourist guest's disinterested viewing and a director's or photographic designer's cinematic interpretation, as that the latter take their time (across several seasons of the drama) to superimpose the city's social makeup over its geomorphological and environmental profiling. This allows them to expose a hierarchy of 'nested units' (Gibson, 1979, p. 22), which leads us all the way down to the politics of bordering and biopolitical classification. This is precisely what Walter, Jesse and Gustavo's sociocultural blueprints do as expositions of 'borders within borders', the multiplicity of sites, in which flourishing is entrapped, constrained and disciplined in everyday life (see Sheller, 2020, p. 31 on intersectional [gendered and racialised] migrations and kinopolitics). Looking past the story's key characters, we see other male, and mostly Black anti-heroes, who evade border control to smuggle drugs into the United States. These small plots within the main plot occur repeatedly across seasons, transforming *BB* camera's 'expert eye' into a figment of biometric control and biopolitical sorting: a non-human Leviathan, ascribing criminal algorithmic identities to human types (Amoore, 2006).

Thus, what at first may appear to scientific experts to be an arbitrary atmospheric game is, in fact, a nicely concealed popcultural critique of the 'needs' and 'wants' that define Albuquerque's design ecologies: its vulnerability to cross-border crime, such as human and drug trafficking; its racial and class inequalities and its struggle to transform its physical, cultural and geographical hybridity into an internationally recognised identity that moves. To make my point clearer, it is inaccurate to say that the *BB* film and tourist projects had the same objectives from the outset; on the contrary, the cinematic industry's project in phase 1 could potentially sabotage Albuquerque's tourism profile as a civilised and hospitable city of arts and culture. Only when the *BB's* cinematic saga was transformed into an *exoscape* (when its cruel realist atmospheres were tamed into tourism walks, sweets and film souvenirs), did it produce a cinematic *exopolis* as a creative project. To explore this *BB* tourist design, I now turn to Albuquerque's filmed locations and tourist *BB* performances.

Phase 2: The Structural Violence of Terrestrial Sorting: Edgework Vs. Biographical Death

Little 'miracles' happen: the TV series captured the hearts of American and international audiences and the ensued *BB* anti-hero worship transformed the principal filming locales in Albuquerque, into tourist attractions, prompting the city's Tourist Bureau to advertise *BB* tours on its website (under the umbrella of 'film tourism' that also includes other recent production shots in the city – Visit Albuquerque, 2014), and local business associated with the series to brand and market various *BB* products accordingly. As Dredge and Jamal (2013) aptly explain, there is no way one can fix the factors that contribute to sustainable film-induced tourism in today's hyper-neoliberal destinations. Albuquerque's rise from a post-colonial migration town to a cinematic technological node in the region overflown with human artistic and professional mobilities is a case in point.

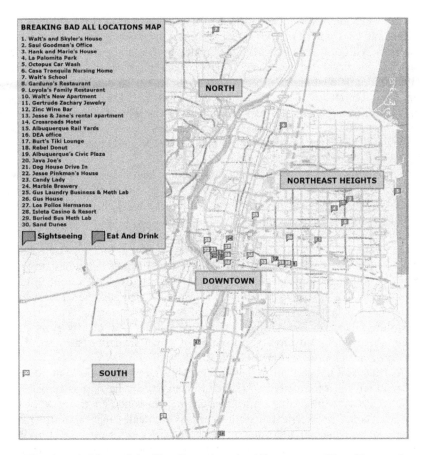

Fig. 4. A Map of the Key Locations in Albuquerque That Featured
in *BB*. *Source:* Shared Wikitravel, CC BY SA 3.0 <https://
creativecommons.org/licenses/by-sa/3.0/> via Wikitravel.

Still, I want to suggest that Albuquerque's transformation into a themed
non-place was certainly supported by a geographical dispersion of its filmed sites
across its four quadrants. The popcultural map of ABQ *BB* locations shows a
remarkable spread of cinematic events and its anti-heroes' dwelling locations
without any reference to the actual locations' historical archives (Fig. 4).
Disambiguating the popcultural from the political is a clever amnesiac strategy,
which allows for the inscription of novel activities on site. As a 'system' in its own
right, 'a single field with multiple attractions to carry out in its complex and
changing totality' (Amendola cited in Savelli, 2009, pp. 150–151), the contemporary city accommodates filmographic narratives of mobility while generating
surprising connections with unlikely industries, such as fashion. In the case of

global fan communities, locations transform into tourist attractions with the help of film and television when tourists begin to enact the fictional heroes' journeys on location. With or without the help of emerging tourist industries, such itineraries institute journeys (see Couldry's (2000) 'media pilgrimages' and Graburn's (1983b) 'tourist pilgrimages') from which urban locales become fashionable destinations. To reiterate Crouch's (2010) and Robert's (2012b, pp. 6–7) points, a map 'is performative insofar as it recodifies the city with the "embodied semiotics" ... and "spacings" of play, affect and everyday creativity', while also representing the accrual of cultural capital, 'a symbolic marker of ... institutional habitus or of conspicuous consumption'.

The erasure of processes of gentrification, crime and in-migration from a map is a form of symbolic violence: no mention of their structural presence ghosts those whose biographies are of no use (Agamben, 2007). If anyone considers popular cultural design as a-political, I can remind them that *BB* location mapping eventually made its way back into Albuquerque's local cultural and political planning. Once known mainly for its annual International Balloon Fiesta and a swastika-decorated movie theatre, today Albuquerque boasts that it has attracted Bryan Cranston and Aaron Paul to buy homes (Gray Faust, 2013; Grout, 2013b). Significantly, the *Albuquerque Journal* (17 July 2011) celebrated the series' success early on, by highlighting the involvement of some of its principal actors (Bryan Cranston, Giancarlo Esposito) in community politics, local charity events and other activities that advertise the presence of urban solidarity (see also Albuquerque convention & visitor's bureau, 2013).

As much as it has been noted that unemployment, crystal meth and murder are 'a tough sell for a tourist board' (ShortList.com, 2013), the very assemblage of fictional *BB* mobilities (drug trafficking, driving across borders to 'cook' or the various characters' experiential meth journeys) eventually aligned with the language of experimental tourism that we associate with 'New Age' travellers (D'Andrea, 2004, 2006). As Dann (1996) explains, tourist industries are framed around specific cultural tropes enabling the tourist to 'buy' their tangible and intangible products. Ideas and souvenirs are thus enmeshed into filmed landscapes and architecture with apparent ease to produce ideal types of tourist and traveller (Urry & Larsen, 2011, pp. 24–25). This para-linguistic framework gives new tourist meaning to banal locales and practices in Albuquerque, when these practices are performed by *BB* fans. In reality, there is nothing 'apparent' in such processes of commodification that enable the production of global brands such as that of *BB*. Liberated from the burden of stores and product manufacturing, such brands 'are free to soar, less as the dissemination of goods and services than as collective hallucinations' (Klein, 2000, pp. 21–22).

This does not mean that *BB* is not embedded in ideas of place and its industries but that its ideas and cosmologies can be universalised and streamlined into deterritorialised fan communities who can live the 'bad' life for a day before returning to their everyday routines (see also Seaton & Yamamura, 2022, pp. 6–7). More correctly, the shift in the design of such tourism partly conforms to what Emmison (2003) recognised as a confluence of established patterns of 'cultural omnivorism' with 'cultural mobility'. With reference to Australian social and cultural change, he purports that a 'new knowledge class' of professionals and managers attempt to playfully bridge high with low cultural registers, thus demonstrating 'the capacity to navigate between and across cultural realms' (Emmison, 2003, p. 231). Nevertheless, his evaluation of new forms of capital can be further revised in the age of platformisation, which allows less affluent or socially distinguished subjects to enter popular cultural domains and simulate such styles of distinction (Meyers, 2012). Without denying the presence of social privilege in the design and performance of tourism, I maintain that the original thesis on 'cultural omnivorism' (Peterson, 1992) has some relevance in the fields of virtual and embodied cinematic tourist performance. Part of the issue relates to conflicting visions of omnivorousness in communities of researchers and consuming subjects (de Vries & Reeves, 2022), so once again I need to contextualise: the observation applies particularly to cinematic tourist fandom, because its enactment requires the minimum cultural capital one can acquire by watching the said film or TV programme. To refer back to Fig. 4, by claiming cultural capital within the *BB* universe, cinematic tourist fans shift the very value of 'knowing' about place to the enactment of 'an architectural and perceptual enclave whose apparently distinct locales (and locals) convey inhabitants to a singular place' – what Woods (2005, p. 318) calls an 'omnitopia'. As capitalist assemblages of meaning that flatten local histories, omnitopias are easily transferable to digispheres, cinespheres and then back to real locations. Hence, although I explore the inscription of tourist performances on location, I cannot ignore the role of new media in their global dissemination as post-historical or indeed distorted historical ('distorical'- Hollinshead, 1998a) examples in my research into a global *BB* industry.

Because *BB* centres on an assemblage of mobilities (from doing science to selling and tasting it), my study invites the employment of mobile methodologies to address the impact of sociocultural (de-)territorialisation on fan communities and practices (Hall, 2008; Hannam, 2008). I examine how the fan structures of *BB* itineraries and consumption rituals are packaged and marketed to global TV fans-come-tourists by Albuquerque's businesses and tourist administration. Incidentally, before condemning such local practices of growth, we may need to remind ourselves that such agency is a scarce resource during the recession, in which these events unfold. In order to scrutinise the production of locally orchestrated and officially sanctioned public presentation of the series' consumer-tourist impact, materials were collected from Albuquerque's Convention & Visitors' Bureau official site. This site works today as a node in which materials on *BB* consumption modes converge and are stored. Additional press and Internet data were selected for its compatibility or explicit connection to Albuquerque's self-presentation as a global televisual tourist destination. Following Dredge and Jamal's (2013, p. 561) reflections on new visions of community in sustainable tourist business, I note that the idea of a uniform locality or a so-called 'community consensus' might distract from 'the intense complexity or micro-politics that all sides are inevitably imbricated within and shaped by' (Meethan, 2001, p. 61).

Topophilic art such as the one involved in the making of *BB* means business: the economic effect of the show has been such that new legislation (known as 'The Breaking Bad Bill') was passed to provide tax breaks to productions filming in

New Mexico – an initiative harmonised with the Albuquerque Film Office's decision in 2002 to offer tax incentives to film industries (Gray Faust, 2013). Albuquerque studios figure today amongst the most attractive filming destinations with a record of hosting series such as *In Plain Sight* and blockbusters such as *Avengers Assemble, Transformers* and the *Lone Ranger* (ShortList.com, 2013). It is therefore unsurprising that sites advertising Albuquerque tourism insert the city into a global urban network directed by America's media centres: close enough to one of the foremost digital hubs, Los Angeles, Albuquerque is already well connected. In addition, a 2013 exhibition by the Museum of the Moving Image in New York featured an exhibit entitled 'From Mr. Chips to Scar-face: Walter White's Transformation in *Breaking Bad*, further proving the same point (Gray Faust, 2013). This is not an insignificant town but a glamorous node in America's cultural network.

And yet, defining a city's iconicity on the basis of drug trafficking is at best risky. The fact that *BB's* staging in Albuquerque came dangerously close to *The Wire's* depiction of Baltimore as the city of crack presented local administration with a challenge. As a representative of the local Tourist Board noted, the fear was that all this grimness 'would put people off . . . I mean, you know, it was still a show about drugs' (Kelly, 2013). Albuquerque mayor Richard Berry ameliorated anticipated criticism by flagging the city's drop-in serious crime rates: 'I'm confident viewers have no difficulty distinguishing fiction from reality', he says (Gray Faust, 2013). The fear was not merely about associations of the city with drug trafficking but also with the endless trail of crimes committed in their name.

The relationship between crime, landscape and the media spans several decades. Prominent amongst the early offerings of British mass culture were the 'penny dreadfuls', cheap publications that serialised lurid and sensational stories about banditry, theft and murder, often inspired by notorious real-life characters such as Jack the Ripper, Ned Kelly and Charles Peace (Springhall, 1998). In the United States of America, similar 'dime novels' and 'pulp fictions' became a staple of popular consumption, serving up a heady brew of sex, crime and violence (Denning, 1986). Crime narratives went on to feature in twentieth-century popular culture in the form of novels, comic books, movies and television shows (Carrabine, 2008, pp. 106–118; Yar, 2010, 2014). Moreover, as Jarvis (2007, p. 327) notes, consumption of mass media representation of crime is now supplemented by a burgeoning industry of 'murderbilia', spanning art, T-shirts, calendars, trading cards, board games and action figures centred on notorious real-life killers. Inspired by the avant-garde filmmaker Kenneth Anger's book *Hollywood Babylon* (1959) (which detailed murders, suicides and grisly accidental deaths involving famous stars), in the 1980s, the likes of *Grave Line Tours* began offering guided trips around Hollywood in a vintage hearse, stopping to view the sites at which the famous met their untimely and undignified ends (Besten, 2000).

A notable feature of such tours is the interweaving of sightseeing that involves both fictional and factual crimes; one of *Grave Line's* successors, *Oh Heavenly Tour*, included within its itinerary the sites associated with actual deaths alongside settings where fictional crimes were filmed in movies such as *Halloween* and *L.A. Confidential*. A more recent iteration of the same type of guided tour, *Dearly*

Departed: The Tragical History Tour of Los Angeles, 'unravels some of the most gruesome and notorious cases that made headlines and takes a look at where these events actually unfolded' (dearlydepartedtours.com, 2013). Other tour operators likewise 'seamlessly combine the sites of real crimes and movie locations', such as the *Sopranos Tour* of New York and New Jersey (Sacco and Horton, 2013), and the *Untouchables Tour* of Chicago (Gangster Tour, n.d.). Other couplings of crime and tourism include the conversion of penitentiaries into visitor attractions and even hotels (as with the *HI Ottawa Jail Hostel*, formerly the *Carlton County Gaol* – 'steeped in history and built on fun, we guarantee that you'll agree that the Jail is the best place to Hang!' – hishostels.com, 2013). The kinds of tourist experience (of sights, locations, goods and services) I explore in this chapter, centred around the TV series, can thus be placed within this wider span of crime-related travel and consumption that has grown notably in recent decades (see, for example, Gibson, 2006; Klein, 1998; Wilbert & Hansen, 2009).

Crime enhances topophilia, producing a unique aesthetics we often associate with European tours to sites ready to be visually consumed (Tzanelli, 2013a; Urry, 1995). As explored in Reijnders' (2009) exposition of Dutch writer Armando's writings, landscapes riddled with horrific crimes harbour a feeling of guilt. It is precisely this lingering feeling that underscores the fascination of *BB* fans, who turn tourists of the cinematic Albuquerque. Reijnders borrows from the buoyant literature on 'thanatourism' or 'dark tourism' to reinterpret Armando's (1998 in Reijnders, 2009, p. 175) conception of 'guilty landscapes'. Armando grew up in a Police Transit Camp and had the opportunity to reflect on the clash between the locality's tourism – inducing landscapes – and the war crimes committed in the local concentration camp. Generally, thanatourism focuses on human visits to locations wholly or partially motivated by the desire for actual or symbolic encounters with death (Lennon & Foley, 2000). The consumerist desire to visit and consume the exotic essence of such sites reinvents them as tourist and media-ethnographic topographies (Cohen, 2005; Laing & Frost, 2012). Dann and Seaton (2001) note that slavery as 'dissonant heritage' has left its mark on tourism across the world. Within one or more transnational networks of such dark tourism, different types of dark heritage may dissolve, or even swap places (Korstanje & Baker, 2018) – note, for example, how the tours to Hollywood Forever, Forest Lawn in Glendale, Forest Lawn in Hollywood, and Pierce Brothers Westwood Village Memorial Park Cemetery, all cemeteries in L.A., which involve popcultural pilgrimages to the graves of celebrities (Soligo & Dickens, 2020), and the *Oh Heavenly Tours*, share the same topophilic drive to real death.

The Freudian couple of *eros* and *thanatos*, the collective social drive to death that underlines most of this scholarship (Korstanje, 2022; Martini & Buda, 2020), nicely complements the consumerist drive of *BB* tourism. But I would claim that the *BB* consumer drive has the opportunity to reinvent thanatourism's historic links. Unlike Reijnders, I identify the allure of *BB's* Albuquerque in the male heroes' overall ethos or social habitus, which framed the first phase of *BB* tourism design. Especially, Walter's double life (as a loving father and teacher/polymath on the one hand and a ruthless drug lord on the other) has been explicitly identified with Albuquerque as a cinematic site. His firm association with a deadly trade might serve as link to an alternative type of tourism. Commonly known as 'drug tourism', this countercultural trend stresses the inner, experiential dimensions of travel, which are enhanced by hallucinatory substances. Hallucination is etymologically connected to the act of wandering like a vagabond and the need to satisfy one's need for purpose in life. Walter and Jesse are neither tourists nor vagabonds in the traditional sense, but producers of substances that allow new tourist industries such as that of *BB* to interpellate a new ideal type of tourist: an *alitis* or privileged vagabond. This ideal type of tourist etymologically derives from *aláomai* (to wander (Vardiabasis, 2002) and calls into being a Simmelian peripatetic stranger in Albuquerque's guilty urban lifeworlds, who is in search for new stimuli through 'photographic' elicitations of memory (Wolff & Simmel, 1959). Incidentally, the series' final season concludes with White's memorial travels back in time before his crimes dissolved his family and he became a true criminal outcast.

Fig. 5.   Jesse's RV, With Its Peculiar Ventilation System, Is Today a Site of Tourist Fascination. *Source:* Pom' from France, European Union, CC BY-SA 2.0 <https://creativecommons.org/licenses/by-sa/2.0> via Wikimedia Commons.

White is representative of the modalities of new, extreme urbanisation: taking ideas of edgework to their realist extremes and some more (risk of emotional and physical injury, plus reckless harm of those for whom one cares deeply – Lyng, 1990, p. 857), we watch him first splitting into two personas by necessity and then even enjoying breaking away from America's hypocritical middle-class 'goodness', which is based on economic success and impeccable 'fronts'. His necessary emasculation in the company of pharmaceutical giants he has to pay to stay alive is 'repaired' in the worlds of crime and risk defining the trafficking of illegal substance. In them, he is a maker and ruler of the world of illicit leisure: an entrepreneurial version of the tourist state (Hollinshead, 2009a) that 'authors' or co-creates with illicit capitalist networks mobilities of harmful pleasure and crime. Having designed his own global microstructure of mobility (Knorr Centina, 2005), first in his collaborator's decrepit RV and thereafter in the clinical space of a meth lab, he has achieved to enter a global order of things that move, amidst personal uncertainty. And if *he* can manage to stage this fictional for a series theatre of violence, *BB* fans should be able to enjoy an anodyne version of his 'frisk society': a model of social planning, in which surveillance and control technologies do not just transform into mundane characteristics of urban everyday life (as Urry (2007, p. 149) suggests), but are creatively internalised by a death drive to master one's own fears. For leisure industries trading in playfulness and seriousness in various degrees, faking the commitment 'to get as close as possible to the edge without going over it' (Lyng, 1990, p. 562) is a goldmine. Today, Jesse's notorious RV is a must-stop in the BB tours of Albuquerque (*see* Fig. 5).

Such controlled recklessness brings *BB* tourism design even closer to what Franklin et al. (2000) discussed as an enactment of safety through performances that preserve global ordering, by attending to *effects* (feeling safe), rather than *causes* (who/what induces insecurity in the first place). The very urban profile of Albuquerque as a spatio-temporal compressor of histories of mobility and activities speaks the language of such hypermobile planning: dubbed America's 'high desert Hollywood', Albuquerque is packaged today even in 'two-night getaways at $500 including airfare' lodging at Parq Central (a former mental hospital featured in the show) and some better-known filmed sites (Jones, 27 July 2013). The BaD Tour, which is run by Jesse Heron and Mike Silva of the Albuquerque Trolley Company, is described as 'a 3.5 h open-air joyride'. The tour featured in *USA Today*, *People* magazine, *The LA Times*, *The Huffington Post* and is sponsored by Albuquerque's own *Back Alley Draft House*, a popular local brewery. It covers 38 miles and 13 main locations from the series, including the exteriors of Walter, Jesse and Gus' houses, the car wash and laundry facilities that act as the meth-maker's storefronts, Tuco's headquarters, the Crossroads Motel and the infamous railroad tracks. A complimentary drink is provided during a stop at *Twisters Grill*, the restaurant that doubles as *Los Pollos Hermanos* on the show (*see* Fig. 6; Conforti, 2013).

Fig. 6.   The Notorious *Los Pollos Hermanos*. *Source:* Pom' from France, European Union, CC BY-SA 2.0 <https://creativecommons.org/licenses/by-sa/2.0>, via Wikimedia Commons.

When the tour is fully booked, an alternative is provided that combines visits to some *BB* locations with cultural sightseeing. The 85-min long 'Best of ABQ City Tour' features a peek at Jesse's house and Hank's DEA office during a trip through Historic Old Town, Museum Row, Nob Hill, the University of New Mexico, the historic Barelas neighbourhood and along Historic Route 66. This itinerary capitalises on the city's long road to colonisation, migration and successive gentrification, suggesting to visitors a different 'bad' process of inscription, erasure and re-inscription of ethnic memories and human mobilities – a convergence of ethnoscapes, mediascapes and ideoscapes (Appadurai, 1990). The blended option better enmeshes the series' story into Albuquerque's real biography, producing a marketable urban palimpsest: as Huyssen (2003) reminds us, 'many of the mass-marketed memories we consume are "imagined memories" to begin with, and thus more easily forgettable'.

Combined use of clips and music from the series contributes to this safe hallucinatory tourist adventure. As D'Andrea (2006, p. 106) notes in the case of global counter-cultural journeys (Ibiza, Goa, Bali, Ko Pangnan, Bahia, Byron Bay, Pune, Marrakech, etc.), DJs describe their task as 'taking the crowd on a journey', whereas the tourists' psychedelic experiences are described as 'intergalactic journeys' inducing self-transformation (D'Andrea, 2004). Again, their hallucinogenic musical travels refer to the ancient Greek 'hallucinogen' as 'wandering practice'. Little attention is paid to the fact that Albuquerque tours are organised by trusted operators, as the aim is to sustain the illusion of demediation, the idea that nothing mediates between experience and reality 'out there' (Strain, 2003): tourists are supposed to be on a dangerous adventure at all times. I would also add that constant distancing from the televisual heroes' evil core partakes in traditional differentiations between 'authentic' travel and 'inauthentic' mass tourism experience: McCabe's (2005) emic approach to authenticity prioritises the experiential dimension of vacationing that can be 'valid and fulfilling, no matter how "superficial" it may seem to the social scientist' (Gottlieb, 1982, p. 167). This is reiterated in online testimonies of the BaD tour, which may be pre-packaged but can still be constantly redrafted by individual visitors.

Such tourist hermeneutics centre on the potential of performances in *BB*'s guilty landscapes, whose evident banality does not affect their cinematic value. Individual performances of landscapes have become sine qua non in touring, especially where photographing places is involved (Bærenholdt et al., 2004). But note that Bærenholdt et al. (2004, p. 69) dutifully quote Edward Said, when they stress that 'the very idea of representation ... is a theatrical one': tours become dynamic accounts of the city, thus opening wide a gateway to post-truth itineraries in Albuquerquean memory archives (Crang, 2001, 2002). Hence, instead of stressing the banality of such encapsulations of the everyday, tourist photographs of *BB* locations enhance the sense of media pilgrimage, adding to the conviction of visitors (Kelly, 2013) that they partake in extraordinary rituals (Campbell, 2005, p. 202; Haldrup & Larsen, 2010; Tzanelli, 2013a). As artist Grayson Perry said in this context, 'television is now our literature, the tour is like a walk around the pages of your favourite book' (Kelly, 2013). Clever tourist marketing by the city's official representatives has included the incorporation of the series into *Albuquerque Museum of Art and History* exhibits (Dibdin, 2013). Framed *BB* posters and stills promote a story about drugs as tourist art that can only be consumed by knowledgeable, 'aesthetically reflexive' agents, rather than visitors suffering from lack of conspicuous consumption skills or indeed an addiction (Beck, 2002; Giddens, 1991, 1994; Norris, 2013, p. 3.2).

The *BB* industry also enables convergences between mind-walking through cinematic narrative and terrestrial travel promoting alternative hedonist consumption and countering the 'dictatorship' of drug speed (Ingold, 2010; Virilio, 2006). *The Biking Bad Tour* proffers a philosophy of 'slow travel' that might even allow 'bad' cyclists to be 'good' and enjoy landscape away from the strains of post-modern consumerist imperatives (Rojek, 2010; Fullagar, 2012, pp. 99–101).

The 'Guided Biking Bad Tours' showcase 'vivid southwestern landscapes of [the] city (and the show) . . . in stunning detail from the comfortable seats of our unique bicycles'. They market 'intimate' and 'interactive' engagement with the filmed locations with the help of professional tour guides through 'character montage detailing one of our five distinct tour routes, each with a unique perspective and sequence of locations to be explored' (Routes – Rentals & Tours, 2013). Merging 'dangerous' media pilgrimage with the aesthetic principles of an alternative hedonism in which slowness is both beautiful and beneficial ennobles the series' 'bad' heroes as aesthetic products, ready to be consumed by tourists (Couldry, 2000; Haybron, 2008). All in all, a critical social scientist may acknowledge that *BB's* 'cult geographies' of place articulate fan consumption rituals (Hills, 2002) in fictionally 'bad' but in reality, harmless ways, only up to a point. The turning point is when harm is problematised in ecstatic terms that transcend Berger's (1967) phantasmagorical imaginaries of consumption. As the *Borat 1 & 2* case of satire attests, 'harm' emerges in transitions from political and cultural metaphor to real social difference, or through mere fusion of dreamworlds with real life-worlds in need. The bridge is realised not by the 'wants' of popcultural pilgrims, but the urgency to cater first for them in an era of multispecies extinction.

Phase 3: Designing Painless Endangering in the Age of Extremes

Undoubtedly, Albuquerque's guilty landscapes partake in the production of a tourist fan community that simulates the use of intoxicating elements such as drugs and music. Yet, by teasing more than one sense (tasting candies, bathing in bath salts, visiting, scrutinising and touching props and residences), the *BB* tourist experience dissolves established boundaries between ideas of cooking drugs, eating branded foodstuff and being photographed in guilty landscapes ('People take 30–40 pictures a day', says *Twisters* manager (Gray Faust, 2013)). Deleuze and Guattari's differen-tiation between architecture and cooking (as manifestations of the State machine (Deleuze & Guattari, 1988, p. 402)), and music and drugs (as manifestations of the 'nomadic machine' of tourism (Deleuze & Guattari, 1988, pp. 381–382)) is not sustained in *BB* consumption rituals. With an emphasis on the senses, such rituals invite tourists to indulge in safe hedonist acts that enable them to be(come) more than heroes for a day. Musical stimuli in the tour tie the *BB* narrative to the global project of urban regeneration with the help of music events (Cohen, 2002). For example, as the *ABQ BaD* tour commences, passengers listen to 'Crystal Blue Persuasion' by Tommy James & the Shondells – soundtrack to a fantastic montage in series five (Kelly, 2013). The practice complements the introduction of relevant clips from the series in subsequent stops – that is, outside the house belonging to Jesse, a relevant clip plays in the trolley on a screen overhead. Instant transitions from the role of simulated drug tourist to that of fast-food consumer and the (anti-) hero of *Los Pollos Hermanos* (Gus) enable first distant enactments of mediated archetypes (akin to what Seaton (2002, pp. 237–238) calls tourist 'metempsychosis') and finally proximate engagement with the plurality of *BB* lives (Seaton's (2002, pp. 150–154) 'tourist metensomatosis').

There is a long history of mass media-inspired moral panics about drug 'epi-demics' – for example, marijuana as 'the weed of madness' in the 1950s (Goode & Ben-Yehuda, 1994); 'crack' cocaine in the 1980s (Reinarman & Levine, 1997); heroin and 'heroin chic' in the 1990s (Denham, 2008) and 'ecstasy' in the 2000s (Hier, 2002). In recent years, 'crystal meth' has been featured heavily in press reportage as the new drug 'epidemic', with stories about its supposedly destructive power supported with arresting before-and-after images of the users' broken faces (Ayres & Jewkes, 2012). The drug's users are depicted in a state of 'zombie-like corporeal ruin – scarred sunken faces, blisters, and broken rotting teeth' (Lin-neman & Wall, 2013, p. 316). *BB* draws upon this public awareness of 'crystal meth' as the 'death drug' of the moment, trading upon its notorious reputation. However, I should also note that media constructions of drug 'epidemics' draw upon associations of different substances with particular social class, ethnic and gender identities. Thus, for example, the 1950s panic about 'reefer madness' drew heavily upon marijuana's associations with African-American jazz and 'Beatnik' cultures; the representation of 'crack' was closely linked to associations with urban crime, poverty and African-American culture –a ghetto landscape popu-lated with 'crack dens' and 'crack whores' (Meyers, 2004).

In the case of 'crystal meth', the drug has been closely allied to constructions of rural 'white trash' in America (Linneman & Wall, 2013). In contrast, however, one of *BB's* innovations is to subvert this association through its protagonists who represent identifiable stereotypes of 'respectable' middle-class America – scientist and schoolteacher Walter; the dapper, punctilious and precisely spoken entre-preneur Gustavo; even Jesse, his 'slacker' demeanour notwithstanding, hails from a suburban middle-class family. This ambivalent figure of the familiar drug stranger is in fact constitutive of the *BB* consumption rituals. There is no way a penniless *BB* pilgrim would prioritise such pilgrimages in their life; the social isomorphism between the *BB* pilgrims and the three key anti-heroes takes us on the bridge of harm. But the pilgrim only steps to other side when their visual knowledge of a criminal world is transformed into a multi-sensory experience.

Significantly, sensory *BB* experiences are more self-guided and independently organised than the standard *ABQ* tours. For such self-guided tours, suggestions are made of some of the series' hotspots such as *Los Pollos Hermanos* and the *Octopus Car Wash*. Tasting the show figures prominently in such self-guided consumption: the free drink during the stop at *Twisters Grill* extends to safe DIY cooking with branded *Los Pollos Hermanos* herbs, which can also be bought online (Greatfaceandbody.com, 2013). The shift from public sightseeing to one's private kitchen is suggestive of the ways tourism can extend to traditionally feminised, ordinary workspaces (Tzanelli, 2012) – only now these can be occupied by Heisenberg wannabes. A 'Rebel Donut' (2013) has also been released as the winner of The Food Network's new show *Donut Showdown* for consumption by *BB* clientele. It is reported that the Rebel Donut shop gets orders for their *BB Blue Sky donuts* from all over the country. Topped with 'blue meth' sugar crystals, the donut is the first to sell out at weekends, beating out all of Rebel's other offerings. The product, which according to assistant manager Dylan Mettling makes 'rabid fans' drive cross-country just to buy it, is supported by Aaron Paul, who declares himself a 'sweet addict' (Grout, 2013a). The sweet trade has picked up also with Albuquerque folk artist, Steve White, who has been crafting custom Pez dispensers of everyone from Frida Kahlo and Kim Kardashian to the Beatles and Elvis Pez-ley since 1999, but his bestsellers are the characters from *BB*.

However, 'die hard' fans are mostly prompted on the site to buy the iconic blue ice candy, a coloured rock candy resembling White's special meth mix, from *The Candy Lady*, a specialty sweet shop located in Albuquerque's Historic Old Town (*see* Figs. 7 and 8; Conforti, 2013). Debbie Ball, (aka Candy Lady), has been dubbed by the Albuquerque tourist board 'a character' (Kelly, 2013) – an ambivalent nomination given her TV-inspired trade. Her sweet shop on Old Town's Romero Road rose to local notoriety in the 1980s when she started selling erotic confectionery. Her 'meth' is now sold for a dollar each in little 'drug dealer' bags that were used as props in the series' first two seasons. 'We really didn't think it was going to take off like it did. At least now I can say that we sell sex and drugs' (Kelly, 2013), she explains. Her business is another moot point in *BB's* guilty industry because critics consider that it cynically glamorises crystal meth. Ball's response to such accusations is that not only do buyers not 'see it as a drug – they see it as a prop' but also the sweets 'are never, ever sold to children' (Kelly, 2013). Centring on fusions of erotica and crime souvenirs, Ball's business comes close to ideas that frame dark cinematic genres (Langford, 2005; Tudor, 1989, p. 167) in which embodied 'threats' and 'risks' are never quite managed by civilising

Fig. 7.   *The Candy Lady*, Old Town of Albuquerque. *Source:* John Phelan, CC BY-SA 4.0 <https://creativecommons.org/licenses/by-sa/4.0> via Wikimedia Commons.

Fig. 8.   Cooking Meth at The Candy Lady, Old Town of
Albuquerque. *Source:* Pom' from France, European Union, CC BY-SA 2.0
<https://creativecommons.org/licenses/by-sa/2.0>, via Wikimedia
Commons.

technologies. Just like *BB's* fictional risks, her 'bad candy' enterprise seems ready
to corrupt one's soul and body but is too sweet to be resisted.

The defence is shared by Keith and Andre West-Harrison, whose spa, *Great
Face & Body*, also offers *Bathing Bad*, a line of blue bath salts in 8 oz plastic bags.
They claim that they received only one email outlining the dangers of crystal
meth. 'But real meth isn't even blue', Keith argues, 'I know what meth looks like,
and that's not it' (Kelly, 2013). The business does not hesitate to use the series'
plot in its advertising that promises customers lifestyle luxury in crime's stead.
Focusing on caring for the body, Keith and Andre remark on their website that
'it's hard to believe 'Heisenberg' himself isn't on our payroll, cooking the cerulean
soap somewhere. Cooked right in downtown Albuquerque, *Bathing Bad* is what

happens when two fans of *BB* buy a 9,000 sq. ft building that had been vacant for 10 years. They needed major money to renovate and asked themselves 'What would Walter White do? *Bathing Bad* was a much better option than meth' (Greatfaceandbody.com, 2013). The product line, which features blue bathing organic products (lotions, soaps and scrubs), targets consumers with an interest in cosmetic rituals. Stressing that *Bathing Bad* chemistry 'isn't breaking any laws' (Greatfaceandbody.com, 2013) allows space for associations with celebrity cultures that promote equations between looking healthy with feeling self-confident and glamorous (Featherstone, 1991, p. 182; Plummer, 1995, pp. 124–125).

Fig. 9.   *Breaking Bad* Merchandise at a Gift Shop in the Albuquerque International Sunport. *Source:* Perry Planet, CC BY-SA 2.0 <https://commons.wikimedia.org/wiki/File:Breaking_bad_merchandise_sunport.jpg> via Wikimedia Commons.

Other merchandise appears less menacing to consumers or is presented in acceptable terms – for example, BaD Trolley organisers were quick to note on the tour's website that children are brought at the visitors' 'own discretion' (ABQ Trolley Co., 2013). Similarly, *BB* T-shirts and other merchandise including Walter White's signature black hat are less offensive to the public (*see* Fig. 9). Likewise, the branding of Albuquerque's alcoholic drinks by *Marble Brewery* that sells 'Walt's White Lie' and 'Heisenberg's Dark Ale' or O'Neil's that offers a *Blue BB*-themed cocktail attract less negative commentary as they are addressed to adult fans (Albuquerque convention & visitor's bureau, 2013). Ironically, the ubiquitous critical focus on consumables enhances established connections between food and travel (du Rand & Heath, 2006) with anecdotal travel stories connected to the filmed locations – and hence the televisual script. The visit to Walter's house, whose owner is rumoured to have pocketed around $500,000 from filming, is marked by one such story: apparently, the tour guide explains, 'the guy who owns the place goes out to pick up his newspaper some days and has to remove a giant pizza a fan has thrown [on the roof]' (ShortList.com, 2013). Food items are treated in such media pilgrimages as fetishistic props that add to the tourist experience – but this time not by tasting but gazing at their place in the media text.

On the whole, the packaging of safe risk in *BB* products never lets consumer pass the second stage of Mortlock's (1984) schema of adventure experience, which commences with play (the subject is required to show minimal involvement in skills and emotions in leisure), proceeds with adventure (they use their skills to overcome a 'problem' in alien environments) and frontier adventure (when insecurity and fear of emotional/physical harm become a possibility) and concludes with misadventure (when challenges are beyond one's control and capabilities). All *BB* products seem to operate within the parameters of commodified adventure, taking on board questions of risk, responsibility but also consumer commitment, not facilitating the freedom or personal transcendence one encounters in 'peak experiences' (Mitchell, 1983, p. 154; Varley, 2006, pp. 177–179). The organic fragility of human nature is not put at risk, as would be the case with immediate confrontations of death; on the contrary, it is pushed back to a secondary phase of mediation that already mediates crime (in a TV series). As a pilgrimage suspended between frames, it tempers edgework to such an extent that *BB* consumers are left to enjoy a distillation of the spectacular (Best, 1989; Debord, [1967] 1994). Yet, even such distillation maintains connections to *ekstasis* as an embodied extension of experience outside reality, into the world of dreams and the ludic (Berger, 1967, p. 43). This *ekstasis* lands the soft *BB* edgeworkers nowhere near the worlds of *ZG*, where unprotected sex and macho dancing test one's limits and competencies. In fact, its commercialised links to adventure facilitate the civilisation of the inner self, who is allowed to transgress within legitimised regions of what Wang (2010, p. 130) called 'the Eros-space' of modernity.

So, what is harmful in all these? Real crime thrives on silence, conspiracy and suspicions that may repress or exacerbate emotions, as Heisenberg's tale attests. *BB* adventurers/edgeworkers are boxed into this unorthodox muting of emotions in a culture of control under which they spend their real lives. Whilst it comes with a promise of playful liberation from it, Candy Lady's faux blue meth remains a dark tourist reminder of its grip to the real: even though *BB* consumption is pictured, photographed and verbally articulated in fan, tourist and the televisual artists' narratives, there is always something left unsaid in these rituals. This invisible suspension of meaning, layers class with the aesthetics and politics of gendered and racial representation. It is well established in social analysis that women who take risks especially in leisure activities dominated by men, mitigate gendered constraints by strategically drawing upon middle class and liberal notions of female empowerment (Laurendeau & Shahara, 2008). Similar results are yielded where edgework involves extreme sexual play, such as BDSM (Newmar, 2011) or extreme activities, such as staged kidnappings (Tzanelli & Yar, 2020). Framed as a series of soft middle-class activities, the *BB* consumption industry relocates harm risks to the emotional domain (Olstead, 2010). Filmed landscape and its consumables partake in a non-representational game: new media technologies such as digital cameras, video cameras, You Tube films and relevant materials stored in Internet repositories and press sites reinterpret them as playscapes by transforming emotions such as fear, guilt, anger or remorse into leisure/pleasure (Lefebvre, 2006; Thrift, 2008).

On the one hand, online journals' readers are encouraged to post their own experiences of *BB* tours that are pictured, google-mapped and cross-referenced with production stills and professional celebrity photography. In websites such as OLV (Christine, 2013), photos of the cast filming and *BB* actors' tweets thus figure as integral testimony of terrestrial tours by anonymous individual tourists who are happy to post memories of their journeys. On the other hand, as the principal actor in the story, Albuquerque's landscape is identified with the rugged White and the damaged Pinkmann or with Gus' professional cover, to communicate what lies beneath their ennobled peaceful surface. This respectability is rife with emotions transferred to the fans who both abhor and are excited by *BB's* criminal travel arc. The shift from non-represented to landscaped emotions turns a banal shopping visit for designer donuts and bathing salts into the core of the experiential journey (also Norris, 2013): tourists commune in emotions painted in New Mexico's red desert and Albuquerque's sweetened donuts. As tokens, souvenirs or gifts from the *BB* tour, cinematically branded products attain a magical relationship with the city's landscape and their producers (Cave & Buda, 2018).

The emergence of new global tourist sensescapes and playscapes in the space of a few filmed neighbourhoods is a big deal in an era dominated by virtual post-tourism. Such safe ontologies of popcultural pilgrimage have expanded after the release of *BB's* televisual prequel and cinematic sequel, which I explore below. But where tourism planning attempts to de-solidify stereotypes, structural technomorphism kicks in to ensure the global dissemination of fixed practices of mobility. Sometimes in cinematic tourism, the pastiche of images and imaginations guiding place myths (Shields, 1991) can come close to sociocultural realities (Kim, 2012; Hao & Ryan, 2013). Structural technomorphism allows for representational replication and extension (*ekstasis*), amplifying the possibilities to consolidate social stereotyping, regardless of the intentions of the creative and technical classes involved in its staging. *BB's* complete success produced a whole franchise, including a sequel film, *El Camino: A Breaking Bad Movie* (dir. V. Gilligan, 2019), following Pinkman's story and a prequel TV series, *Better Call Saul* (dirs. V. Gilligan, B. Obenkirk, P. Gould, T. Schauz, B. Cranston, M. Morris, M. MacLaren, M. Spiro, J. McKay, T. McDonough, M. Slovis, M. McKean & G. Mastras, 2015–2022) focusing on the personal life and career of criminal lawyer Jimmy McGill in the years leading up to his encounter with Walter White and Jesse Pinkman. The equally successful *Better Call Saul*, which was filmed in Albuquerque, brought into sharp focus how the cross-border nature of drug trade impacts on the lives of white middle classes. It did so by using as an example its main anti-hero McGill, and his loved ones, whose imperfect natures are still likeable, in contradistinction to Fring's Latino networks.

The third phase of *BB* tourism design produces a narrative node out of the new *BB* franchise on the web, where race and class become objects of fascination at best. The digital face of the revamped Breaking Bad Store is supported by powerful press networks, such as *US News & World Report* and the *Associated Press*, which advertise it as 'a must-stop destination'. Here is its discursive introduction:

> Located in the historic Albuquerque Old Town district near the Plaza, this is the first physical store of its kind to exclusively feature "Breaking Bad" and "Better Call Saul" merchandise including clothing, unique novelties from around the world and items crafted by local artisans. It also features interactive photo opportunities. Immerse yourself in the world of Walter White and Saul Goodman, and you can become the one who knocks.
> (The Breaking Bad store, n.d.)

A short video does a quick tour of its interior, which is full of *BB's* para-phernalia of violence, complete with Walter and Jesse's blue meth suits, references to Fring's chicken business front, and now also *Better Call Saul's* own criminal characters and universe of violence (Crowe70ec1, 2021). The enterprise revises old approaches to the Other of the colonial expansion, who is fixed in time and almost fossilised in manners. It does so by turning what they allegedly traffic, or help others to traffic (crystal meth) in the now-time, into a metaphor of infection of social and by extension phenotypical borders (Mbembe, 2017). The verdict is not anymore that 'the black man' has never attained consciousness of his own freedom (see Clark & Szerszynski, 2021, pp. 112–114), but that he has managed now to transform what Hegel called his 'arrested development' into an infectious planetary disease. The codification of difference through harmful substances consigns Albuquerque's indigenous pasts and cross-border presents of 'need' to the non-domain of waste: as the real city of Albuquerque is enjoying a spectacular boom, its symbolic expenditure policies also grow, allowing for the planetary crises of credit and defaulted debt to be silenced (Hutnyk, 2004, p. 178).

What I mean is particularly applicable to the United States, in which ever since the country's entrance to World War II, political power used collective affect to navigate through periods of social crisis. To date, the country's permanent state of war with invisible racial others necessitates crafting a liaison between affect-as-excess (patriotism) with providential economies of grief, belief and repair (Clough, 2006). However, this inward-looking strategy is also supplanted with a '"catastrophic" apparatus defined by relations of destruction, damage, and loss' (Anderson, 2010, p. 164). This apparatus allows not just for the crime-effective maintenance of biopolitical networks of surveillance and control but also their extension to the domains of cybernetic and even artistic representation (Clough, 2007). At times, conceptions of the 'public' serve as affective poles of 'population' (Foucault, 2007), which, for practical reasons, are reduced to the 'popular-cultural', as this is what allows for the symbolic scouring for new exotic resources (Moore, 2015, p. 222). Thus, Potts (2012, p. 233) sees in the emergence of a 'Ground Zero souvenir and tourist industry' the endorsement of a voyeuristic visitor economy, which now stands alongside rituals of mourning the loss of loved ones in the terrorist event (Sharpley & Stone, 2009, pp. 8–9). The ensuing trivialisation of collective mourning in '9/11 teddy-bears' and 'Osama Bin-Shot' T-shirts parallels Nazi uses of kitsch to create a sense of shared national sentiment – a 'key element in superficial symbols of national unity' (Sturken, 2007, p. 22).

When placed within America's economies of collective affect, *BB's* tourism mobilities feature 'an indeterminate conversion point between subjective ideality' and a world rife with 'risks' to one's 'subjective integrity' (Terada cited in Anderson, 2010, p. 164). The transposition of the personal/individual experience of risk to the domains of leisure covers its origins in the domain of collective affective labour. The histories of this labour may be vaguely comprehensible, if at all, to the *BB* tourist, who may nevertheless perform them as touristic edgework. Where the serious dark tourist heritage (of war and terrorism) design of Ground Zero seeks to preserve the traces of national grief on American architectural landscapes (Sturken, 2004), *BB's* transposition of fears about leaking borders and darker criminal others in leisure and tourism demotes their etiological and genealogical roots to a spectacle. When all is said, one still has to consider that Albuquerque's crime numbers ('46,391 property crimes and 15,765 violent crimes recorded in 2021') (Albuquerque Police Department, 2021) are listed on websites offering travel advice (Travellers Worldwide, 2022), with a note that the city is one of the most dangerous American urban destinations for travellers. Is it not better to replace architectures of grief and materialities of dust and bombed rubble with the omnitopic business structures of faux meth journeys to a land in which memories of racial invasion are reduced to candies?

Conclusion

In this chapter, I have sought to illuminate how new intersections emerge between the consumption of mediated popular culture and the real and imagined topographies within which those representations are framed. In the case of *BB*, this amounts to an array of tourist experiences (both formally organised and self-guided) focused upon sensory consumption (sights, sounds, tastes and touches) onto which an array of symbolic and narrative meanings have been projected through the success of the show. On the one hand, this hybridised touristic experience partakes of a now conventional form of fan 'pilgrimage' in which the landscapes associated with popular films, and television shows are commercially packaged, exploited and marketed, transforming otherwise largely unremarkable places into 'must see' destinations. On the other hand, given the textual and narrative parameters of the show itself, such tourism actively adduces, aestheticises and domesticates the risk, danger, harm and violence associated with the drug trade. Adducing all these 'bads' can easily be read as the analogue of what Hutnyk (2004) saw in the exercise of 'Bad Marxism', the post-modern scholar's propensity to reduce hybridity to play without consequences such as those involved in the representational commoditisation of already disenfranchised identities. Or, it could be seen as what Costanza-Chock (2020) identified as the exclusion of the same identities from the pool of voices that participate in the design of new ideas. It could also be seen as the discursive counterpart of Jensen's 'dark design' in the leisure sector, which turns darkness into symbolic capital for urban centres without removing the normative stigma of its illicit patina from those who need recognition most. Above all, while enclosing all these, it could be seen as a component of terrestrial endangering in the epoch of extreme urbani-sation and climate catastrophe – themes this chapter cannot cover, but certainly alludes to via the works of Latour (2018), Urry (2016), Sheller (2018b, 2020), and Clark and Szerszynski (2021).

The appeal of *BB* tourism is dependent upon the ability to offer transgression as a point of imaginary identification and vicarious pleasure. Yet, at the same time, for the locality and those who offer it as a consumer experience, it generates notable tensions and the potential for unwelcome associations and moral opprobrium arising from accusations that it 'glamorises' or 'trivialises' crime. Consequently, the selling of *BB* as a form of tourist experience simultaneously activates fans' attachment to the show's depictions of criminality while denying those very meanings by emphasising its status as fiction, simulation and fun.

The management of this apparent conflict by experts allows a tourist industry to thrive on constantly manipulated signs, which are conveniently 'sweetened', 'cooked' or 'softened' – civilised – for the tourist palate. But perhaps we should not forget that Albuquerque's realist geographies partake of a global political economy of crime, pleasure, waste and damaged environments (Opiz & Tellmann, 2012). The city's *BB* industry mirrors its unwanted implication in networks of drug trafficking, illegal migration and the very American justice and prison system, which relocates former criminals in the region under ongoing protection programmes. It is as if the Walter/ Jesse *effect* of 'frisking' social orders (see Urry, 2007) in pleasurable rituals suppresses the real *causes* of the city's turn to cosmetic planning (see Franklin, 2003). Such unorthodox trading of the realist roots of Albuquerque's violence palimpsests for the tourist routes of a crime series could easily be understood *as a softer style of off-shoring*: drug playscapes across the world; popcultural artscapes to the major American urban centres; but also, regional gentrification, which will produce new cross-border economies of labour for the elites' needs (Urry, 2014, p. 195).

Conclusion: Undoing the Cinematic Tourist Provenance, Designing Viable Futures

Scholars like to pretend that they always know from which stance they write before they even begin to argue their thesis. In this book's introductory pages, I explained that it is better to depart on an agnostic scholarly journey with inter-, post- or trans-disciplinary baggage, and a sketchy itinerary. However, the agnostic scholarly traveller also needs a personal notebook, in which they can communicate moments of confusion – never mind any pretensions to certainty in what follows an introduction. The messy notes we take during the journey may earn us the badge of what Rabelais once called 'Residents of the City of Lanterns': literary charlatans and pedantic graduates in the academy, medicine and the *belle arts* who excel above all at projecting a respectable face in their paradigmatic domain/polis. If taken seriously (as I think it should be), this exercise can lead all the way down to a re-evaluation of the internal structure of what Boltanski and Thévenot (1983, p. 647) called 'the stylization of social groups' involved in the nomination of locations as hospitality destinations. For those of us who can bear to be Lanterns instead of respectable intellectual travellers for a while, the significance of the exercise is revealed later. Subversive stylisation can produce hopeful or reproduce problematic (as the *Borat* case attests) vocational and occupational categories on the basis of what Boltanski & Thévenot dub in their work 'regimes of worth' (Boltanski & Thévenot, 1983, p. 653).

This book's land of literary charlatans is ruled by international tourism experts, state officials and regional governance adjudicators. The scholars who decide to study these groups arrive later, to inspect the state of play in the fields these groups may have already generated (consciously or unconsciously) through alliances and rivalries. During their own journeys, they are bound to generate their own lands in which they build homes for their studies (Munar, 2016). This book is where I 'land' to perform my own vocational rituals by asking questions – so, who am I really in relation to my worlds of tourism? To adduce that scholarship operates completely outside my studied fields of action would be a worrying sign of lanternism: a disease that refuses to give way to a more composed approach to truth-making as world-*making*. From their stance, all the aforementioned categories of experts 'enunciate' (a-la Pêcheux, [1975] 1982; Hollinshead & Suleman, 2018, p. 212; also, Hollinshead, Suleman, & Vellah,

The New Spirit of Hospitality, 133–140
Copyright © 2023 Rodanthi Tzanelli
Published under exclusive licence by Emerald Publishing Limited
doi:10.1108/978-1-83753-160-820231006

2021) the field of cinematic tourism as a by-product of contemporary mobilities of labour, expertise, landscapes, representational technologies and represented ecologies, including human and non-human populations.

Because it is based on such complex entanglements of mobilities, cinematic tourism's multi-field is central to the mobilities paradigm's critiques of national territory as a hegemonic socio-political ontology (Manderscheid, 2020, p. 366). However, 'hegemonic' is a very tricky keyword here: such territories come to life as public domains regulated and constantly renovated by stylised groups, which can shift alliances and form oppositions where there was collaboration, simply because there is no such thing as 'a world', but 'worlds-in-the-making' (Tsing, 2015) in which they are thrown to perform their sense-making. A scholar would never escape the lanternist condition, unless they were ready to accept two uncomfortable recurring themes in such sense-making situations: first, that such enunciative categories of stylised human groups comprise the public face of global cultures, which circulates in digispheres, conference rooms and policy domains, bringing the said filmed and thereafter tourismified places to life as worthy reality bites in bytes; and second, that scholars too are public actors and agents of change through critique that may spot injustices and techniques of justification that help to perpetrate them. Note also that these two realities connect to the way that scholars treat the studied stylised categories in their work, apropos to those groups that do the work of hospitality in cinematic tourism in private domains. This juxtaposition or comparison comprises the emotional core of the regimes of worth they propagate in their work (Hollinshead & Kuon, 2013; Hollinshead, Suleman, & Vellah, 2021; Tucker & Akama, 2009).

There is nothing absolutely 'truthful' in my mapping. For example, at times, I seem to attribute the making of cinematic tourism worlds to the calculative 'tourist gaze' (a-la Urry, 1990 – 1st edition) of heartless business – a price one pays, if they blindly follow a particular version of Bourdieu's work on distinction. Because all regimes of worth are built on emotional, cognitive and embodied investment, even business partakes in the most basic form of affective labour (a-la Anderson, 2010) to produce tourism worlds. At other times, I seem to extend this automation of habitus to scholarly research, which in reality, like the business of tourism, is made up of people who will bring myriad heuristic styles to the table of worldmaking, different approaches and justifications of deleting and supplementing, weeding out and recomposing what in this book features as a phased process. Unpacking the process of cinematic tourism worldmaking begins as a 'radical pluralist' venture for all interest groups; even when the detached researcher/expert has to phase and compose it, they need to acknowledge that they deal with different reali*ties*, each of them contextually and discursively as real as the rest in their environment/field (Vervoort et al., 2015). There is no such thing as a 'redemptive truth' (Rorty, 2004, p. 7; Vervoort et al., 2015, p. 64) behind a 'planetary parapet' to unite these world versions, only a researcher, who will have to decide which one (or which group of truths) they can better enunciate as viable and worthy projects (Hollinshead, Suleman, & Lo, 2021). Hence, a travelling researcher is a temporary Lantern also in so far as they are bearers of a light that illuminates different pathways to truth – as truth-makers of sorts (Putnam, 1996).

Back in the worldmaking multi-field, wars continue to be waged – and in the cinematic tourism business, these days they seem to be filtered more and more through a platformised vision, which shapes human actors and their environments as immutable ideas (to borrow from Sheller's (2003) reading of consuming animate worlds in tourism). To clarify again, in this book, I tried to highlight how such filmed locales are shaped by political practices into bounded categories (Olwig, 2002) that overwrite their qualities as material and aesthetic realms gathered 'in the marking' (Tsing, 2017) by different sedentary and mobile groups of tourists and hosts. I also endeavoured to stress what structural techno-morphism does during such wars of attrition and regeneration, not just to the subjects of my study, but also the scholarly ethico-aesthetic compass that has to locate truths in digital fields. Rorty's (2004, p. 9) conviction that, after Kant and Hegel, we transitioned from a philosophical to a literary culture needs updating: we are now prey to the virtualities that the proponents of Deleuze, Barad, Derrida and Latour would see as a new phase of worldmaking mobilities (Büscher et al., 2011). The virtual re-constitutes regimes of worth in ever more complex ways than those we were used to unpack in traditional ethnographies.

My pluralist approach to economies of attention has a very different aim from that of a neoliberal entrepreneur's or an academic relativist's: it seeks to pinpoint areas of *discomfort* in worldmaking projects of cinematic tourism potentiality, as well as the *conditions* under which these projects interact and converge in a social researcher's analysis (Vervoort et al., 2015, p. 68). Elsewhere, I termed those repetitions 'affective refrains', explaining that the role of such formulaic ethico-aesthetic repetitions is to bind researchers into paradigmatic groups, and specific programmes, outlining how planetary futures might or should be (Tzanelli, 2022a, 2022b, 2023). To connect this back to the first chapter of the book, identifying *discomforts* and the *conditions* under which worldmaking projects intersect allows the most stubborn scholarly Lanterns to produce axiological maps. On such maps, they can place the paradigmatic 'constellations' that stand in positions of aversion or attraction to each other (Gregory, 1996).

Once, Goodman (1996, p. 6) stated that 'the nearest pictorial approach to the way the world is, is the way the camera sees it'. I aspired to show that his statement was at best partial because it did not move beyond the first phase of truth-making, which is that of the world picture. Consider how the filmed enunciators (sex labour, digital designers, film actors and regional cities and administrators) come to life in a *second-order field of action*, which is stylised by people like me. One of Gillian Rose's (1993, p. 213) many wise critiques of problematic lanternism focusses on problems generated by silencing this second-order field: consider, she said, not 'how images "themselves" represent "hierarchies and differences"' but 'the ways in which geographers [read here: social scientists] and their images and audiences also intersect in ways that produce hierarchies and differences'. Such a change in perspective allows for the production of a cultural-political poetics of research, which does not concentrate on pictorial 'facts' but explains the role of affective refrains in the making of collective futures.

Cinematic tourism mobilities are cursed to live in a limbo between artistic production and popular-cultural travel: neither category can quite accommodate their quirky in-between-ness, which very much encapsulates the messy world of experts. To resolve ambiguity, examinations of its labour are often pushed to either side of the polar formation, to explore inequalities or distinguished talent (such tilting-both-sides produces at least two homes and two exiles for the area's scholars). This is a pragmatic decision, which commences in the vocational categories of business (tourism design) but does not end there. Currently, cinematic tourism is discussed in popular-cultural terms because it is tourism, only when its artistic affiliations are silenced. Hence (a) this categorical discomfort spills over the subject area's transdisciplinary, interdisciplinary and post-disciplinary examination, (b) making the subject itself a prima facie example of mobilities analysis. The studied mobilities commence with an examination of the regimes of biopolitical worth (i.e., types of labour involved in the business), but soon thereafter must move to the cybernetic domain of production and species endangerment (Latour, 2018, pp. 80–85) and the ecological, including that of natural environments and the media (Fuller, 2012, p. 122). I want to suggest that areas of discomfort and a focus on worldmaking conditions converge behind the silencing of a particular type of labour, which transcends the materialities of vocational categories. This is the affective labour of the Techno-Anthropocene, which is produced in fields of entanglement between humans, technologies, natural habitats and built landscapes.

In the documentary film *The lost Leonardo* (dir. A. Koefoed, 2021), we follow the discovery and successive clandestine sales of *Salvator Mundi*, a painting allegedly produced by Leonardo da Vinci. Broken into perspectival fragments, the documentary, which borrows from the conventions of the thriller genre, lends a sympathetic ear and eye to key characters who became involved in the enunciation of the painting as fake or authentic: Alexander Parish and Robert Simon, the two American art dealers, who bought it as an 'After Leonardo' at a 2005 auction in New Orleans for $1,175, and become convinced that it worths more than what they paid for it; Dianne Modestini, a New York art restorer, who, after an extensive restoration of the painting (2005–2013) that reveals overpainted details, she becomes convinced that this is indeed a lost da Vinci masterpiece; Luke Syson, curator at the National Gallery, who, after a marathon of evaluation exchanges, controversially decides to include it in an exhibition of Leonardo's works under the title 'by Leonardo da Vinci' to evoke reactions; Bernd Lindemann, a Professor of the art museum Gemäldegalerie, Berlin, who is convinced it is just a Leonardo remake; Frank Zöllne, a Leonardo expert, who recognises authentic Leonardo elements in the painting, but becomes convinced that the restored masterpiece should be attributed to Modestini's meticulous 'renovation'; businessman and freeport owner, Yves Bouvier, who tries to pawn the painting to Russian billionaire, Dmitry Rybolovlev, for a much larger amount than that it was originally bought in New York in 2005, only to be legally prosecuted for fraud and Rybolovev himself, who, as part of a sell-out of his artistic collection via Christie's, advertises it as the 'male Mona Lisa' and hires Leonardo di Caprio to feature in a relevant promotional video for it. Rybolovev manages to sell the lost

Leonardo for a price in excess of $400 million (and an additional $50 million commission to Christie's) to then Crown Prince and Prime Minister of Saudi Arabia Mohammed bin Salman Al Saud, who stores it in his yacht. The film concludes with the 2019–2020 Leonardo exhibition at the Louvre, in which, a publication in the museum's shop authenticating the painting, is not recognised by Louvre's curators. There is the expectation that *Salvator Mundi* will feature next to *Mona Lisa* for public inspection. However, the space in which the contested painting was supposed to be hang remains empty during the opening and throughout the exhibition's duration, amidst rumours that it will now be displayed in a new dedicated museum in Saudi Arabia (Gleiberman, 2021).

The thriller's gist is crafted as a 'whodunnit': which documentary fragment or perspectival judgement comprises what is real/authentic for the painting. A multimodal semantics of world-making collapses into a social semantics of labour, which turns the contested artefact (*Salvator Mundi*) into an attractor of different enunciations of worth: who did the painting gives way to who will buy it (a private investor for his private collection?), enjoy it (global audiences, lovers of art?) and conserve or preserve it – and to what ends (a shady Crown Prince or a group of international artistic institutions?). We discern elements of individuality in the delivery of such judgements over what is real and authentic in a strangely Adornoesque now thriller: Modestini's decision to set up a website, in which she shares all 'evidence' of authentication and restoration; Lindemann and Zöllne's associations of authenticity with different types of expertise; Syson's strategy of eliciting authentication in the public spheres of art and heritage and Bouvier and Rybolovlev's reduction of the same to discourses of monetary loss or profit. All agents filter their judgements through *mediations within the film's secondary mediation* (video clips, photographs, exhibition posters, internet posting), constantly deferring the frame of absolute reality. The film contains several direct references to post-truth in the age of mediation and transaction, which are surrounded by stunning imagery of the painting itself as Leonardo's vanished presence. We cannot disregard other inventories of signs in it, which frame the very institutions that make the story's economy of cultural goods function in licit and illicit modes: not only art galleries, museums and auction houses but also film studios and freeports – non-places of illegal transaction, in which the rules of law have no hold over mobility agents. Forming the opposing pole of all other aforementioned 'institutions of consecration' (Bourdieu, 1993, p. 260), freeports and studios enunciate a new modality of movement with ontogenetic consequences. These do not preclude the emergence of unauthenticated pictorial art – not as the *manifattura* ('individual manual style') of an artistic pioneer, but the mediatised aggregate of contemporary enunciations about his labour. But also note that the documentary's 'whodunnit' prioritises discourses of greed over discourses of affective labour, which are endowed with historical and synchronic depth. Whispers of them are atmospherically irradiated from Modestini, who wonders in a more composed manner which parts of the painting belong to Leonardo's apprentices and whether these should be erased altogether. Modestini, the in-betweener of art and technical-scientific craft and not Syson or the other art experts in the multi-field of truth-making is the only one who wants to preserve the labour of love that went into making *Salvator Mundi's* memory palimpsest and thus its cumulative biographical aura, never mind the status of expertise.

Modestini is a sure aggregate of regimes of worth in fields of mediated mediation – the new modality's digital palimpsest that best describes what structural technomorphism does or does not do to cinematic tourism hosting in the eras of immaterial labour. I use 'modality' in modernity's stead because it allows me to talk about tourism in the era of terrestrial endangering, as well as engendering. Note that the most basic temporal model propagated by modern-isers (pre-modernity vs. modernity) replicates the binary construction of tourism imaginaries as economies of spectacular attention. The sociological objectivisa-tion of actors and actants in the book's story-telling suggests that my epistemo-logical perspective capitalises on existential traces (experiences) to produce constructivist phenomenologies (of hosting, visiting and touring). Such phenom-enologies defect to a post-material land, where objects and subjects of travel and hosting are co-constituted as seamless fields of action: playscapes for tourists but also *exoscapes* for the hosts. Now speaking of post-phenomenologies, a researcher troubled by the absence of concrete categories of affective labour that used to define tourist and tourism fields, may ask what the so-called Techno-Anthropocene has to offer to the art of being human, non-human or post-human in the natural and cultural worlds.

The three case studies of this book provide grim prognostications, but there are also some positive observations to be made. The vanishing of particular versions of affective-embodied labour in tourism seems to be supplemented or replaced with digital valorisations of the labour of national memory across all three cases (Zorba as Greek-land; Borat as ennobled Kazakh-branded eco-tourism; Walter White as the hard-done-by American Everyman) supplanting thanatourist urbanism – a localised form of spatial cleansing in the race for urban excellence, which seeks to restore the institutional and territorial agency of the state vis-à-vis the management of terrestrial life (immigrants, natural environments and heritage materialities alike in contexts of neoliberal fragmentation) (Herzfeld, 2006b, 2016). The cinematic tourist becomes a means to an end, when their role is supposed to be of disinterested play and relaxation – surely a right all of us should enjoy. In fact, this globetrotter's functionalisation in economies of sign rather than bio-engendering, reflects a particular functionalisation of activity. Tourism itself loses its specificity as a form of leisure and is consigned to the governance of mobilities. To refer back to *Salvatore Mundi's* story, the vitalist, rather than artistic, aspects of creativity as well as the possibility for them to be granted a place in public cultures (a-la Hollinshead), survive only and if they authenticate the provenance of a land.

Addressing the things to come (a-la Barad, 2010), a provenance is both a place of origin and a way forward (*pro*: forth + *venire*: to come). As an aesthetic category, a provenance is always exposed to public inspection and judgement (*kategorein*: to accuse in public). When it comes to public-cultural enunciations of worthy provenances, Bourdieu (1993, p. 262) stressed that technical rules allow for settling scores and conflicts in what really is real: for provenances to be realised, we need experts, who decree who is an artist, what is authentic, who is a technician and who is common labour. At this point, one must have recourse to post-phenomenologies of cinematic tourism fields of worth. The human judges of worth display intentionality in the ways they fashion cinematic tourist sites as 'popcultural' or heritage locales, because past experience suggests that they may actually become heritage in the future. The very mediation of all intentionality via technologies controlled by particular interest groups has already shaped the texture of these locales' public presence as a hegemonic version of reality via the assignation of judging roles to certain groups (Descola, 2016; Salazar & Zhu, 2015). Or, more correctly, cinematic and new digital media platforms have assumed the role of a 'phenomenal transparency' (Metzinger, 2018; Vindenes & Wasson, 2021), allowing for their content to be presented not as a subjective experience but a representation. Such 'representations' are based on expert opinion that is already shaped by a post-human mode of co-creating futures (Verbeek, 2015).

Does this not expose a circular logic in who gets to speak and be in human public fora? Like *Salvator Mundi*, who is now preserved in the recesses of a desert as both a territorially bounded statement on ecological rationalisation in the Anthropocene and Saudi Arabia's global texture of cultural capital, the new cinematic tourist destinations feature more and more as a parable of an onto-genetic bifurcation. Neither 'local' nor naturally and ecologically rooted, they are techno-creative processes with dubious origins in a cinematic 'event': the release and success of a film. Their subsequent reinstitution as touristic imaginaries *de jure* rooted in a land (their *territoirisation* to follow Lapointe, 2021) – is engineered by the tourist expert, who wants to design alternative mobility futures. The design itself will enter a new transmodal discursive cycle in the Critical Zone of public commons, in which it may be contested as unsustainable, ecocidal or otherwise. Herein we can situate a fortuitous merger between points of discomfort and attraction across critical tourism and critical mobilities studies, which tends to sharply separate them from the categories of business experts: a critical scholar's vocational commitment to sympathetic imagining prompts them to surmise what those who are not granted a voice in this process may think, experience or have to say. To reverse Bauman's (2021, p. 179) reflections on the Borgesian imaginary of (radical) otherness (regardless of whether this draws on class, gender, race or disability): when the critical scholar begins to believe in its presence, it comes to life and has to be acknowledged in public.

However, even such a bleak conclusion merits some critical filtering. I suppose this suggests the introduction of yet another post-truthful teaser: What would have happened without such post-Anthropocenic tools at our disposal during the ravaging COVID-19 pandemic? How would out-of-the-way places manage to survive in a competitive tourismified world without their internet windows? More crucially, how would even proponents of de-growing tourism effectively and speedily disseminate sustainable practices to counter the wave of unhelpful image-based tourismification in crowded destinations without new media platforms? Would our evolving cyborg ontologies of hosting on and offline global strangers not provide the first, if flawed, solution to the excessive carbonisation and environmental pollution that are currently beckoning over-tourismified locales? It seems then that the solution to unjust mobilities may not be to shut down technological ontogenesis, but to target the circular logic of professionalised *technopoesis* (see Introduction & Chapter 1) as a zone of unjust distinction and territorial endangering. And just so I am not accused of generalisation, endangering life is in itself a multi-field and a plural project, which must begin with situated definitions of capabilities, talents and limitations to flourishing on our crowded multi-species planet.

Bibliography

ABQ Trolley Co. (2013, October 10). The BaD Tour. http://www.abqtrolley.com/index.php/TheBaDTour

Adams, K. A. (2006). *Art as politics*. University of Hawaii Press.

Adey, P. (2017). *Mobility* (2nd ed.). Routledge.

Agamben, G. (2007). *Profanations* (J. Fort, Trans.). Zone Books.

Agamben, G. (2009). *What is an apparatus and other essays*. Stanford University Press.

Agarwal, S., & Shaw, G. (2017). *Heritage, screen and literary tourism*. Channel View Publications.

Agnew, J. A., Livingstone, D. N., & Rogers, A. (1996). Nature, culture and landscape. In J. A. Agnew, D. J. Livingstone, & A. Rogers (Eds.), *Human geography* (pp. 233–246). Blackwell.

Ahmed, S. (2007). Phenomenologies of whiteness. *Feminist Theory, 8*(2), 149–168. https://doi.org/10.1177/1464700107078139

Albuquerque Police Department. (2021). Crime trends in Albuquerque (2018–2021). https://www.cabq.gov/police/documents/2018-2021-year-crime-stats.pdf

Albuquerque Convention & Visitor's Bureau. (2013, October 10). Breaking Bad filming locations in Albuquerque. http://www.itsatrip.org/albuquerque/arts/breaking-bad-in-albuquerque.aspx

Albuquerque city, New Mexico. (2020). 2020 census. *United States Census Bureau*. https://www.census.gov.quickfacts/fact/table/albuquerquecitynewmexico/POP010220

Alderson, A. S., & Beckfield, J. (2004). Power and position in the world city system. *American Journal of Sociology, 109*(4), 811–851. https://doi.org/10.1086/378930

Alexander, C. (2020). A chronotope of expansion: Resisting spatio-temporal limits in a Kazakh nuclear town. *Ethnos*. https://doi.org/10.1080/00141844.2020.1796735

Alma de Creta 1. (2022). About us. https://www.almadecreta.com/en/about-us/

Alma de Creta 2. (2022). Zorba the Greek. https://www.almadecreta.com/en/tour-item/zorba-the-greek/

AlSayyad, N. (2006). *Cinematic urbanism*. Routledge.

Amoore, L. (2006). Biometric borders: Governing mobilities in the war on terror. *Political Geography, 25*(3), 336–351. https://doi.org/10.1016/j.polgeo.2006.02.001

Anastasiou, D., & Schäler, R. (2010). Translating vital information: Localisation, internationalization and globalisation. *Syn-Théses, 3*, 11–25. https://doi.org/10.26262/st.v0i3.5150

Anderman, N., & Haaretz Staff. (2006, November 20). Posters advertising Borat movie sanitized for Israeli consumption. *Haaretz*. https://web.archive.org/web/20070226204340/http://www.haaretz.com/hasen/spages/790394.html

Anderson, B. (2009). Affective atmospheres. *Emotion, Space and Society, 2*(2), 77–81. https://doi.org/10.1016/j.emospa.2009.08.005

Anderson, B. (2010). Modulating the excess of affect: Morale in a state of 'total war'. In M. Gregg & G. J. Seigworth (Eds.), *The affect theory reader* (pp. 161–185). Duke University Press.

Anderson, B. (2014). *Encountering affect*. Ashgate.

Anderson, B. (2015). What kind of thing is resilience? *Politics, 35*(1), 60–66. https://doi.org/10.1111/1467-9256.12079

Anderson, B., & Ash, J. (2015). Atmospheric methods. In P. Vannini (Ed.), *Non-representational methodologies* (pp. 34–51). Routledge.

Anger, K. (1959). *Hollywood Babylon*. Simon & Schuster.

Appadurai, A. (1990). Disjuncture and difference in the global cultural economy. *Public Culture, 2*(2), 1–24. https://www.jstor.org/stable/23266798

Arendt, H. (1958). *The human condition*. University of Chicago Press.

Arendt, H. (1972). *Cries of the Republic*. Harcourt & Brace.

Ash, J., & Turner, J. (1976). *The golden hordes*. St. Martin's Press.

Ashworth, L. M., & Swatuk, L. A. (1998). Masculinity and the fear of emasculation in international relations theory. In M. Zalewski & J. Parpart (Eds.), *The 'man' question in international relations* (pp. 73–93). Routledge.

Askarbekov, Y. (2016, October 28). What Kazakhstan really thought of Borat. *BBC*. https://www.bbc.com/culture/article/20161028-what-kazakhstan-really-thought-of-borat

Associated Press. (2020, October 24). The latest: Trump calls 'Borat' star an unfunny 'creep'. https://wtop.com/arts/2020/10/the-latest-harris-insists-biden-wont-ban-fracking/

Ateljevic, I. (2008). Transmodernity: Remaking our (tourism) world? In J. Tribe (Ed.), *Philosophical issues in tourism* (pp. 278–300). Channel View Publications.

Ateljevic, I., Hollinshead, K., & Ali, N. (2009). Special issue note: Tourism and worldmaking – Where do we go from here? *Tourism Geographies, 11*(4), 546–552. https://doi.org/10.1080/14616680903262794

Ateljevic, I., Morgan, N., & Pritchard, A. (2013). *The critical turn in tourism studies*. Routledge.

Augé, M. (2008). *Non-places*. Verso.

Ayres, T. C., & Jewkes, Y. (2012). The haunting spectacle of crystal meth: A media-created mythology? *Crime, Media, Culture, 8*(3), 315–332. https://doi.org/10.1177/1741659012443234

Bajracharya, P., Lippitt, C. D., & Sultana, S. (2020). Modeling urban growth and land cover change in Albuquerque using SLEUTH. *The Professional Geographer, 72*(2), 181–193. https://doi.org/10.1080/00330124.2019.1674668

Baker, T., & Ruming, K. (2014). Making 'Global Sydney': Spatial imaginaries, worlding and strategic plans. *International Journal of Urban and Regional Research, 39*(1), 62–78. https://doi.org/10.1111/1468-2427.12183

Banet-Weiser, S. (2018). *Empowered*. Duke University Press.

Banio, A., & Malchrowicz-Mósko, E. (2019). Dance in tourism from an anthropological perspective: An introduction to the research issue. *Sciendo, 29*(1), 15–21. https://doi.org/10.2478/tour-2019-0002

Barad, K. (2007). *Meeting the universe halfway*. Duke University Press.

Barad, K. (2010). Quantum entanglements and hauntological relations of inheritance: Dis/continuities, spacetime enfoldings, and justice-to-come. *Derrida Today, 3*(2), 240–268. https://doi.org/10.3366/drt.2010.0206

Barber, B. (2003). *Jihad versus McWorld*. Corgi Books.
Bærenholdt, J. O. (2013). Governmobility: The powers of mobility. *Mobilities, 8*(1), 20–34. https://doi.org/10.1080/17450101.2012.747754
Bærenholdt, J. O., Haldrup, M., Larsen, J., & Urry, J. (2004). *Performing tourist places*. Ashgate.
Barkin, S. J. (2020). *The social construction of state power*. Bristol University Press.
Bartucci, M. E., Hayes, J., & James, P. (2018). *Constructivism reconsidered*. University of Michigan Press.
Basea, E. (2015). Zorba the Greek, sixties exotica and a new cinema in Hollywood and Greece. *Studies in European Cinema, 12*(1), 60–76. https://doi.org/10.1080/17411548.2015.1015830
Baudrillard, J. (1973). *Toward a critique of the political economy of the sign*. Telos.
Bauman, Z. (1992). *Modernity and ambivalence*. Cambridge: Polity.
Bauman, Z. (1996a). From pilgrim to tourist—Or a short history of identity. In S. Hall & P. Du Gay (Eds.), *Questions of cultural identity* (pp. 18–36). SAGE.
Bauman, Z. (1996b). Tourists and vagabonds. Institut für Höhere Studien (IHS), Wien, Abt. *Politikwissenschaft, 30*, 7–15. http://nbn-resolving.de/urn:nbn:de:0168-ssoar-266870
Baumann, Z. (1998). *Work, consumerism and the new poor*. Open University Press.
Bauman, Z. (2007). *Consuming life*. Polity.
Bauman, Z. (2021). *Culture and art* (K. Bartoszyńska, Trans.). Polity.
Bauman, Z., & Lyon, D. (2013). *Liquid surveillance*. Polity.
Bauriedl, S., & Strüver, A. (2011). Strategic staging of urbanity: Urban images in films and film images in Hamburg's city marketing. In H. Schmid, W.-D. Sahr, & J. Urry (Eds.), *Cities and fascination* (pp. 169–186). Routledge.
Beck, U. (2002). *Individualization*. SAGE.
Beeton, S. (2005). *Film-induced tourism*. Channel View Publications.
Beeton, S. (2006). Understanding film-induced tourism. *Tourism Analysis, 11*(3), 181–188. https://doi.org/10.3727/108354206778689808
Beeton, S. (2010). The advance of film tourism. *Tourism and Hospitality Planning & Development, 7*(1), 1–6. https://doi.org/10.1080/14790530903522572
Beeton, S. (2015). *Travel, tourism and the moving image*. Channel View Publications.
Beeton, S. (2016). *Film-induced tourism* (2nd ed.). Channel View Publications.
Belhassen, Y., & Caton, K. (2009). Advancing understandings: A linguistic approach to tourism epistemology. *Annals of Tourism Research, 36*, 335–333. https://doi.org/10.1016/j.annals.2009.01.006
Belhassen, Y., & Caton, K. (2011). On the need for critical pedagogy in tourism education. *Tourism Management, 32*(6), 1389–1396. https://doi.org/10.1016/j.tourman.2011.01.014
Bell, D. (2007). Moments of hospitality. In J. Germann Molz & S. Gibson (Eds.), *Mobilizing hospitality* (pp. 29–46). Ashgate.
Benhabib, S. (1992). *Situating the self*. Polity.
Benson, M. (2010). The context and trajectory of lifestyle migration – The case of the British residents in Southwest France. *European Societies, 12*(1), 45–64. https://doi.org/10.1080/14616690802592605
Benson, M., & O'Reilly, K. (2003). *Lifestyle migration*. Ashgate.
Berger, P. (1967). *The sacred canopy*. Anchor Books.
Bergson, H. (1941). *Creative evolution*. Henry Holt & Co.

Berman, M. (2010). *All that is solid melts into air* (Rev. ed.). Verso.

Best, S. (1989). The commodification of reality and the reality of commodification: Jean Baudrillard and postmodernism. *Current Perspectives in Social Theory, 19,* 23–25.

Besten, M. (2000). L.A. death trip – Death is a star attraction in the City of Angels. Hollywood Underground. http://www.hollywood-underground.com/grave linearticle.htm

Bialski, P. (2011). Technologies of hospitality: How planned encounters develop between strangers. *Hospitality & Society, 1*(3), 245–260. http://doi.org/10.1386/hosp.1.3.245_1

Bialski, P. (2012). *Becoming intimately mobile.* Peter Lang.

Bialski, P. (2013). Online to offline social networking: Contextualising sociality today through Couchsurfing.org. In D. Picard & S. Buchberger (Eds.), *Couchsurfing cosmopolitanisms* (pp. 161–172). Transcript.

Bianchi, R. V. (2009). The 'critical turn' in tourism studies: A radical critique. *Tourism Geographies, 11*(4), 484–504. https://doi.org/10.1080/14616680903262653

Bianchi, R. V. (2018). The political economy of tourism development: A critical review. *Annals of Tourism Research, 70,* 88–102. https://doi.org/10.1016/j.annals.2017.08.005

Bingel, H. (2010). Fictional narratives and their ways of spiritual worldmaking. In V. Nünning & A. Nünning (Eds.), *Cultural ways of worldmaking* (pp. 287–308). de Gruyter.

Birtchnell, T., & Caletrio, J. (2014). Introduction: The movement of the few. In T. Birtchnell & J. Caletrio (Eds.), *Elite mobilities* (pp. 1–20). Routledge.

Blackwelder, C. (2020, October 24). Sacha Baron Cohen responds to Borat 2 scene with Rudy Giuliani: 'He did what he did'. *Good Morning America.* https://www.goodmorningamerica.com/culture/story/sacha-baron-cohen-responds-borat-scene-rudygiuliani-73783279

Böhme, G. (2016). *The aesthetics of atmospheres.* Routledge.

Böhme, G. (2017). *Critique of aesthetic capitalism.* Berlin Mimesis International/Suhrkamp Verlag.

Boltanski, L., & Chiapello, E. (2018). *The new spirit of capitalism* (2nd ed.). Verso.

Boltanski, L., & Thévenot, L. (1983). Finding one's way in social space: A study based on games. *Social Science Information, 22*(4–5), 631–680. https://doi.org/10.1177/053901883022004003

Boltanski, L., & Thévenot, L. (2000). The reality of moral expectations: A sociology of situated judgement. *Philosophical Explorations, 3*(3), 208–231. https://doi.org/10.1080/13869790008523332

Boltanski, L., & Thévenot, L. (2006). *On justification.* Princeton University Press.

Bonawitz, A. (2006, November 28). Did 'Borat' cause Pam and Kid's split? *CBS.* https://web.archive.org/web/20101118044203/; http://www.cbsnews.com/stories/2006/11/28/entertainment/main2211673.shtml

Boorstin, D. (1961). *The image.* New York, NY: Vintage.

Boorstin, D. (1962). *The image.* Penguin.

Bornstein, E. (2008). Our Borats, our Selves: Yokels and cosmopolitans on the global stage. *Slavic Review, 67*(1), 1–7. https://doi.org/10.2307/27652762

Botterill, D. (2000). Social scientific ways of knowing hospitality. In C. Lashley & A. Morrison (Eds.), *In search of hospitality* (pp. 177–197). Butterworth Heinemann.

Bourdieu, P. (1977). *Outline of a theory of practice* (R. Nice, Trans.). Polity.

Bourdieu, P. (1984). *Distinction* (R. Nice, Trans.). Harvard University Press.

Bourdieu, P. (1993). In R. Johnson (Ed.), *The field of cultural production*. Polity.

Bowers, A. M. (2004). *Magic realism*. Routledge.

Bowman, G. (1996). Passion, power and politics in a Palestinian tourist market. In T. Selwyn (Ed.), *The tourist image* (pp. 83–103). John Wiley and Sons.

Boyd, S. (2002). Media constructions of illegal drugs, users, and sellers: A closer look at *Traffic*. *International Journal of Drug Policy*, *13*(5), 397–407. https://doi.org/10.1016/S0955-3959(02)00079-8

Braidotti, R. (2013). *The posthuman*. Polity.

Bramwell, B., & Lane, B. (2014). The 'critical turn' and its implications for sustainable tourism research. *Journal of Sustainable Tourism*, *22*(1), 1–8. https://doi.org/10.1080/09669582.2013.855223

Brandellero, A., & Janssen, S. (2014). Popular music as cultural heritage: Scoping out the field of practice. *International Journal of Heritage Studies*, *20*(3), 224–240. https://doi.org/10.1080/13527258.2013.779294

Brennan, E. (2013, August 6). Albuquerque's Pole on 'Breaking Bad'. *The New York Times*. https://www.nytimes.com/2013/08/11/travel/albuquerques-role-on-breaking-bad.html

Britton, S. G. (1982). The political economy of tourism in the third world. *Annals of Tourism Research*, *9*(3), 331–358. https://doi.org/10.1016/0160-7383(82)90018-4

Brodsky-Porges, E. (1981). The Grand Tour: Travel as an educational device, 1600–1800. *Annals of Tourism Research*, *8*(2), 171–186. https://doi.org/10.1016/0160-7383(81)90081-5

Brown, R. H. (1977). *A poetic of sociology*. Cambridge University Press.

Brown, R. H. (1987). *Society as text*. University of Chicago Press.

Bruner, M. (2001). The Masai and the lion king: Authenticity, nationalism, and globalisation in African tourism. *American Ethnologist*, *28*(4), 881–908. https://doi.org/10.1525/ae.2001.28.4.881

Buchmann, A. (2006). From Erewhon to Edoras: Tourism and myths in New Zealand. *Tourism Culture & Communication*, *6*(3), 181–189. https://doi.org/10.3727/109830406778134090

Buck-Morss, S. (1986). The flaneur, the sandwichman and the whore: The politics of loitering. *New German Critique*, *39*, 99–140. https://doi.org/10.2307/488122

Buda, D. M. (2015). *Affective tourism*. Routledge.

Bulkens, M., Minca, C., & Muzaini, H. (2015). Storytelling as method in spatial planning. *European Planning Studies*, *23*(11), 2310–2326. https://doi.org/10.1080/09654313.2014.94260

Bunten, A. C., & Graburn, N. H. H. (2018). *Indigenous tourism movements*. University of Toronto Press.

Burawoy, M. (2004). Public sociologies: Contradictions, dilemmas, and possibilities. *Social Forces*, *82*(4), 1603–1618. https://doi.org/10.1353/sof.2004.0064

Burawoy, M. (2005). For public sociology. *American Sociological Review*, *70*, 4–28. https://doi.org/10.1177/000312240507000102

Burawoy, M. (2008). Open the social sciences: To whom and for what? *Portuguese Journal of Social Science*, *6*, 137–146. https://doi.org/10.1386/pjss.6.3.137_1

Burgess, J. (1982). Perspectives on gift and exchange in hospitable behaviour. *International Journal of Hospitality Management*, *1*(1), 49–59. https://doi.org/ 10.1016/0278-4319(82)90023-8

Busby, G., & O'Neill, K. (2006). Cephallonia and Captain Corelli's mandolin: The influence of literature and film on British visitors. *Acta Turistica*, *18*(1), 30–51.

Buscema, C. (2011). The harvest of Dionysus: Mobility/proximity, indigenous migrants and relational machines. In G. Pellegrino (Ed.), *The politics of proximity* (pp. 43–60). Ashgate.

Büscher, B., & Fletcher, R. (2017). Destructive creation: Capital accumulation and the structural violence of tourism. *Journal of Sustainable Tourism*, *25*(5), 651–667. https://doi.org/10.1080/09669582.2016.1159214

Büscher, M., Urry, J. & Witchger, K. (2011). Introduction: Mobile methods. In M. Büscher, J. Urry, & K. Witchger (Eds.), *Mobile methods* (pp. 1–19). Routledge.

Butler, R. (1980). The concept of a tourism area cycle of evolution: Implications for management of resources. *The Canadian Geographer [Le Géographe Canadien]*, *24*(1), 5–12. https://doi.org/10.1111/j.1541-0064.1980.tb00970.x

Butler, J. (1990). *Gender trouble*. Routledge.

Butler, R. (2006). *The tourism area life cycle*. Channel View Publications.

Butler, R. (2011). *Tourism area life cycle*. Goodfellow.

Cacoyannis, M. (2010, June). Interview with Dimitris Koutoulas held in Athens.

Calhoun, C. (2002). The class consciousness of frequent travelers: Toward a critique of actually existing cosmopolitanism. *South Atlantic Quarterly*, *101*(4), 869–897.

Campbell, N. (2005). Producing America: Redefining post-tourism in the global media age. In D. Crouch, R. Jackson, & F. Thompson (Eds.), *The media and the tourist imagination* (pp. 198–214). Routledge.

Campbell, C. (2018). *The romantic ethic and the spirit of modern consumerism*. SAGE.

Canguilhem, G. (1991). *The normal and the pathological*. Zone Books.

Capra, F. (1997). *The web of life*. Flamingo.

Carlson, J., & Stewart, K. (2014). The legibilities of mood work. *New Formations*, *82*(autumn), 114–133. https://doi.org/10.3898/NewF.82.07.2014

Carr, N. (2010). The shallows. *Atlantic*.

Carrabine, E. (2008). *Crime, culture and the media*. Polity.

Caton, K. (2012). Taking the moral turn in tourism. *Annals of Tourism Research*, *39*(4), 1906–1928. https://doi.org/10.1016/j.annals.2012.05.021

Cave, J., & Buda, D. (2018). Souvenirs in dark tourism: Emotions and Symbols. In R. P. Stone, R. Hartmann, T. Seaton, R. Sharpley, & L. White (Eds.), *The Palgrave handbook of dark tourism studies* (pp. 707–726). Palgrave Macmillan.

Cecchine, R. (2009, November 23). Borat's aftermath: A Romanian town seeks damages. *The Independent*. https://independent-magazine.org/2009/11/23/carmen/

Chakrabarti, D. (2000). *Provincializing Europe*. Princeton University Press.

Chambers, D., & Buzinde, C. (2015). Tourism and decolonisation: Locating research and self. *Annals of Tourism Research*, *51*, 1–16. https://doi.org/10.1016/ j.annals.2014.12.002

Cheer, J. M., Lapointe, D., Mostafanezhad, M., & Jamal, T. (2021). Tourism in crisis: Global threats to sustainable tourism futures. *Journal of Tourism Futures*, *7*(3), 278–294. https://doi.org/10.1108/JTF-09-2021-227

Christine. (2013, August 11). Breaking Bad filming in Albuquerque. *OLV*. https:// www.onlocationvacations.com/tag/breaking-bad-filming-in-albuquerque/

Christopherson, S., & Rightor, N. (2010). The creative economy as 'big business': Evaluating state strategies to lure filmmakers. *Journal of Planning Education and Research, 29*(3), 336–352. https://doi.org/10.1177/0739456X09354381

City of Albuquerque, Charter. (n.d.). Charter of the city of Albuquerque. http://www.cabq.gov/council/documents/charter-review-task-force/ciy_charter.pdf

City of Albuquerque, Planning. (n.d.). *Historic landmarks.* https://www.cabq.gov/planning/boards-commissions/landmarks-commission/historic-landmarks

City of Albuquerque, Technology and Innovation. (n.d.). Strategic plans. https://www.cabq.gov/technology-innovation/technology-innovation

Clark, N., & Szerszynski, B. (2021). *Planetary thought.* Polity.

Clough, P. T. (2006). Sacrifice, mimesis and the theorizing of victimhood (a speculative essay). *Representations, 94,* 131–149. https://doi.org/10.1525/rep.2006.94.1.131

Clough, P. T. (2007). Introduction. In P. T. Clough & J. Halley (Eds.), *The affective turn* (pp. 1–33). Duke University Press.

Clough, P. T., Goldberg, G., Schiff, R., Weeks, A., & Wilse, C. (2007). Notes towards a theory of affect itself. *Ephemera, 7*(1), 60–77. https://ephemerajournal.org/sites/default/files/2022-01/7-1cloughetal.pdf

Cohen, E. (1986). Lovelorn farangs: The correspondence between foreign men and Thai girls. *Anthropological Quarterly, 59*(3), 115–127. https://doi.org/10.2307/3317198

Cohen, E. (1996). A phenomenology of tourist experiences. In Y. Apostolopoulos, S. Leivadi, & A. Yannakis (Eds.), *The sociology of tourism* (pp. 90–114). Routledge.

Cohen, E. (2002). Authenticity, equity and sustainability in tourism. *Journal of Sustainable Tourism, 10*(4), 267–276. https://doi.org/10.2307/3317198

Cohen, E. (2001). Thai tourism: Trends and transformations. In E. Cohen (Ed.), *Thai tourism: Hill tribes, islands and open-ended prostitution* (2nd ed., pp. 1–28). White Lotus Press.

Cohen, S. (2002). Paying one's dues: The music business, the city and urban regeneration. In M. Talbot (Ed.), *The business of music* (pp. 263–291). University of Liverpool Press.

Cohen, E. (2003). Transnational marriage in Thailand: The dynamics of extreme heterogamy. In K. S. Chon, T. Bauer, & B. Mckercher (Eds.), *Sex and tourism* (pp. 57–82). The Haworth Hospitality Press.

Cohen, S. (2005). Screaming at the Moptops: Convergences between tourism and popular music. In D. Crouch, R. Jackson, & F. Thompson (Eds.), *The media and the tourist imagination* (pp. 76–91). Routledge.

Cohen, E. (2019). Posthumanism and tourism. *Tourism Review, 74*(3), 416–427. https://doi.org/10.1108/TR-06-2018-0089

Cohen, E., & Cohen, S. A. (2012). Current sociological theories and issues in tourism. *Annals of Tourism Research, 39*(4), 2177–2202. https://doi.org/10.1016/j.annals.2012.07.009

Cohen, E., & Cohen, S. A. (2015). Beyond Eurocentrism in tourism: A paradigm shift to mobilities. *Tourism Recreation Research, 40*(2), 157–168. https://doi.org/10.1080/02508281.2015.1039331

Cohen, S. A., & Cohen, E. (2019). New directions in the sociology of tourism. *Current Issues in Tourism, 22*(2), 153–172. https://doi.org/10.1080/13683500.2017.1347151

Cohen, S. A., Duncan, T., & Thulemark, M. (2013). Introducing lifestyle mobilities. In T. Duncan, S. A. Cohen, & M. Thulemark (Eds.), *Lifestyle mobilities* (pp. 1–20). Ashgate.

Coleman, S., & Eade, J. (2004). *Reframing pilgrimage*. Routledge.

Coleman, S., & Eade, J. (2018). *Pilgrimage and political economy*. Berghahn.

Collins, N., & Bekenova, K. (2017). Fuelling the New Great Game: Kazakhstan, energy policy and the EU. *Asia Europe Journal, 15*, 1–20. https://doi.org/10.1007/s10308-016-0451-4

Combined statistical areas – 2020 census. (2020). *TIGERweb Redirect*. https://tigerweb.geo.census.gov/tigerwebmain/Files/bas22/tigerweb_bas22_csa_2020_tab20_us.html

Conforti, K. (2013, October 11). 4 ways Breaking Bad fans can get their fix. Budget Travel. http://www.budgetravelonline.com/blog/budget-tavel-vacation-ideas-breaking-bad-tours,13006/

Connell, R. W. (1987). *Gender and power*. Stanford University Press.

Connell, R. W. (1995). *Masculinities*. University of California Press.

Connell, J. (2012). Film tourism – Evolution, progress and prospects. *Tourism Management, 33*(5), 1007–1029. https://doi.org/10.1016/j.tourman.2012.02.008

Córdoba-Azcárate, M. (2020). *Stuck with tourism*. University of California Press.

Corrigan, P. (1997). *The sociology of consumption*. SAGE.

Costanza-Chock, S. (2020). *Design justice*. MIT Press.

Couldry, N. (2000). *The place of media power*. Routledge.

Cowan, J. (1990). *Dance and the body politic in Northern Greece*. Princeton University Press.

Crang, M. (2001). Rhythm of the city, temporalized pace and motion. In J. May & N. Thrift (Eds.), *Timespace* (pp. 187–207). Routledge.

Crang, M. (2002). Between places: Producing hubs, flows and networks. *Environment and Planning A, 34*, 569–574. https://doi.org/10.1068/a34154

Cresswell, T. (2001). The production of mobilities. *New Formations, 43*(1), 11–25.

Cresswell, T. (2006). *On the move*. Routledge.

Cresswell, T. (2010). Towards a politics of mobility. *Environment and Planning D, 28*(1), 17–31. https://doi.org/10.1068/d11407

Cresswell, T. (2015). *Place*. Wiley Blackwell.

Cresswell, T., & Merriman, P. (2011). Introduction. In T. Cresswell & P. Merriman (Eds.), *Geographies of mobilities* (pp. 1–19). Ashgate.

Cretetravel.com. (2022). Zorba from Crete – Private tour. https://www.cretetravel.com/en/activity/41/Zorba_from_Crete_-_Private_Tour

Cronin, A. M. (2004). *Advertising myth*. Routledge.

Cronin, A. M. (2010). *Advertising, commercial spaces and the urban*. Palgrave Macmillan.

Cronin, A. M. (2018). *Public relations capitalism*. Springer.

Crouch, D. (2010). *Flirting with space*. Ashgate.

Crowe70ec1. (2021). The Breaking Bad store ABQ advertisement. You Tube. https://www.youtube.com/watch?v=hEcRQ-MVwPQ&t=47s

Croy, G. W. (2010). Planning for film tourism: Active destination management. *Tourism and Hospitality Planning & Development, 7*(1), 21–30. https://doi.org/10.1080/14790530903522598

Croy, G. W., Kersten, M., Mélinon, A., Bowen, D. (2019). Film tourism stakeholders and impacts. In C. Lundberg & V. Ziakas (Eds.), *The Routledge handbook of popular culture and tourism* (pp. 391–403). Routledge.

Czeglédy, A. P. (2003). The words and things of Ernest Gellner. *Social Evolution & History, 2*(2), 6–33.

D'Andrea, A. (2004). Global nomads: Techno and new age as transnational countercultures in Ibiza and Goa. In G. Saint-John (Ed.), *Rave culture and religion* (pp. 256–272). Routledge.

D'Andrea, A. (2006). Neo-nomadism: A theory of post-identitarian mobility in the global age. *Mobilities, 1*(1), 95–119. https://doi.org/10.1080/17450100500489148

Dann, G. M. S. (1977). Anomie, ego-enhancement and tourism. *Annals of Tourism Research, 4*(4), 184–194. https://doi.org/10.1016/0160-7383(77)90037-8

Dann, G. M. S. (1996). *The language of tourism.* CABI.

Dann, G. M. S. (1997). Research note: Paradigms in tourism research. *Annals of Tourism Research, 24*(2), 472–474. https://doi.org/10.1016/S0160-7383(97)80022-9

Dann, G. M. S., & Parrinello Liebman, G. (2009). Setting the scene. In G. M. S. Dann & G. Liebman Parrinello (Eds.), *The sociology of tourism* (pp. 1–65). Emerald Publishing Limited.

Dann, G. M. S., & Seaton, A. V. (2001). Slavery, contested heritage and thanatourism. In G. M. S. Dann & A. V. Seaton (Eds.), *Slavery, contested heritage and thanatourism* (pp. 1–29). Haworth Hospitality Press.

Davis, M. (1990). *City of quartz: Excavating the future in Los Angeles.* Haymarket.

Dawe, K. (2008). Arcadia calling: Cretan music and the popular imagination. *Journal of Intercultural Studies, 28*(2), 227–236. https://doi.org/10.1080/07256860701236633

de Sousa Santos, B. (1995). *Towards a new common sense.* Routledge.

de Sousa Santos, B. (2007). From an epistemology of blindness to an epistemology of seeing. In B. de Sousa Santos (Ed.), *Cognitive justice in a global world* (pp. 407–439). Lexington Books.

de Vries, R., & Reeves, A. (2022). What does it mean to be a cultural omnivore? Conflicting visions of omnivorousness in empirical research. *Sociological Research Online, 27*(2), 292–312. https://doi.org/10.1177/13607804211006109

Deadline Hollywood. (n.d.). 101 Best written TV series of all time from WGA/TV Guide: Complete list. http://www.deadline.com/2013/06/wgas-101-best-written-tv-series-of-all-time-complete-listdearlydepartedtours.com

Dearly departed: The tragical history tour. (2013, October 17). http://www.dearly departedtours.com/

Debord, G. ([1967] 1994). *Society of the spectacle.* Zone Books.

Degen, M., & Rose, G. (2022). *The new urban aesthetic.* Bloomsbury.

DeLanda, M. (2002). *Intensive science and virtual philosophy.* Continuum.

DeLanda, M. (2006). *The new philosophy of society.* Bloomsbury.

Delanty, G. (2001). *Challenging knowledge.* Open University Press.

Delanty, G. (2009). *The cosmopolitan imagination.* Cambridge University Press.

Delanty, G., & O'Mahony, P. (2002). *Nationalism and social theory.* SAGE.

Deleuze, G. (1990). *The logic of sense.* Columbia University Press.

Deleuze, G. (2002). The actual and the virtual. In *Dialogues* (E. R. Albert, Trans.) (Vol. II, pp. 148–152). Columbia University Press.

Deleuze, G., & Guattari, F. (1987). *A thousand plateaus: Capitalism and schizophrenia.* University of Minnesota Press.

Deleuze, G., & Guattari, F. (1988). *A thousand plateaus*. Athlone.

Denham, B. E. (2008). Folk devils, news icons and the construction of moral panics: Heroin chic and the amplification of drug threats in contemporary society. *Journalism Studies, 9*(6), 945–961. https://doi.org/10.1080/14616700802227811

Denning, M. (1986). Cheap stories: Notes on popular fiction and working-class culture in nineteenth-century America. *History Workshop Journal, 22*(1), 1–17. http://www.jstor.org/stable/4288715

Derrida, J. (1981). *Positions* (A. Bass, Trans). University of Chicago Press.

Derrida, J. (1994). *Spectres of Marx*. Routledge.

Derrida, J. (2000). Hostipitality. *Angelaki, 5*(3), 3–18. https://doi.org/10.1080/09697250020034706

Derrida, J. (2000). Hostipitality. *Angelaki, 5*(3), 3–18. https://doi.org/10.1080/09697250020034706

Derrida, J., & Dufourmantelle, A. (2000). *Of hospitality*. Stanford University Press.

Dervin, F., & Jacobsson, A. (2021). *Teacher education for critical and reflexive interculturality*. Palgrave Macmillan.

Descola, P. (2016). Landscape as transfiguration. Edward Westermarck Memorial Lecture, October 2015. *Suomen Antropologi, 41*(1), 3–14. https://journal.fi/suomenantropologi/article/view/59038

Desforges, L. (2000). Traveling the world: Identity and travel biography. *Annals of Tourism Research, 27*(4), 926–945. https://doi.org/10.1016/S0160-7383(99)00125-5

Dibdin, E. (2013, May 31). 'Breaking Bad': Digital Spy goes on location with the AMC drama. *Digital Spy*. http://www.digitalspy.co.uk/ustv/s166/breaking-bad/news/a485880/breaking-bad-digital-spy-goes-on-location-with-the-amc-drama.html

Dicken, B., & Laustsen, C. B. (2004). Sea, sun, sex and the discontents of pleasure. *Tourist Studies, 4*(2), 99–114. https://doi.org/10.1177/1468797604054376

Diekmann, A., & Hannam, K. (2012). Touristic mobilities in India's slum places. *Annals of Tourism Research, 39*(3), 1315–1336. https://doi.org/10.1016/j.annals.2012.02.005

Douglas, J. A. (2014). What's political ecology got to do with tourism? *Tourism Geographies, 16*(1), 8–13. https://doi.org/10.1080/14616688.2013.864324

Dredge, D., & Jamal, T. (2013). Mobilities on the Gold Coast, Australia: Implications for destination governance and sustainable tourism. *Journal of Sustainable Tourism, 21*(4), 557–579. https://doi.org/10.1080/09669582.2013.776064

du Bois, W. E. B. ([1899] 1903). *Souls of black folk*. A.C. McLurg & Co.

du Rand, G. E., & Heath, E. (2006). Towards a framework for food tourism as an element of destination marketing. *Current Issues in Tourism, 9*(3), 206–234. https://doi.org/10.2164/cit/226.0

Dunn, D. (2015). Those people were a kind of solution: Post-tourists and grand narratives. In T. V. Singh (Ed.), *Challenges in tourism research* (pp. 26–33). Channel View Publications.

Durant, H. (1938). *The problem of leisure*. George Routledge and Son.

Durkheim, E. (1982). In S. Lukes (Ed.), *The rules of sociological method*. The Free Press.

Dussel, E. (1985). *Philosophy of liberation*. Orbis.

Echter, C. M., & Jamal, T. (1997). The disciplinary dilemma of tourism studies. *Annals of Tourism Research, 24*(4), 868–883. https://doi.org/10.1016/S0160-7383(97)00060-1

Edensor, T. (1998). *Tourists at the Taj.* Routledge.

Edensor, T. (2002). *National identity, popular culture and everyday life.* Berg.

Edensor, T. (2005a). *Industrial ruins.* Berg.

Edensor, T. (2005b). Mediating William Wallace: Audio-visual technologies in tourism. In D. Crouch, R. Jackson, & F. Thompson (Eds.), *The media and the tourist imagination* (pp. 105–118). Routledge.

Eisenstadt, S. (1998). The construction of collective identities. *European Journal of Social Theory, 1*(2), 229–254. https://doi.org/10.1177/136843198001002008

Eisenstadt, S. (1999). *Fundamentalism, sectarianism and revolution.* Cambridge University Press.

Eisenstadt, S., & Giesen, B. (1995). The construction of collective identity codes. *European Journal of Sociology, 26*(1), 72–102. https://doi.org/10.1017/S0003975600007116

Eisner, R. (1991). *Travelers to an antique land.* MIT Press.

Ek, R. (2011). Creating the creative postcolonial citizen? *Culture Unbound, 3,* 167–186. http://www.cultureunbound.ep.liu.se. Accessed on January 27, 2023.

Elias, N. (2000). *The civilizing process (Vols. 1 & 2).* Blackwell.

Elliott, A., & Urry, J. (2010). *Mobile lives.* Routledge.

Emmison, M. (2003). Social class and cultural mobility: Reconfiguring the cultural omnivore thesis. *Journal of Sociology, 39*(3), 211–230. https://doi.org/10.1177/00048690030393001

Encyclopaedia Britannica. (n.d.). Sacha Baron Cohen (British actor). https://www.britannica.com/biography/Sacha-Baron-Cohen

Enzensberger, H. M. (1974). *The consciousness industry.* Seabury Press.

Escobar, A. (1999). After nature: Steps to an antiessentialist political ecology. *Current Anthropology, 40*(1), 1–30. https://doi.org/10.1086/515799

Escobar, A. (2001). Culture sits in places: Reflections on globalization and subaltern strategies of localization. *Political Geography, 20*(2), 139–174. https://doi.org/10.1016/S0962-6298(00)00064-0

Escobar, A. (2004). Actor networks and new knowledge producers: Social movements and the paradigmatic transition in the sciences. In B. de Sousa Santos (Ed.), *Para além das guerras da ciência.* Afrontamento. www.unc.edu/escobar

Escobar, A. (2018). *Designs for the pluriverse.* Duke University Press.

Esposito, R. (2011). *Immunitas.* Polity.

Everingham, P., & Motta, S. C. (2022). Decolonising the 'autonomy of affect' in volunteer tourism encounters. *Tourism Geographies, 24*(2–3), 223–243. https://doi.org/10.1080/14616688.2020.1713879

Fatima, Q., & Zafar, S. (2014). New Great Game: Players, interests, strategies and Central Asia. *South Asian Studies, 29*(2), 623–652.

Favell, A., Feldblum, M., & Smith, M. P. (2007). The human face of global mobility: A research agenda. *Society, 44*(2), 25–55. https://doi.org/10.1007/BF02819922

Featherstone, M. (1991). The body in consumer culture. In M. Featherstone (Ed.), *The body* (pp. 170–196). SAGE.

Feifer, M. (1985). *Going places.* Macmillan.

Fennell, D. (2006). *Tourism ethics.* Channel View Publications.

Fennell, D. (2009). Ethics and tourism. In J. Tribe (Ed.), *Philosophical issues in tourism* (pp. 211–226). Channel View Publications.

Fenton, M., & Pearce, P. (1988). Multidimensional scaling and tourism research. *Annals of Tourism Research, 15*(2), 236–254. https://doi.org/10.1016/0160-7383(88) 90085-0

Fleming, M. (2020, October 15). How Sacha Baron Cohen's plan to use Borat sequel to combat Facebook & Twitter Holocaust denier policies evolved with abrupt about face & surprise lawsuit. Yahoo.com. https://uk.style.yahoo.com/sacha-baron-cohen-planborat-192749803.html

Fletcher, S. (2011). Sustaining tourism, sustaining capitalism? The tourism industry's role in global capitalist expansion. *Tourism Geographies, 13*(3), 443–461. https://doi.org/10.1080/14616688.2011.570372

Foucault, M. (1979). *Discipline and punish*. Vintage.

Foucault, M. (1980). *Power/knowledge*. Harvester.

Foucault, M. (1997). The birth of biopolitics. In P. Rabinow (Ed.), *Michel Foucault: Ethics* (pp. 73–79), New Press.

Foucault, M. (2003). *Society must be defended*. Penguin.

Foucault, M. (2007). *Security, territory and population*. Palgrave Macmillan.

Foucault, M. (2010). *The birth of biopolitics*. Palgrave Macmillan.

Franklin, A. (2003). *Tourism*. SAGE.

Franklin, A. (2009). The sociology of tourism. In T. Jamal & M. Robinson (Eds.), *The SAGE handbook of tourism studies* (pp. 65–82). SAGE.

Franklin, S., Lusry, C., & Stacey, J. (2000). *Global nature, global culture*. Routledge.

Freudendal-Pedersen, M. (2020). Mobilities and values. In M. Büscher, M. Freudendal-Pedersen, S. Kesselring, & N. Grauslund Kristensen (Eds.), *Handbook of research methods and applications for mobilities* (pp. 21–27). Edward Elgar.

Friedberg, A. (1995). Cinema and the postmodern condition. In L. Williams (Ed.), *Viewing positions* (pp. 59–86). Rutgers University Press.

Friedman, R. (2006, November 2). Dharma and...Borat? A 'victim' complains. *Fox News*. https://web.archive.org/web/20070321062110/http://www.foxnews.com/story/0,2933,226960,00

Friese, H. (2004). Spaces of hospitality. *Angelaki, 9*(2), 67–79. https://doi.org/10.1080/0969725042000272753

Frost, W. (2010). Life changing experiences: Film and tourists in the Australian outback. *Annals of Tourism Research, 37*(3), 707–726. https://doi.org/10.1016/j.annals.2010.01.001

Fullagar, S. (2002). Narratives of travel: Desire and the movement of feminine subjectivity. *Leisure Studies, 21*(1), 57–74. https://doi.org/10.1080/02614360110119546

Fullagar, S. (2012). Gendered cultures of slow travel. In S. Fullagar, K. Markwell, & E. Wilson (Eds.), *Slow tourism* (pp. 99–112). Channel View Publications.

Fullagar, S., & Wilson, E. (2012). Critical pedagogies: A reflexive approach to knowledge creation in tourism and hospitality studies. *Journal of Hospitality and Tourism Management, 19*(1), 1–6. https://doi.org/10.1017/jht.2012.3

Fuller, S. (2006). *The new sociological imagination*. SAGE.

Fuller, S. (2011). *Humanity 2.0*. Palgrave Macmillan.

Fuller, S. (2012). The art of being human: A project for general philosophy of science. *Journal of General Philosophy of Science, 43*, 113–123. https://doi.org/10.1007/s10838-012-9181-5

Fuller, S. (2018). *Post-truth: Knowledge as a power game*. Anthem.

Fürsich, E., & Kavoori, A. (2001). Mapping a critical framework for the study of travel journalism. *International Journal of Cultural Studies, 4*(2), 149–171. https:// doi.org/10.1177/136787790100400202

Fussell, P. (1980). *Abroad.* Oxford University Press.

Fyfe, G., & Law, J. (1988). Introduction: On the invisibility of the visible. In G. Fyfe & J. Law (Eds.), *Picturing power* (pp. 1–14). Routledge.

Gangster Tour. (n.d.). Untouchable tours: It's a blast!. http://www.gangstertour.com/

Geertz, C. (1973). *The interpretation of cultures.* Basic Books.

Geertz, C. (2000). *Available light.* Princeton University Press.

Genova, A., & Hatcher-Moore, P. (2017, October 13). This is what nuclear weapons leave in their wake. National Geographic. https://www.nationalgeographic.com/ photography/article/nuclear-ghosts-kazakhstan

Geraghty, L. (2019). Passing through: Popular media tourism, pilgrimage, and narratives of being a fan. In C. Lundberg & V. Ziakas (Eds.), *The Routledge handbook of popular culture and tourism* (pp. 203–213). Routledge.

Germann Molz, J. (2006a). Getting a 'flexible eye': Round-the-world travel and scales of cosmopolitan citizenship. *Citizenship Studies, 9*(5), 517–531. https://doi.org/ 10.1080/13621020500301288

Germann Molz, J. (2006b). Watch us wander: Mobile surveillance and the surveillance of mobility. *Environment and Planning A, 38*(2), 377–393. https://doi.org/10.1068/ a3727

Germann Molz, J. (2014). Toward a network hospitality. *First Monday, 19*(3). https:// doi.org/10.5210/fm.v19i3.4824

Germann Molz, J. (2018). Discourses of scale in network hospitality: From the Airbnb home to the global imaginary of 'belong anywhere'. *Hospitality & Society, 8*(3), 229–951. https://doi.org/10.1386/hosp.8.3.229_1

Germann Molz, J., & Buda, D.-M. (2022). Attuning to affect and emotion in tourism studies. *Tourism Geographies, 24*(2–3), 187–197. https://doi.org/10.1080/ 14616688.2021.2012714

Germann Molz, J., & Gibson, S. (2007). Mobilizing and mooring hospitality. In J. Germann Molz & S. Gibson (Eds.), *Mobilizing hospitality* (pp. 1–28). Ashgate.

Ghermezian, S. (2020. October 15). Estate of late Holocaust survivor sues creators of Borat over appearance in upcoming sequel. *The Allgemeiner.* https://www.algemeiner.com/ 2020/10/15/estate-of-late-holocaust-survivor-sues-borat-creators-over-appearance-insequel/

Gibson, J. J. (1979). *The ecological approach to visual perception.* Houghton Mifflin.

Gibson, D. C. (2006). The relationship between serial murder and the American tourism industry. *Journal of Travel & Tourism Marketing, 20*(1), 45–60. https:// doi.org/10.1300/J073v20n01_04

Giddens, A. (1990). *The consequences of modernity.* Polity.

Giddens, A. (1994). Living in a post-traditional Society. In U. Beck, A. Giddens, & S. Lash (Eds.), *Reflexive modernization* (pp. 110–173). Polity.

Giddens, A. (1991). *Modernity and self-identity.* Polity.

Gill, R. (2007). Postfeminist media culture: Elements of a sensibility. *European Journal of Cultural Studies, 10*(2), 147–166. https://doi.org/10.1177/1367549407075898

Gleiberman, O. (2021, August 11). 'The Lost Leonardo' review: An enthralling art-world mystery that only starts by asking: Is it, or isn't it? *Variety.* https:// variety.com/2021/film/reviews/the-lost-leonardo-review-1235039350/

Gomez, A. (2011, July 11). Breaking Bad' puts city in spotlight. *Albuquerque Journal.* http://www.abqjournal.com/43799/living/breaking-bad-puts-city-in-spotlight.html

Goode, E., & Ben-Yehuda, N. (1994). Moral panics: Culture, politics, and social construction. *Annual Review of Sociology, 20,* 149–171. https://www.jstor.org/stable/2083363

Goodman, N. ([1968] 1999). *Languages of art.* Hackett.

Goodman, N. (1978). *Ways of worldmaking.* Hackett.

Goodman, N. (1996). The way the world is. In P. J. McCormick (Ed.) *Starmaking* (pp. 1). MIT.

Gössling, S., Scott, D., & Hall, M. C. (2021). Pandemics, tourism and global change: A rapid assessment of COVID-19. *Journal of Sustainable Tourism, 29*(1), 1–20. https://doi.org/10.1080/09669582.2020.1758708

Gottdiener, M. (2001). *Theming America.* Westview.

Gottlieb, A. (1982). Americans' vacations. *Annals of Tourism Research, 9,* 165–187. https://doi.org/10.1177/004728758302200166

Graburn, N. H. H. (1977). Tourism: The sacred journey. In V. Smith (Ed.), *Hosts and guests* (pp. 17–32). University of Pennsylvania Press.

Graburn, N. H. H. (1983a). The anthropology of tourism. *Annals of Tourism Research, 10*(1), 9–33. https://doi.org/10.1016/0160-7383(83)90113-5

Graburn, N. N. H. (1983b). *To pray, pay and play.* Centre des Hautes Etudes Touristiques.

Graff, H. J. (2015). *Undisciplining knowledge.* JHU Press.

Gravari-Barbas, M., & Graburn, N. H. H. (2012). Tourist imaginaries. *International Interdisciplinary Review of Tourism, 1*(1). https://journals.openedition.org/viatourism/1180?lang=en

Gray Faust, C. (2013, August 1). Albuquerque welcomes fans of 'Breaking Bad'. Go Escape.

Greatfaceandbody.com. (2013, October 10). Freshly 'cooked' products for every Breaking Bad fan. http://www.greatfaceandbody.com/bathingbad

Gregory, W. (1996). Discordant pluralism: A new strategy for critical systems thinking? *Systems Practice, 9,* 605–625. https://doi.org/10.1007/BF02169216

Griffero, T. (2014). *Atmospheres.* Routledge.

Grimwood, B. S. R., Caton, K., & Cooke, L. (2018). *New moral natures in tourism.* Routledge.

Grosz, E. (1994). Women, chora, dwelling. *ANY: Architecture New York, 4,* 22–27.

Grout, P. (2013a, March 11). Breaking Bad fans get additional fixes in Albuquerque. *People.* http://www.people.com/people/article/0.20720780.00.html

Grout, P. (2013b, May 8). Only in Albuquerque: The top five things you can't find anywhere else. Huff Post Travel. http://www.huffpost.com/pam-grout/only-in-albuquerque-the-t_b_3224880.html

Guardian Film News. (2006, November 20). Birds get the best of Bond. https://web.archive.org/web/20071225171531/http://film.guardian.co.uk/news/story/0,1952548,00.html?gusrc=rss&feed=16

Guattari, F. ([1989] 2014). *Three ecologies.* Semiotext(e).

Habermas, J. ([1962] 1982). *The structural transformation of the public sphere.* Polity.

Habermas, J. (1989). *The theory of communicative action (Vol. 2: Lifeworld and system).* Beacon Press.

Haldrup, M., & Larsen, J. (2010). *Tourism, performance and the everyday.* Routledge.

Hall, M. C. (2008). Of time and space and other things: Laws of tourism and the geographies of con-temporary mobilities. In P. Burns & M. Novelli (Eds.), *Tourism and mobilities* (pp. 15–32). CABI.

Hannam, K. (2008). The end of tourism? Nomadology and the mobilities paradigm. In J. Tribe (Ed.), *Philosophical issues in tourism* (pp. 101–116). Channel View Publications.

Hannam, K., & Diekmann, A. (2016). 'Absolutely not smelly': The political ecology of disengaged slum tours in Mumbai, India. In M. Mostafanezhad, R. Norum, E. J. Shelton, & A. Thompson-Carr (Eds.), *Political ecology of tourism* (pp. 270–283). Routledge.

Hannam, K., Mostafanezhad, M., & Rickly, J. (2016). Introduction. In K. Hannam, M. Mostafanezhad, & J. Rickly (Eds.), *Event mobilities* (pp. 1–14). Routledge.

Hannam, K., Sheller, M., & Urry, J. (2006). Mobilities, immobilities and moorings. *Mobilities, 1*(1), 1–22. https://doi.org/10.1080/17450100500489189

Hanquinet, L. (2017). Inequalities: When culture becomes capital. In D. O'Brien, T. Miller, & V. Durer (Eds.), *Routledge companion to global policy* (pp. 327–340). Routledge.

Hao, X., & Ryan, C. (2013). Interpretation, film language and tourist destinations: A case study of Hibiscus Town, China. *Annals of Tourism Research, 42*, 334–358.

Hardt, M., & Negri, A. (2004). *Multitude*. Penguin.

Harvey, D. (1982). *The limits to capital*. Basil Blackwell.

Harvey, D. (1989). *The condition of postmodernity*. Blackwell.

Harvey, D. (2006). *Spaces of global capitalism*. Verso.

Hasan, L. (2008, 8 July). If I see Borat, I will kill him with my own hands. *ABC News.* https://abcnews.go.com/International/Entertainment/story?id=2659018&page=2

Hassard, J., & Law, J. (1999). *Actor network theory and after*. Blackwell.

Haybron, D. (2008). Philosophy and the science of subjective wellbeing. In M. Eid & R. Larsen (Eds.), *The science of subjective wellbeing* (pp. 17–43). Guildford Press.

Hays, S. (2007). Stalled at the altar? Conflict, hierarchy, and compartmentalization in Burawoy's public sociology. In D. Clawson, R. Zussman, J. Misra, N. Gerstel, R. Stokes, D. L. Anderton, & M. Burawoy (Eds.), *Public sociology* (pp. 79–90). University of California Press.

Heal, F. (1990). *Hospitality in early modern England*. Clarendon Press.

Hegel, G. W. F. (1977). *The phenomenology of spirit*. Oxford University Press.

Heitmann, S. (2010). Film tourism planning and development: Questioning the role of stakeholders and sustainability. *Tourism and Hospitality Planning & Development, 7*(1), 31–46. https://doi.org/10.1080/14790530903522606

Herzfeld, M. (1980). Honour and shame: Problems in comparative analysis of moral systems. *Man, 15*(2), 339–351.

Herzfeld, M. (1985). *The poetics of manhood*. Princeton University Press.

Herzfeld, M. (2002). The absent presence: Discourses of crypto-colonialism. *South Atlantic Quarterly, 101*(4), 899–926. https://doi.org/10.1215/00382876-101-4-899

Herzfeld, M. (2005). *Cultural intimacy*. Routledge.

Herzfeld, M. (2006a). Practical Mediterraneanism. In W. V. Harris (Ed.), *Rethinking the Mediterranean* (pp. 45–64). Oxford University Press.

Herzfeld, M. (2006b). Spatial cleansing: Monumental vacuity and the idea of the West. *Journal of Material Culture, 1*(1/2), 127–149.

Herzfeld, M. (2016). *The siege of spirits*. University of Chicago Press.

Herzfeld, M. (2019). What is a polity? Subversive archaism and the bureaucratic nation-state. 2018 Lewis H. Morgan Lecture. *HAU: Journal of Ethnographic Theory, 9*(1), 23–35. https://doi.org/10.1086/703684

Hess, J. (1975). Godfather II: A seal Coppola couldn't refuse. *Jump Cut: A Review of Contemporary Media, 7,* 1–11.

Hexhagen, M., Ziakas, V., & Lundberg, C. (2022). Popular culture tourism: Conceptual foundations and state of play. *Journal of Travel Research.* https://doi.org/10.1177/00472875221140903

Hibberd, J. (2013, September 30). 'Breaking Bad' series finale ratings smash all records. *Entertainment Weekly.* https://ew.com/article/2013/09/30/breaking-bad-series-finale-ratings/

Hier, S. P. (2002). Raves, risks and the ecstasy panic: A case study in the subversive nature of moral regulation. *Canadian Journal of Sociology, 27*(1), 33–57. https://doi.org/10.2307/3341411

Higgins-Desbiolles, F. (2010). The elusiveness of sustainability in tourism: The culture-ideology of consumerism and its implications. *Tourism and Hospitality Research, 10*(2), 116–129. https://doi.org/10.1057/thr.2009.31

Hills, M. (2002). *Fan cultures.* Routledge.

Hishostels.com. (2013). HI-Ottawa jail. http://www.hihostels.ca/Ontario/1166/HI-Ottawa-Jail.hoste

Hobson, P. J. S., & Dietrich, U. C. (1995). Tourism, health and quality of life. *Journal of Travel & Tourism Marketing, 3*(4), 21–38. https://doi.org/10.1177/004728759503400275

Holland, P., & Huggan, G. (2000). *Tourists with typewriters.* University of Michigan Press.

Holliday, R., & Potts, T. (2012). *Kitsch!* Manchester University Press.

Hollinshead, K. (1998a). Disney and commodity aesthetics: A critique of Fjellman's analysis of 'distory' and the 'historicide' of the past. *Current Issues in Tourism, 1*(1), 58–119. https://doi.org/10.1080/13683509808667833

Hollinshead, K. (1998b). Tourism, hybridity and ambiguity: The relevance of Bhabha's 'third space' cultures. *Journal of Leisure Research, 30*(1), 121–156. https://doi.org/10.1080/00222216.1998.11949822

Hollinshead, K. (1999a). Surveillance of the worlds of tourism: Foucault and the eye-of-power. *Tourism Management, 20*(1), 7–23. https://doi.org/10.1016/S0261-5177(98)00090-9

Hollinshead, K. (1999b). Tourism as public culture: Horne's ideological commentary on the legerdemain of tourism. *International Journal of Tourism Research, 1*(4), 267–292. https://doi.org/10.1002/(SICI)1522-1970(199907/08)1:4<267::AID-JTR171>3.0.CO;2-Z

Hollinshead, K. (2003). Symbolism in tourism: Lessons from 'Bali 2002' – Lessons from Australia's dead heart. *Tourism Analysis, 8*(2), 267–295. https://doi.org/10.3727/108354203774077129

Hollinshead, K. (2008). Tourism and the social production of culture and place. *Tourism Analysis, 13*(5–6), 639–660. https://doi.org/10.3727/108354208788160540

Hollinshead, K. (2009a). 'Tourism state' cultural production: The re-making of Nova Scotia. *Tourism Geographies, 11*(4), 526–545. https://doi.org/10.1080/14616680903262737

Hollinshead, K. (2009b). The 'worldmaking' prodigy of tourism: The reach and power of tourism in the dynamics of change and transformation. *Tourism Analysis, 14*(1), 139–152. https://doi.org/10.3727/108354209788970162

Hollinshead, K. (2009c). Theme parks and the representation of nature and culture: The consumer aesthetics of representation and performance. In T. Jamal & M. Robinson (Eds.), *The SAGE handbook of tourism studies* (pp. 269–289). SAGE.

Hollinshead, K. (2010). Tourism studies and confined understanding: The call for a 'new sense' postdisciplinary imaginary. *Tourism Analysis, 15*(4), 499–512. https://doi.org/10.3727/108354210X12864727693669

Hollinshead, K., Ateljevic, I., & Ali, N. (2009). Worldmaking agency–worldmaking authority: The sovereign constitutive role of tourism. *Tourism Geographies, 11*(4), 427–443. https://doi.org/10.1080/14616680903262562

Hollinshead, K., & Kuon, V. (2013). The scopic drive of tourism. In O. Moufakkir & Y. Reisinger (Eds.), *The host gaze in global tourism* (pp. 1–18). CABI.

Hollinshead, K., Kuon, V., & Alajmi, M. (2015). Events in the liquid modern world: The call for fluid acumen in the presentation of peoples, places, pasts, and presents. In O. Moufakkir & T. Pernecky (Eds.), *Ideological, social and cultural aspects of events* (pp. 12–27). CABI.

Hollinshead, K., & Suleman, R. (2018). The everyday instillations of worldmaking: New vistas of understanding on the declarative reach of tourism. *Tourism Analysis, 23*(2), 201–213. https://doi.org/10.3727/108354218X15210313504553

Hollinshead, K., Suleman, R., & Nair, B. B. (2021). Trilogy of strategies of disruption in research methodologies: Article 1 of 3: The unsettlement of tourism studies: Positive decolonization, deep listening, and dethinking today. *Tourism Culture & Communication, 21*(2), 143–160.

Hollinshead, K., Suleman, R., & Vellah, A. (2021). Trilogy of strategies of disruption in research methodologies: Article 2 of 3: The Reimagination of tourism studies: Positive renewal, restoration, and revival today. *Tourism Culture & Communication, 21*(3), 259–276.

Hollinshead, K., Suleman, R., & Yu Lo, C. (2021). Trilogy of strategies of disruption in research methodologies: Article 3 of 3: The evocative power of tourism studies: Positive interruption, interdependence, and imaging forward today. *Tourism Culture & Communication, 21*(4), 355–373.

Hollinshead, K., & Vellah, A. B. (2020). Dreaming forward: Postidentity and the generative thresholds of tourism. *Journal of Geographical Research, 3*(4). https://doi.org/10.30564/jgr.v3i4.2299

Holmwood, J. (2010). Sociology's misfortune: Disciplines, interdisciplinarity, and the impact of audit culture. *British Journal of Sociology, 61*(4), 639–658. https://doi.org/10.1111/j.1468-4446.2010.01332.x

Honneth, A. (2007). *Disrespect*. Polity.

Horne, D. (1992). *The intelligent tourist*. Margaret Gee.

Huang, R. (2008). Critical thinking: Discussion from Chinese postgraduate international students and their lecturers. *Hospitality, Leisure, Sport and Tourism Network*. http://citeseerx.ist.psu.edu/viewdoc/download?doi=10.1.1.498.4104&rep=rep1&type=pdf

Huffpost. (2013, October 4). Walter White's obituary: Albuquerque honors 'Breaking Bad' antihero in local newspaper. Huffpost TV. https://www.huffpost.com/entry/walter-white-obituary-albuquerque_n_4044193

Hunziker, W. (1973). *Le système de la doctrine touristique*. Gurten.

Hutnyk, J. (1996). *The rumour of Calcutta*. Zed.

Hutnyk, J. (2000). *Critique of exotica*. Pluto Press.

Hutnyk, J. (2004). *Bad Marxism*. Pluto Press.

Hutnyk, J. (2022). Comparative urbanism and collective methodologies: Restoration projects in West Bengal and Southeast London. *HAU: Journal of Ethnographic Theory, 12*(1), 184–197. https://doi.org/10.1086/718528

Hutnyk, J. (2022). Comparative urbanism and collective methodologies: Restoration projects in West Bengal and South East London. *Hau: Journal of Ethnographic Theory, 12*(1). https://doi.org/10.1086/718528

Huyssen, A. (2000). Present pasts: Media, politics, amnesia. *Public Culture, 12*(1), 21–38. https://doi.org/10.1215/08992363-12-1-21

Huyssen, A. (2003). *Present pasts*. Stanford University Press.

ICAP. (2020). *Leading women in business*. ICAP. https://dir.icap.gr/mailimages/icap.gr/Posts/LWB_Study_Oct2020.pdf

Ihde, D. (1990). *Technology and the lifeworld*. Indiana University Press.

Ihde, D. (2022). *Material hermeneutics*. Routledge.

Ingold, T. (2010). Ways of mind-walking: Reading, writing, painting. *Visual Studies, 25*(1), 15–23. https://doi.org/10.1080/14725861003606712

Inskeep, M. (2006, September 26). Borat Sagdiyev delivers a message to Washington. NPR. https://web.archive.org/web/20131214234756/http://www.npr.org/templates/story/story.php?storyId=6165663

International Atomic Energy Agency. (2016, November 8). IAEA reviews Kazakhstan's nuclear power infrastructure development. www.iaea.org

Isaac, R. K., Platenkamp, V., Higgins-Desbiolles, F., & Hall, M. C. (2016). Giving Palestinian tourism(s) a voice. In R. K. Isaac, C. Michael Hall, & F. Higgins-Desbiolles (Eds.), *The politics and power of tourism in Palestine* (pp. 244–259). Routledge.

Iwashita, C. (2003). Media construction of Britain as a destination for Japanese tourists: Social constructionism and tourism. *Tourism and Hospitality Research, 4*(4), 331–340. http://www.jstor.org/stable/23745921

Iwashita, C. (2008). Roles of films and television dramas in international tourism: The case of Japanese tourists to the UK. *Journal of Travel & Tourism Marketing, 24*(2–3), 139–151. https://doi.org/10.1080/10548400802092635

Jafari, J. (1987). Tourism models: The sociocultural aspects. *Tourism Management, 8*(2), 151–159. https://doi.org/10.1016/0261-5177(87)90023-9

Jamal, T. (2019). *Justice and ethics in tourism*. Routledge/Earthscan.

Jamal, T., & Hollinshead, K. (2001). Tourism and the forbidden zone: The underserved power of qualitative inquiry. *Tourism Management, 22*(1), 63–82. https://doi.org/10.1016/S0261-5177(00)00020-0

Jang, K., & Kim, S. (2022). Staging mediatized tourism places as imagined playscapes: The crucial role of a tour designer. *Journal of Hospitality & Tourism Research.* https://doi.org/10.1177/10963480221130997

Jansson, A. (2002). Spatial phantasmagoria: The mediatization of tourism experience. *European Journal of Communication, 17*(4), 429–443. https://doi.org/10.1177/0267323102017004020

Jansson, A. (2018). Rethinking post-tourism in the age of social media. *Annals of Tourism Research, 69*, 101–110. https://doi.org/10.1016/j.annals.2018.01.005

Jarness, V., & Friedmann, S. (2017). 'I'm not a snob, but…': Class boundaries and the downplaying of difference. *Poetics, 61*, 14–25. https://doi.org/10.1016/j.poetic.2016.11.001

Jarvis, B. (2007). Monsters Inc.: Serial killers and consumer culture. *Crime, Media, Culture, 3*(3), 326–344. https://doi.org/10.1177/1741659007082469

Jay, M. (1994). *Downcast eyes: The denigration of vision in twentieth-century French thought.* University of California Press.

Jayathilaka, G. K. (2020). The worldmaking agency of the Sri Lankan travel blogger. *Tourism Culture & Communication, 20*(2–3), 117–127. https://doi.org/10.3727/109830420X15894802540197

Jenkins, H. (2008). *Convergence culture.* New York University Press.

Jenkins, H., Ford, S., & Green, J. (2013). *Spreadable media.* New York University Press.

Jensen, O. B. (2013). *Staging mobilities.* Routledge.

Jensen, O. B. (2014). *Designing mobilities.* Aalborg University Press.

Jensen, O. B. (2016). New 'Foucauldian boomerangs': Drones and urban surveillance. *Surveillance and Society, 14*(1), 20–33. https://doi.org/10.24908/ss.v14i1.5498

Jensen, O. B. (2019). Dark design: Mobility injustice materialized. In N. Cook & D. Butz (Eds.), *Mobilities, mobility justice and social justice* (pp. 116–128). Routledge.

Jensen, O. B. (2020). Atmospheres of Rejection: How Dark Design Rejects Homeless in the City. In Paper for the 4th International Congress on Ambiences, Ambiences, Alloæsthesia: Senses, Inventions, Worlds, e-conference organized by the Ambiences Net, 2–4 December.

Jensen, O. B. (2021). Pandemic disruption, extended bodies, and elastic situations: Reflections on COVID-19 and mobilities. *Mobilities, 16*(1), 66–80. https://doi.org/10.1080/17450101.2021.1867296

Jensen, O. B. (2022). *Re-designing World-making and mobilities in the Techno-Anthropocene.* In Conference Presentation, Designing the Techno-Anthropocene, København, Denmark (pp. 1–14).

Jensen, O. B., & Morelli, N. (2011). Critical points of contact: Exploring networked relations in urban mobility and service design. *Danish Journal of Geoinformatics and Land Management, 46*(1), 36–49.

Joas, H. ([1995] 2005). *The creativity of action.* Polity.

Jones, J. (2013, July 27). Albuquerque is Hollywood in the high desert. *Los Angeles Times.* http://www.articles.latimes.com/2013/jul/27/travel/la-tr-albuquerque-escape-20130728

Katz, J. (1988). *Seductions of crime.* Basic Books.

Kaufmann, E. (2000). *The delirium of praise.* John Hopkins University Press.

Kazakhstan Travel. (2020, October 25). 'Very Nice!' Kazakh tourism official new slogan Borat response. You Tube. https://www.youtube.com/watch?v=eRGXq4t9wY4

Kazig, R., Masson, D., & Thomas, R. (2017). Atmospheres and mobility: An introduction. *Mobile Culture Studies – The Journal, 3*, 7–20. https://hal.univ-grenoble-alpes.fr/hal-01882685v1

Kelly, S. (2013, August 10). The Breaking Bad tours driving a tourist boom in Albuquerque. *The Guardian.* https://www.theguardian.com/travel/2013/aug/11/breaking-bad-tour-albuquerque

Kim, S. S. (2012). Audience involvement and film tourism experiences: Emotional places, emotional experiences. *Tourism Management, 33*, 376–387. https://doi.org/10.1016/j.tourman.2011.04.008

Kim, W. D. (2017). Nikos Kazantzakis's ZORBA the GREEK: Another echo of Henri Bergson. *The Explicator, 75*(3), 181–184. https://doi.org/10.1080/00144940.2017.1346575

Kim, S. K., Kim, S. S., & Oh, M. (2017). Film tourism town and its local community. *International Journal of Hospitality & Tourism Administration, 18*(3), 334–360. https://doi.org/10.1080/15256480.2016.1276005

Kirschenblatt-Gimblett, B. (1997). *Destination culture.* University of California Press.

Klein, N. M. (1998). Staging murders: The social imaginary, film, and the city. *Wide Angle, 20*(3), 85–96. https://muse.jhu.edu/pub/1/article/36218N1

Klein, N. (2000). *No logo.* Flamingo.

Knorr-Cetina, K. (2005). The rise of a culture of life. *EMBO Reports, 6*, 76–80.

Knox, D., & Hannam, K. (2007). Embodying everyday masculinities in heritage tourism. In A. Pritchard, N. Morgan, I. Ateljevic, & A. Harris (Eds.), *Tourism and gender* (pp. 263–272). CABI.

Kohso, S. (2020). *Radiation and revolution.* Duke University Press.

Kolehmainen, M., & Mäkinen, K. (2021). Affective labour of creating atmospheres. *European Journal of Cultural Studies, 24*(2), 448–463. https://doi.org/10.1177/1367549419886021

Korstanje, M. E. (2012). Reconsidering cultural tourism: An anthropologist's perspective. *Journal of Heritage Tourism, 7*(2), 179–184. https://doi.org/10.1080/1743873X.2011.639883

Korstanje, M. E. (2017). *The rise of thana-capitalism and tourism.* Routledge.

Korstanje, M. E. (2018a). *Critical essays in tourism research.* Nova Science.

Korstanje, M. E. (2018b). *The mobilities paradox.* Edward Elgar.

Korstanje, M. E. (2022). New morbid forms of tourism: The case of dark tourism in perspective. In M. E. Korstanje, V. G. Gowreesunkar, & S. W. Maingi (Eds.), *Tourism in crisis* (pp. 79–92). Nova Science.

Korstanje, M. E., & Baker, D. (2018). Politics of dark tourism: The case of Cromañón and ESMA, Buenos Aires, Argentina. In *The Palgrave handbook of dark tourism studies* (pp.533–552). Palgrave.

Korstanje, M. E., Cisneos Mustelier, L., & Herrera, S. (2016). Understanding the indiscipline of tourism: A radical critique of the current state of epistemology. In N. Papas & I. Bregoli (Eds.), *Global dynamics in travel, tourism, and hospitality* (pp. 208–221). IGI Global.

Korstanje, M. E., & Séraphin, H. (2020). *Tourism, terrorism and security.* Emerald Publishing Limited.

Koutoulas, A. (1998). *O Mousikos Theodorakis.* Ekdoseis Livani.

Koutoulas, D. (2006). The market influence of tour operators on the hospitality industry: The case of Greek resort hotels. In A. Papatheodorou (Ed.), *Corporate rivalry and market power* (pp. 94–123). I.B. Tauris.

Krippendorf, J. (1986). Tourism in the system of industrial society. *Annals of Tourism Research, 13*(4), 517–532. https://doi.org/10.1177/004728758702500429

Kuhn, T. (1970). *The structure of scientific revolutions* (2nd ed.). University of Chicago Press.

Kumm, B. E., Berbary, L., & Grimwood, B. S. R. (2019). For those to come: An introduction to why posthumanism matters. *Leisure Sciences*, *41*(5), 341–347. https://doi.org/10.1080/01490400.2019.1628677

Laing, J., & Frost, W. (2012). *Books and travel*. Channel View Publications.

Langford, B. (2005). *Film genre*. Edinburgh University Press.

Lapointe, D. (2021). Tourism territory/territoire(s) touristique(s): When mobility challenges the concept. In M. Stock (Ed.), *Progress in French tourism geographies* (pp. 105–116). Springer.

Lapointe, D., & Coulter, M. (2020). Place, labour and (im)mobilities: Tourism and biopolitics. *Tourism Culture & Communication*, *20*(2–3), 95–106. https://doi.org/ 10.3727/109830420X15894802540160

Lapointe, D., Sarrasin, B., & Lagueux, J. (2020). Management, biopolitics and foresight: What looks for the future of the world? *Téoros*. http://journals.openedition.org/teoros/ 8407. Accessed on February 1, 2022.

Larsen, J. (2023). The tourist gaze 1.0, 2.0, 3.0 and 4.0. In A. Lew, M. Hall, & A. Williams (Eds.), *The Wiley Blackwell companion to tourism*. Wiley-Blackwell. (in press)

Larsen, J., & Urry, J. (2008). Networking in mobile societies. In J. O. Bærenholdt, B. Granås, & S. Kesserling (Eds.), *Mobility and place* (pp. 89–101). Ashgate.

Lashley, C. (2000). Towards a theoretical understanding. In C. Lashley & A. Morrison (Eds.), *In search of hospitality* (pp. 1–17). Butterworth Heinemann.

Lash, S., & Urry, J. (1987). *The end of organized capitalism*. University of Wisconsin Press.

Lash, S., & Urry, J. (1994). *Economies of signs and space*. SAGE.

Latour, B. (1987). *Science in action*. Open University Press.

Latour, B. (1993). *We have never been modern*. Harvard University Press.

Latour, B. (2005). *Re-assembling the social*. Oxford University Press.

Latour, B. (2018). *Down to earth*. Polity.

Laurendeau, J., & Shahara, N. (2008). 'Women could be every bit as good as guys'. Reproductive and resistant agency in two 'action' sports. *Journal of Sport & Social Issues*, *32*(1), 24–47. https://doi.org/10.1177/0193723507307819

Law, J. (2015). What's wrong with a one-world world? *Distinktion: Journal of Social Theory*, *16*(1), 126–139. https://doi.org/10.1080/1600910X.2015.1020066

Law, J., & Mol, A. (2002). *Complexities*. Routledge.

Lazaridis, G. (2001). Trafficking and prostitution: The growing exploitation of migrant women in Greece. *European Journal of Women's Studies*, *8*(1), 67–102. https://doi.org/10.1177/1350506801008001

Lazarsfield, P. F., Sewell, W. H., & Wilensky, H. L. (1967). *The uses of sociology*. Basic Books.

Lazzarato, M. (2004). From capital-labor to capital-life. *Ephemera Theory Multitude*, *4*(3), 187–208. https://ephemerajournal.org/sites/default/files/2022-01/4-3lazzarato.pdf

Lazzarato, M. (2011). The misfortunes of the 'artistic critique' and cultural employment. In G. Raunig, G. Ray, & U. Wuggenig (Eds.), *Critique of creativity* (pp. 41–56). MayFly Books.

Lazzarato, M. (2013). Art, work and politics in disciplinary societies and societies of security. In E. Alliez & P. Osborne (Eds.), *Spheres of action* (pp. 87–97). Tate Publishing.

Lefebvre, M. (2006). *Landscape and film*. Routledge.

Lehman-Wilzig, C. (2004). The natural life cycle of new media evolution: Inter-media struggle for survival in the internet age. *New Media & Society*, *6*(6), 707–730. https://doi.org/10.1177/146144804042524

Lennon, J., & Foley, M. (2000). *Dark tourism*. Continuum.

Lew, A. A., Cheer, J. M., Haywood, M., Brouder, P., & Salazar, N. B. (2020). Visions of travel and tourism after the global COVID-19 transformation of 2020. *Tourism Geographies*, *22*(3), 455–466. https://doi.org/10.1080/14616688.2020.1770326

Light, D. W. (2005). Contributing to scholarship and theory through public sociology. *Social Forces*, *83*, 1647–1655. https://www.jstor.org/stable/3598407

Lindström, K. N. (2019). Destination development in the wake of popular culture tourism. In C. Lundberg & V. Ziakas (Eds.), *The Routledge handbook of popular culture and tourism* (pp. 477–495). Routledge.

Lin, C.-C. T., Minca, C., & Ormond, M. (2018). Affirmative biopolitics: Social and vocational education for Quechua girls in the postcolonial "affectsphere" of Cusco, Peru. *Environment and Planning D: Society and Space*. https://doi.org/10.1177/0263775817753843

Linneman, T., & Wall, T. (2013). 'This is your face on meth': The punitive spectacle of 'white trash' in the rural war on drugs. *Theoretical Criminology*, *17*(3), 315–334. https://doi.org/10.1177/1362480612468934

Lister, R. (1997). *Citizenship*. Macmillan.

Logothetis, M. (1992). *Tourism statistics of the Dodecanese*. Institute of Tourist and Hotel Research.

Loizos, P., & Papataxiarchis, E. (1991a). Introduction: Gender and kinship in marriage and alternative contexts. In P. Loizos & E. Papataxiarchis (Eds.), *Contested identities* (pp. 3–25). Princeton University Press.

Loizos, P., & Papataxiarchis, E. (1991b). Gender, sexuality, and the person in Greek culture. In P. Loizos & E. Papataxiarchis (Eds.), *Contested identities* (pp. 221–234). Princeton University Press.

Lorimer, H. (2005). Cultural geography: The busyness of being 'more-than-representational'. *Progress in Human Geography*, *29*(1), 83–94. https://doi.org/10.1191/0309132505ph531p

Lövbrand, E., Beck, S., Chilvers, J., Forsyth, T., Hödren, J., Hulme, M., & Lidskog, R. (2015). Who speaks for the future of Earth? How critical social science can extend the conversation on the Anthropocene. *Global Environmental Change*, *32*, 211–218. https://doi.org/10.1016/j.gloenvcha.2015.03.012

Loyd, J. M., & Mountz, A. (2014). Managing migration, scaling sovereignty and islands. *Island Studies*, *9*(1), 23–42. https://islandstudiesjournal.org/files/ISJ-9-1-LoydMountz.pdf

Lugosi, P. (2014). Mobilising identity and culture in experience co-creation and venue operation. *Tourism Management*, *40*, 165–179. https://doi.org/10.1016/j.tourman.2013.06.005

Lynch, P., Germann Molz, J., McIntosch, A., Lugosi, P., & Lashley, C. (2011). Theorizing hospitality. *Hospitality & Society*, *1*(1), 3–24. https://doi.org/10.1386/hosp.1.1.3_2

Lynch, P., & MacWhannel, D. (2000). Home and commercialized hospitality. In C. Lashley & A. Morrison (Eds.), *In search of hospitality* (pp. 100–117). Butterworth Heinemann.

Lyng, S. (1990). Edgework: A social psychological analysis of voluntary risk taking. *American Journal of Sociology*, *95*(4), 851–886.

Macarthur, J. (2007). *The picturesque*. Routledge.

MacCannell, D. (1973). Staged authenticity: Arrangements of social space in tourist settings. *American Journal of Sociology*, *79*(3), 589–603. https://doi.org/10.1086/225585

MacCannell, D. ([1976] 1989). *The tourist*. Schocken Books.

MacCannell, D. (2011). *The ethics of sightseeing*. University of California Press.

MacCannell, D. (2012). On the ethical stake in tourism research. *Tourism Geographies*, *14*(1), 183–194. https://doi.org/10.1080/14616688.2012.639387

Macionis, N. (2004). Understanding the film induced tourist. In W. Frost, G. W. Croy, & S. Beeton (Eds.), *First international tourism and media conference* (pp. 86–97). Monash University.

MacKenzie, D. (2017). Capital's geodesic: Chicago, New Jersey, and the material sociology of speed. In J. Wajcmann & N. Dodd (Eds.), *The sociology of speed* (pp. 55–71). Oxford University Press.

Mair, H., & Reid, D. G. (2007). Leisure research and social change: A millennial state of the art. *Leisure/Loisir: Journal of the Canadian Association for Leisure Studies*, *31*(2), 417–426. https://doi.org/10.1080/14927713.2007.9651393

Malbon, B. (1999). *Clubbing*. Routledge.

Manderscheid, K. (2020). Critical mobilities – Mobilities as critique? In M. Büscher, M. Freudendal-Pedersen, S. Kesselring, & N. Grauslund Kristensen (Eds.), *Handbook of research methods and applications for mobilities* (pp. 365–373). Edward Elgar.

Mangan, D. (2013, June 25). Medical bills are the biggest cause of US bankruptcies: Study. *CNBC*. http://www.cnbc.com/id/100840148

Månsson, M. (2015). *Mediatized tourism: The convergence of media and tourism performances*. Media-Tryck, Lund University.

Månsson, M., Cassinger, C., Eskilsson, E., & Buchmann, A. (2020). Introduction: In the juncture of media convergence and tourism – A research agenda. In M. Månsson, A. Buchmann, C. Cassinger, & L. Eskilsson (Eds.), *The Routledge companion to media and tourism* (pp. 1–9). Routledge.

Markin, P. B. (2012). Global cities as sites of economic, social, and cultural interdependence. In *Aestheticization, postmodernity, and globalization with regard to the Shanghai Biennale for Contemporary Art*. https://www.researchgate.net/publication/299469720_Global_Cities_as_Sites_of_Economic_Social_and_Cultural_Interdependence

Marques, J. F. (2016). Sun, sand, sea, and sex. In J. Jafari & H. Xiao (Eds.), *Encyclopedia of tourism*. Springer.

Martini, A.-C., & Buda, D. M. (2020). Dark tourism and affect: Framing places of death and disaster. *Current Issues in Tourism*, *23*(6), 679–692. https://doi.org/10.1080/13683500.2018.1518972

Massey, D. (1994). *Space, place and gender*. Polity.

Mbembe, A. (2017). *Critique of black reason* (L. Dubois, Trans.). Duke University Press.

McCabe, S. (2005). 'Who is a tourist?': A critical review. *Tourist Studies*, *5*(1), 85–106. https://doi.org/10.1177/1468797605062716

McGrath, B. (2021). Island as urban artifact/archipelago as urban model. *Island Studies Journal, 16*(1), 81–100. https://doi.org/10.24043/isj.140

McRobbie, A. (2009). *The aftermath of feminism.* SAGE.

McRobbie, A. (2010). Reflections on feminism and immaterial labour. *New Formations, 70*, 60–76. https://doi.org/10.3898/NEWF.70.04.2010

Meethan, K. (2001). *Tourism in global society.* Palgrave.

Mennel, S., Murcott, A., & van Otterloo, A. H. (1992). *The sociology of food.* SAGE.

Merton, R. K. (1938). Social structure and anomie. *American Sociological Review, 3*(5), 672–682. https://doi.org/10.2307/2084686

Metzinger, T. K. (2018). Why is virtual reality interesting for philosophers? Frontiers in Robotics and AI, *5*, 1–19. https://doi.org/10.3389/frobt.2018.00101

Meyers, M. (2004). Crack mothers in the news: A narrative of paternalistic racism. *Journal of Communication Inquiry, 28*(3), 194–216. https://doi.org/10.1177/0196859904264685

Meyers, E. (2012). 'Blogs give regular people the chance to talk back': Rethinking "professional" media hierarchies in new media. *New Media & Society, 14*(6), 1022–1038. https://doi.org/10.1177/1461444812439052

Meyrowitz, J. (1986). *No sense of place.* Oxford University Press.

Michael, M. (2022). *The research event.* Routledge.

Mignolo, W. D. (2009). Epistemic disobedience, independent thought and decolonial freedom. *Theory, Culture & Society, 26*(7–8), 159–181. https://doi.org/10.1177/0263276409349275

Milbourne, P., & Kitchen, L. (2014). Rural mobilities: Connecting movement and fixity in rural places. *Journal of Rural Studies, 34*, 326–336. https://doi.org/10.1016/j.jrurstud.2014.01.004

Mills, C. W. (1959). *The sociological imagination.* Oxford University Press.

Minca, C. (2007). Agamben's geographies of modernity. *Political Geography, 26*, 78–97. https://doi.org/10.1016/j.polgeo.2006.08.010

Minca, C. (2010). The island: Work, tourism and the biopolitical. *Tourist Studies, 9*(2), 88–108. https://doi.org/10.1177/1468797609360599

Minca, C. (2013). The cultural geographies of landscape. *Hungarian Geographical Bulletin, 62*(1), 47–62.

Ministry of Justice of the Republic of Kazakhstan. (2017, June 30). *On approval of the concept of tourism industry development of the Republic of Kazakhstan until 2023.* Decree No. 406. http://adilet.zan.kz/eng/docs/P1700000406

Mitchell, R. (1983). *Mountain experience.* University of Chicago Press.

Mitra, A., & Cohen, E. (1999). Analyzing the web: Directions and challenges. In S. Jones (Ed.), *Doing internet research* (pp. 179–202). SAGE.

Moore, R. (1995). Gender and alcohol in a Greek tourist town. *Annals of Tourism Research, 22*(2), 300–313. https://doi.org/10.1016/0160-7383(94)00078-6

Moore, J. W. (2015). *Capitalism and the web of life.* Verso.

Moore, J. W. (2016). *Anthropocene or capitalocene?* Kairos/PM Press.

Moore, K., Buchmann, A., Månsson, M., & Fisher, D. (2021). Authenticity in tourism theory and experience. Practically indispensable and theoretically mischievous? *Annals of Tourism Research, 89*(3), 103208. https://doi.org/10.1016/j.annals.2021.103208

Morgan, D. (2019). *Snobbery.* Policy Press.

Morley, D., & Robins, K. (1995). *Spaces of identity.* Routledge.

Mortlock, C. (1984). *The adventure alternative*. Cicerone Press.

Morton, T. (2013). *Hyperobjects*. University of Minnesota Press.

Morton, T. (2018). Third stone from the sun. *SubStance, 47*(2), 107–118. https://doi.org/10.1353/sub.2018.0023

Mostafanezhad, M. (2017). *Volunteer tourism*. Routledge.

Mostafanezhad, M., & Norum, R. (2019). *Anthropocene ecologies*. Routledge.

Mostafanezhad, M., Norum, R., Shelton, E. J., & Thompson-Carr, A. (2016). *Political ecology of tourism*. Routledge.

Mostafanezhad, M., & Promburom, T. (2018). Lost in Thailand': The popular geopolitics of film-induced tourism in Northern Thailand. *Social & Cultural Geography, 19*(1), 81–101. https://doi.org/10.1080/14649365.2016.1257735

Mowforth, M., & Munt, I. (2016). *Tourism and sustainability*. Routledge.

Mulvey, L. (2006). Visual pleasure and narrative cinema. In M. G. Durham & D. M. Kellner (Eds.), *Media and cultural studies* (pp. 342–352). Blackwell.

Munar, A. M. (2016). The house of tourism studies and the systemic paradigm. In A. M. Munar & T. Jamal (Eds.), *Tourism research paradigms* (pp. 131–153). Emerald Publishing Limited.

Munar, A. M., Pernecky, T., & Feighery, W. (2016). An introduction to tourism postdisciplinarity. *Tourism Analysis, 21*(4), 343–347. https://doi.org/10.3727/108354216X14600320851578

Munt, I. (1994). The 'other' postmodern tourism: Culture, travel, and the new middle classes. *Theory, Culture & Society, 11*(3), 101–123. https://doi.org/10.1177/02632769401100300

Muzaini, H., & Minca, C. (2018). Rethinking heritage, but 'from below'. In H. Muzaini & C. Minca (Eds.), *After heritage: Critical perspectives on heritage from below* (pp. 1–18). Edward Elgar.

Najibullah, F., & Akaeva, K. (2019, November 23). Victims of Kazakhstan's Soviet-Era nuclear tests feel 'abandoned' by government. Radio Free Europe/Radio Liberty. https://www.rferl.org/a/victims-of-kazakhstan-s-soviet-era-nuclear-tests-feel-abandoned-by-government/30288299.html

Nakano Glenn, E. (2007). Whose public sociology? The subaltern speaks, but who is listening? In D. Clawson, R. Zussman, J. Misra, N. Gerstel, R. Stokes, D. L. Anderton, & M. Burawoy (Eds.), *Public sociology* (pp. 213–230). University of California Press.

Nederveen Pieterse, J. (2006). Emancipatory cosmopolitanism: Towards an agenda. *Development and Change, 37*(6), 1247–1257. https://doi.org/10.1111/j.1467-7660.2006.00521.x

Nederveen Pieterse, J. (2008). Globalization as hybridization. In M. G. Durham & D. M. Kellner (Eds.), *Media and cultural studies key works* (pp. 658–680). Blackwell.

Nederveen Pieterse, J. (2019). *Globalization & culture* (4th ed.). Rowman & Littlefield.

Neumann, B., & Zierold, M. (2010). Media as ways of worldmaking: Media-specific structures and intermedial dynamics. In V. Nünning & A. Nünning (Eds.), *Cultural ways of worldmaking* (pp. 103–118). de Gruyter.

Newmahr, S. (2011). Chaos, order and collaboration: Toward a feminist conceptualization of edgework. *Journal of Contemporary Ethnography, 40*(6), 682–712. https://doi.org/10.1177/0891241611425177

Nichols, L. (2017). Public Sociology. In O. Korgen (Ed.), *The Cambridge handbook of sociology (Vol. 2: Specialty and interdisciplinary studies)* (pp. 313–321). Cambridge University Press.

Nietzsche, F. (2020). About truth and lie in the extra-moral sense. In *Nietzsche's seven notebooks from 1876* (D. F. Ferrer, Trans.) (pp. 119–128). https://archive.org/details/nietzsches-seven-notebooks-from-1876

Nixon, R. (2011). *Slow violence and the environment of the poor.* Harvard University Press.

Norris, C. (2013). A Japanese media pilgrimage to a Tasmanian bakery. *Transformative Works and Cultures, 14*, 1.1–11.4. https://doi.org/10.3983/twc.2013.0470

Nünning, A., & Nünning, V. (2010). Ways of worldmaking as a model for the study of culture. In V. Nünning & A. Nünning (Eds.), *Cultural ways of worldmaking: Media and narratives* (pp. 215–244). de Gruyter.

Nussbaum, M. (2011). *Creating capabilities.* Cambridge University Press.

Nye, Jr., J. S. (2004). *Soft power.* Public Affairs.

Obadare, E. (2009). On the uses of ridicule: Humour, 'infrapolitics' and civil society in Nigeria. *African Affairs, 108*(431), 241–261. https://www.jstor.org/stable/27667121

Ohlsson, J., Lindell, J., & Arkhede, S. (2017). A matter of cultural distinction: News consumption in the online media landscape. *European Journal of Communication, 32*(2), 116–130. https://doi.org/10.1177/0267323116680131

Oksala, J. (2016). Affective labour and feminist politics. *Signs, 41*(2), 281–303. https://doi.org/10.1086/682920

Olstead, R. (2010). Gender, space and fear: A study of women's edgework. motion. *Space and Society, 4*(2), 86–94. https://doi.org/10.1016/j.emospa.2010.12.004

Olwig, K. R. (2002). *Landscape, nature and the body politic.* University Wisconsin Press.

Ong, A. (2011). Worlding cities, or the art of being global. In A. Roy & A. Ong (Eds.), *Worlding cities* (pp. 1–26). Blackwell.

Opiz, S., & Tellmann, U. (2012). Global territories: Zones of economic and legal dis/connectivity. *Distinktion, 13*, 261–282.

Osman, H., Johns, N., & Lugosi, P. (2013). Commercial hospitality in destination experiences: McDonald's and tourists' consumption of space. *Tourism Management, 42*, 238–247. https://doi.org/10.1016/j.tourman.2013.12.009

Ousby, I. (1990). *The Englishman's land.* Cambridge University Press.

Pachucki-Włosek, K. (2022). Political and socio-economics reforms of Kassym Tokayev from 2019 to 2021. *Central Asia & the Caucasus Institute Silk Road Studies, 23*(1), 235–243.

Page, S., & Connell, J. (2010). *Leisure.* Pearson.

Pangrazio, L., Godhe, A.-L., & Ledesma, A. G. L. (2020). What is digital literacy? A comparative review of publications across three language contexts. E-Learning and Digital Media, *17*(6), 442–459. https://doi.org/10.1177/2042753020946291

Paolucci, G. (1998). Time shattered: The postindustrial city and women's temporal experience. *Time & Society, 7*(2–3), 265–281. https://doi.org/10.1177/0961463X98007002006

Papadimitriou, L. (2000). Traveling on screen: Tourism and the Greek film musical. *Journal of Modern Greek Studies, 18*(1), 95–104. https://doi.org/10.1353/mgs.2000.0015

Papanek, V. (1991). *Design for the real world: Human ecology and social change* (2nd ed.). Thames and Hudson.

Papatheodorou, A., & Karpathiotaki, T. (2007). Film induced tourism, development and policymaking: The case of Crete. Paper presented at the First Conference of the International Association for Tourism Economics, 25–27 October 2007. Palma de Mallorca.

Patterson, M. (2020). Red or green? Gentrification in Albuquerque, New Mexico. WWU Honors Program Senior Projects. 375. https://cedar.wwu.edu/wwu_honors/375

Peaslee, R. M. (2010). 'The man from New Line knocked on the door': Tourism, media power, and Hobbiton/Matamata as boundaried space'. *Tourist Studies*, *10*(1), 57–73. https://doi.org/10.1177/1468797610390993

Pêcheux, M. ([1975] 1982). *Language, semantics and ideology* (H. Nagpal, Trans.). St Martin's Press.

Peirce, C. S. (1896). The logic of mathematics: An attempt to develop my categories from within. In C. S. Peirce (Ed.), *The collected papers* (Vol. I, pars. 417–519). Harvard University Press.

Penfold-Mounce, R. (2010). *Celebrity culture and crime*. Palgrave-Macmillan.

Peterson, R. A. (1992). Understanding audience segmentation: From elite and mass to omnivore and univore. *Poetics*, *21*, 243–258. https://doi.org/10.1016/0304-422X(92)90008-Q

Piketty, T. (2014). *Class in the twenty-first century*. Harvard University Press.

Plummer, K. (1995). *Telling sexual stories*. Routledge.

Porter, B. A., Heike, A., Schänzel, H. A., & Cheer, J. M. (2021). Introduction. In B. A. Porter, H. A. Schänzel, & J. M. Cheer (Eds.), *Masculinities in the field*. Channel View Publications.

Powers, J. L. (2017). Collecting kinship and crafting home: The souveniring of Self and Other in Diaspora homeland tourism. In S. Marschall (Ed.), *Tourism and memories of home* (pp. 132–156). Channel View Publications.

Pratt, S. (2015). The Borat effect: Film-induced tourism gone wrong. *Tourism Economics*, *21*(5), 977–993. https://doi.org/10.5367/te.2014.0394

Prince, S. (2000). Political film in the nineties. In W. W. Dixon (Ed.), *Film genre* (pp. 63–75). SUNY.

Pritchard, A., & Morgan, M. J. (2000). Privileging the male gaze: Gendered tourism landscapes. *Annals of Tourism Research*, *27*(4), 884–905. https://doi.org/10.1016/S0160-7383(99)00113-9

Pritchard, A., Morgan, N., & Ateljevic, I. (2011). Hopeful tourism: A new transformative perspective. *Annals of Tourism Research*, *38*(3), 941–963. https://doi.org/10.1016/j.annals.2011.01.004

Putnam, H. (1996). Reflections on Goodman's ways of worldmaking. In P. J. McCormick (Ed.), *Starmaking* (pp. 11–28). MIT.

Pyyhtinen, O. (2007). Event dynamics: The eventalization of society in the sociology of Georg Simmel. *Distinktion: Scandinavian Journal of Social Theory*, *8*(2), 111–132. https://doi.org/10.1080/1600910X.2007.9672949

Rauch, A. (2018). *Concerning astonishing atmospheres*. Mimesis International.

Rebel Donut. (2013, October 10). http://www.rebeldonut.com

Reijnders, S. (2009). Watching the detectives: Inside the guilty landscapes of inspector Morse, Baantjer & Wallander. *European Journal of Communication, 24*(2), 165–181. https://doi.org/10.1177/0267323108101830

Reijnders, S. (2010). On the Trail of 007: Media pilgrimages into the world of James Bond. *Area, 42*(3), 369–377. https://doi.org/10.1111/j.1475-4762.2009.00930.x

Reijnders, S. (2011). *Places of the imagination*. Ashgate.

Reinarman, C., & Levine, H. G. (1997). *Crack in America*. University of California Press.

Reiter, B. (2018). *Constructing the pluriverse*. Duke University Press.

Relph, E. (1976). *Place and placelessness*. Pion.

Revil, G. (2014). Histories. In P. Adey, D. Bissel, K. Hannam, P. Merriman, & M. Sheller (Eds.), *The Routledge handbook of mobilities* (pp. 506–516). Routledge.

Ricoeur, P. (1995). *Figuring the sacred*. Augsburg Fortress Press.

Ricoeur, P. (2004). *Memory, history, forgetting*. University of Chicago Press.

Ritzer, G. (1993). *The McDonaldization of society*. Pine Forge Press.

Ritzer, G. (2010). *The McDonaldization of society* (6th ed.). Pine Forge Press.

Ritzer, G. (2019). Inhospitable hospitality? In B. Rowson & C. Lashley (Eds.), *Experiencing hospitality* (pp. 73–80). Nova Science.

Ritzer, G., & Liska, A. (1997). 'McDisneyization' and 'post-tourism': Contemporary perspectives on contemporary tourism. In C. Rojek & J. Urry (Eds.), *Touring cultures* (pp. 96–112). Routledge.

Roberts, L. (2010). Projecting place: Location mapping, consumption and cinematographic tourism. In R. Koeck & L. Roberts (Eds.), *The city and the moving image* (pp. 183–204). Palgrave.

Roberts, L. (2012a). Cinematic cartography: Projecting place through film. In L. Roberts (Ed.), *Mapping cultures* (pp. 68–84). Palgrave Macmillan.

Roberts, L. (2012b). Mapping cultures: A spatial anthropology. In L. Roberts (Ed.), *Mapping cultures* (pp. 1–28). Palgrave Macmillan.

Roberts, L., & Cohen, S. (2015). Mapping cultures: Spatial anthropology and popular cultural memory. In N. Duxbury, W. F. Garrett-Petts, & D. MacLennan (Eds.), *Cultural mapping as cultural inquiry* (pp. 170–192). Routledge.

Robinson, M. (2012). The emotional tourist. In D. Picard & M. Robinson (Eds.), *Emotion in motion* (pp. 21–46). Routledge.

Roelofsen, M., & Minca, C. (2018). The Superhost. Biopolitics, home and community in the Airbnb dream-world of global hospitality. *Geoforum, 91*(February), 170–181. https://doi.org/10.1016/j.geoforum.2018.02.021

Rojek, C. (1993). *Ways of escape*. Routledge.

Rojek, C. (1998). Cybertourism and the phantasmagoria of place. In G. Ringer (Ed.), *Destinations* (pp. 33–48). Routledge.

Rojek, C. (2010). *The labour of leisure*. SAGE.

Römhild, R. (2003). Practised imagination. Paper presented at the conference Alltag der globalisierung: Perspektiven einer transnationalen Anthropologie, 16–18 January 2003. Frankfurt am Main.

Rorty, R. (2004). Philosophy as a transitional genre. In R. J. Bernstein, S. Benhabib, & N. Fraser (Eds.), *Pragmatism, critique, judgment* (pp. 3–28). MIT Press.

Rose, G. (1993). *Feminism and geography*. Polity.

Rose, N. (1999). *Powers of freedom*. Cambridge University Press.

Rose, G. (2003). On the need to ask how, exactly, is geography 'visual'? *Antipode*, *35*(2), 212–221. https://doi.org/10.1111/1467-8330.00317

Rose, G. (2014). *Visual methodologies*. SAGE.

Rosenberger, R., & Verbeek, P.-P. (2015). A field guide to postphenomenology. In R. Rosenberger & P.-P. Verbeek (Eds.), *Postphenomenological investigations* (pp. 9–41). Lexington Books.

Routes – Rentals & Tours. (2013, October 10). Get your 'Biking Bad' fix by bike. http://www.routesrentals.com/tours/specialty-bike-tours-abq/biking-bad-tour/

Roy, A., & Ong, A. (Eds.). (2011). *Worlding cities*. Blackwell.

Ryan, C., & Hall, M. C. (2001). *Sex tourism*. Routledge.

Ryan, C., Yanning, Z., Huimin, G., & Song, L. (2009). Tourism, a Classic Novel, and Television: The Case of Cáo Xuĕqin's Dream of the Red Mansions and Grand View Gardens, Beijing. *Journal of Travel Research*, *48*(1), 14–28. https://doi.org/10.1177/0047287508328796

Sacco, V. F., & Horton, A. D. (2013, October 17). *Crook's tour: Crime and crime scene tourism*. Press Americana. http://www.americanpopularculture.com/archive/venues/crook.htm

Said, E. (1978). *Orientalism*. Penguin.

Salazar, N. B. (2009). Imaged or imagined? Cultural representations and the 'tourismification' of peoples and places. *Cashiers d'Études Africaines*, *49*(1–2), 49–71. https://doi.org/10.4000/etudesafricaines.18628

Salazar, N. B. (2010). *Envisioning Eden*. Berghahn.

Salazar, N. B. (2012). Tourism imaginaries: A conceptual approach. *Annals of Tourism Research*, *39*(2), 863–882. https://doi.org/10.1016/j.annals.2011.10.004

Salazar, N. B. (2013). The (im)mobility of tourism imaginaries. In M. Smith & G. Richards (Eds.), *The Routledge handbook of cultural tourism* (pp. 34–39). Routledge.

Salazar, N. B. (2017). The cosmopolitanisation of tourism: An afterthought. In R. Shepherd (Ed.), *Cosmopolitanism and tourism* (pp. 187–194). Lexington Books.

Salazar, N. B., & Graburn, N. H. H. (2016). Towards an anthropology of tourism imaginaries. In N. B. Salazar & N. H. H. Graburn (Eds.), *Tourism Imaginaries* (pp. 1–30). Berghahn.

Salazar, N. B., & Zhu, Y. (2015). Heritage and tourism. In L. Maskell (Ed.), *Global heritage* (pp. 240–259). Wiley Blackwell.

Salgado, S. (2018). Online media impact on politics. Views on post-truth politics and postpostmodernism. *International Journal of Media and Cultural Politics*, *14*(3), 317–331. https://doi.org/10.1386/macp.14.3.317_1

Sandywell, B. (1996). *Logological investigations. (Vol. 1: Reflexivity and the crisis of Western Reason)*. Routledge.

Sandywell, B. (2006). Monsters in cyberspace cyberphobia and cultural panic in the information age. *Information, Community and Society*, *9*(1), 39–61.

Sandywell, B., & Beer, D. (2005). Examining reflexivity: An interview with Barry Sandwell. *Kritikos*. https://intertheory.org/Beer-Sandywell.htm

Sassen, S. (2001). *The global city*. Princeton University Press.

Sassen, S. (2013). When territory deborders territoriality. *Territory, Politics, Governance*, *1*(1), 21–45. https://doi.org/10.1080/21622671.2013.769895

Savage, M., Cunningham, N., Devine, F., Friedman, S., Laurison, D., Mckenzie, L., Miles, A., Snee, H., & Wakeling, P. (2015). *Social class in the 21st century*. Pelican.

Savelli, A. (2009). Tourism in Italian sociological thought and study. In G. M. S. Dann & G. Libemann Parrinello (Eds.), *The sociology of tourism* (pp. 131–168). Emerald Publishing Limited.

Sayer, A. (2011). *Why things matter to people.* Cambridge University Press.

Sayer, A. (2013). Postscript: Elite mobilities and critique. In T. Birtchnell & J. Caletrío (Eds.), *Elite mobilities* (pp. 251–162). Routledge.

Schiavone, R., Reijnders, S., & Brandellero, A. (2022). 'Beneath the storyline': Analysing the role and importance of film in the preservation and development of Scottish heritage sites. *International Journal of Heritage Studies, 28*(10), 1107–1120. https://doi.org/10.1080/13527258.2022.2131876

Schindler, L. (2020). Logbooks of mobilities. In M. Büscher, M. Freudendal-Pedersen, S. Kesselring, & N. Grauslund Kristensen (Eds.), *Handbook of research methods and applications for mobilities* (pp. 102–110). Edward Elgar.

Schmid, H., Sahr, W.-D., & Urry, J. (2011). Cities and fascination. In H. Schmid, W.-D. Sahr, & J. Urry (Eds.), *Cities and fascination* (pp. 1–15). Routledge.

Schmidt, S. J. (2011). *Worlds of communication.* Peter Lang.

Schmitz, H. (2016). Atmospheric spaces. *Ambiances. Environnement Sensible, Architecture et Espace Urbain.* https://doi.org/10.4000/ambiances.711

Scribano, A. (2021). *Colonization of the inner planet.* Routledge.

Scribano, A., Korstanje, M. E., & Timmermann López, F. A. (2019). *Populism and postcolonialism.* Routledge.

Scribano, A., & Sánchez Aguirre, R. (2018). Remarks on the social study of sensibilities through creative practices. In A. Scribano (Ed.), *Politics and emotions* (pp. 143–170). Studium Press LLC.

Seaton, A. V. (2002). Tourism as metempsychosis and metensomatosis: The personae of eternal recurrence. In G. M. S. Dann (Ed.), *The tourist as a metaphor of the social world* (pp. 135–168). CABI.

Seaton, P., & Yamamura, T. (2022). Theorizing war-related contents tourism. In T. Yamamura & P. Seaton (Eds.), *War as entertainment and contents tourism in Japan* (pp. 1–18). Routledge.

Selwyn, T. (2000). An anthropology of hospitality. In C. Lashley & A. Morrison (Eds.), *In search of hospitality* (pp. 18–37). Butterworth Heinemann.

Sen, A. (2009). *Development as freedom.* Oxford University Press.

Sennett, R. (1977). *The fall of Public Man.* Faber.

Sewell, W. (1990). *Three temporalities: Toward a sociology of the event.* CSST Working Paper #58/CRSO Working Paper #448, October 1990.

Sewell, W. (2008). Temporalities of capitalism. *Socio-Economic Review, 6*(3), 517–537. https://doi.org/10.1093/ser/mwn007

Sharpley, R., & Stone, P. (2009). *The darker side of travel.* Channel View Publications.

Sheldon, P., Fesenmaier, D., Woeber, K., Cooper, C., & Antonioli, M. (2008). Tourism education futures, 2010–2030: Building the capacity to lead. *Journal of Teaching in Travel & Tourism, 7*(3), 61–68. https://doi.org/10.1080/1531322080 1909445

Sheller, M. (2003). *Consuming the Caribbean.* Routledge.

Sheller, M. (2004). Demobilizing and remobilizing Caribbean paradise. In M. Sheller & J. Urry (Eds.), *Tourism mobilities* (pp. 13–21). Routledge.

Sheller, M. (2009). The new Caribbean complexity: Mobility systems, tourism and spatial rescaling. *Singapore Journal of Tropical Geography, 30*(2), 189–203. https://doi.org/10.1111/j.1467-9493.2009.00365.x

Sheller, M. (2012). *Citizenship from below*. Duke University Press.

Sheller, M. (2014). The new mobilities paradigm for a live sociology. *Current Sociology, 62*(6), 789–811. https://doi.org/10.1177/0011392114533211

Sheller, M. (2018a). Following. In O. B. Jensen, S. Kesselring, & M. Sheller (Eds.), *Mobilities and complexities* (pp. 33–38). Routledge.

Sheller, M. (2018b). *Mobility justice*. Verso.

Sheller, M. (2020). *Island futures*. Duke University Press.

Sheller, M. (2021). The geopolitics of offshore infrastructure-space: Remediating military bases, tourist resorts, and alternative island futures. In M. Mostafanezhad, M. Cordoba Azcarate, & R. Norum (Eds.), *Tourism geopolitics: Assemblages of infrastructure, affect, and imagination* (pp. 283–306). University of Arizona Press.

Sheller, M., & Urry, J. (2003). Mobile transformations of 'public' and 'private' life. *Theory, Culture & Society, 20*(3), 107–125. https://doi.org/10.1177/026327640 30203007

Sheller, M., & Urry, J. (2004). Places to play, places in play. In M. Sheller & J. Urry (Eds.), *Tourism mobilities* (pp. 1–10). Routledge.

Shepherd, R. (2002). Commodification, culture and tourism. *Tourist Studies, 2*(2), 183–201. https://doi.org/10.1177/146879702761936653

Shields, R. (1991). *Places on the margin*. Routledge.

Shoard, C. (2020, October 21). Rudy Giuliani faces questions after compromising scene in new Borat film. *The Guardian*. https://www.theguardian.com/film/2020/oct/21/rudy-giuliani-faces-questions-after-compromising-scene-in-new-borat-film

ShortList.com. (2013). The Breaking Bad industry. http://www.shortlist.com/entertainment/tv/the-breaking-bad-industry

Simmel, G. ([1903] 1997). The metropolis and mental life. In D. Frisby & M. Featherstone (Eds.), *Simmel on culture* (pp. 174–186). SAGE.

Simmel, G. (1991). Money in modern culture. *Theory, Culture & Society, 8*(3), 17–31. https://doi.org/10.1177/026327691008003002

Simoni, V. (2012). Dancing tourists: Tourism, party and seduction in Cuba. In D. Picard & M. Robinson (Eds.), *Emotion in motion* (pp. 267–281). Routledge.

Simoni, V. (2016). *Tourism and informal encounters in Cuba*. Berghahn.

Simpson, I., & Sheller, M. (2022). Islands as interstitial encrypted geographies: Making (and failing) cryptosecessionist exits. *Political Geography, 99*, 102744. https://doi.org/10.1016/j.polgeo.2022.102744

Singh, S. (2019). *Rethinking the anthropology of love and tourism*. Rowman and Littlefield.

Skeggs, B. (2004). *Class, self, culture*. Routledge.

Skeggs, B. (2010). The value of relationships: Affective scenes and emotional performances. *Feminist Legal Studies, 18*(1), 29–51. https://doi.org/10.1007/s10691-010-9144-3

Skocpol, T. (1979). *States and social revolutions*. Cambridge University Press.

Smith, A. D. (1999). *Myths and memories of the nation*. Oxford University Press.

Soja, E. W. (2000). *Postmetropolis*. Blackwell.

Soligo, M., & Dickens, D. R. (2020). Rest in fame: Celebrity tourism in Hollywood cemeteries. *Tourism Culture & Communication, 20*(2–3), 141–150. https://doi.org/10.3727/109830420X15894802540214

Solomon, R. C. (1993). *The passions.* Hackett Publishing.

Sorkin, M. (1992). *Variations on a theme park.* Noonday.

Spierenburg, P. (2008). *A history of murder.* Polity.

Spode, H. (2009). Tourism research and theory in German speaking countries. In G. M. Dann & G. Parrinello (Eds.), *The sociology of tourism* (pp. 65–94). Emerald Publishing Limited.

Springhall, J. (1998). *Youth, popular culture and moral panics.* Macmillan.

Stawkowski, M. E. (2016). 'I am a radioactive mutant': Emergent biological subjectivities at Kazakhstan's Semipalatinsk Nuclear test site. *American Ethnologist, 43*(1), 144–157. https://doi.org/10.1111/amet.12269

Stebbins, R. A. (1992). *Amateurs, professionals and serious leisure.* McGill-Queen's University Press.

Stebbins, R. A. (1996). Volunteering: A serious leisure perspective. *Nonprofit and Voluntary Action Quarterly, 25,* 211–224. https://doi.org/10.1177/0899764096252005

Stein, J. (2020, October 26). Kazakhstan, reversing itself, embraces 'Borat' as 'Very Nice'. *The New York Times.* https://www.nytimes.com/2020/10/26/business/kazakhstanembraces-borat.html

Stengers, I. (2000). *The invention of modern science.* University of Minnesota Press.

Stengers, I. (2010). *Cosmopolitics I.* University of Minnesota Press.

Stiegler, B. (2011). *Technics and time (Vol. 3: Cinematic time and the question of malaise).* Stanford University Press.

Still, J. (2004). Language as hospitality: Revisiting intertextuality via monolingualism of the other. *Paragraph, 27*(1), 113–127. https://doi.org/10.3366/para.2004.27.1.113

Still, J. (2006). France and the paradigm of hospitality. *Third Text, 20*(6), 703–710. https://doi.org/10.1080/09528820601069680

Stinson, M., Grimwood, B., & Caton, K. (2020). Becoming common plantain: Metaphor, settler responsibility, and decolonizing tourism. *Journal of Sustainable Tourism, 29,* 234–252. https://doi.org/10.1080/09669582.2020.1734605

Stone, P. (2013). Dark tourism scholarship: A critical review. *Journal of Tourism, Culture and Hospitality Research, 7*(3), 307–318. https://doi.org/10.1108/IJCTHR-06-2013-0039

Stone, P., & Sharpley, R. (2008). Consuming dark tourism: A thanatological perspective. *Annals of Tourism Research, 35*(2), 574–595. https://doi.org/10.1016/j.annals.2008.02.003

Strain, E. (2003). *Public places, private journeys.* Rutgers University Press.

Sturken, M. (2004). The aesthetics of absence: Rebuilding Ground Zero. *American Ethnologist, 31*(3), 311–325. http://www.jstor.org/stable/3805360

Sturken, M. (2007). *Tourists of history.* Duke University Press.

Sullivan, H. (2020, October 28). 'Very nice!': Kazakhstan adopts Borat's catchphrase in new tourism campaign. *The Guardian.* https://www.theguardian.com/world/2020/oct/27/very-nice-kazakhstan-adopts-borats-catchphrase-in-new-tourism-campaign-sacha-baron-cohen

Sumartojo, S., & Pink, S. (2018). *Atmospheres and the experiential world.* Routledge.

Susen, S. (2016). Towards a critical sociology of dominant ideologies: An unexpected reunion between Pierre Bourdieu and Luc Boltanski. *Cultural Sociology, 10*(2), 195–246. https://doi.org/10.1177/1749975515593098

Swain, M. (2009). The cosmopolitan hope of tourism: Critical action and worldmaking vistas. *Tourism Geographies, 11*(4), 505–525. https://doi.org/10.1080/14616680903262695

Swarbrooke, J., Beard, C., Leckie, S., & Pomfre, G. (2003). *Adventure tourism.* Butterworth-Heinemann.

Tefler, E. (1996). *Food for thought.* Routledge.

Tefler, E. (2000). The philosophy of hospitableness. In C. Lashley & A. Morrison (Eds.), *In search of hospitality* (pp. 38–55). Butterworth Heinemann.

Temenos, C., & McCann, E. (2014). Policies. In P. Adey, D. Bissel, K. Hannam, P. Merriman, & M. Sheller (Eds.), *The Routledge handbook of mobilities* (pp. 575–584). Routledge.

Thacker, E. (2004). *Biomedia.* University of Minnesota Press.

Thambinathan, V., & Kinsella, E. A. (2021). Decolonizing methodologies in qualitative research: Creating spaces for transformative praxis. *International Journal of Qualitative Methods, 20.* https://doi.org/10.1177/16094069211014766

The Breaking Bad Store. (n.d.). Overview. https://www.visitalbuquerque.org/listing/the-breaking-bad-store-abq/10105/

The Polygon. (n.d.). Semipalatinsk Test Site. Dark-tourism.com. https://www.dark-tourism.com/index.php/kazakhstan/15-countries/individual-chapters/519-sts-polygon-soviet-nuclear-test-site-kazakhstan

Thelen, T., Kim, S., & Scherer, E. (2020). Film tourism impacts: A multi-stakeholder longitudinal approach. *Tourism Recreation Research, 45*(3), 291–306. https://doi.org/10.1080/02508281.2020.1718338

Theodorakis, M. (2010, July). Interview held by Dimitris Koutoulas in Athens.

The TravelPorter. (2022). A Day in Chania Like Zorba The Greek. https://thetravelporter.com/crete/zorba-the-greek-chania-tour

Thibaud, J.-P. (2011). The sensory fabric of urban ambiances. *The Senses & Society, 6*(2), 203–215. https://doi.org/10.2752/174589311X12961584845846

Thibaud, J.-P. (2014). The backstage of urban ambiances: When atmospheres pervade everyday experience. *Emotion, Space and Society, 15,* 39–46. https://doi.org/10.1016/j.emospa.2014.07.001

Thiel, P. (2009). The education of a libertarian. *Cato Unbound.*

Thrift, N. (1996). *Spatial Formations.* SAGE.

Thrift, N. (2008). *Non-representational theory.* Routledge.

Thrift, N. (2010). Understanding the material practices of glamour. In M. Gregg & G. J. Seigworth (Eds.), *The affect theory reader* (pp. 289–308). Duke University Press.

Tilly, C. (2003). *The politics of collective violence.* Cambridge University Press.

Tönnies, F. (2001). *Community and civil society.* Cambridge University Press.

Touraine, A. (1995). *Critique of modernity.* Blackwell.

Tourism in Kazakhstan. (2017). Film and literary tourism: Analysis and strategy. https://qaztourism.kz/storage/app/media/analytics/tourism.pdf

Towner, J. (1984). The Grand Tour: Sources and a methodology for an historical study of tourism. *Annals of Tourism Research, 5*(3), 215. https://doi.org/10.1177/004728758502400256

Towner, J. (1985). The Grand Tour: A key phase in the history of tourism. *Annals of Tourism Research, 12*(3), 293–333. https://doi.org/10.1177/004728758602400426

Trading Economics. (2021). Kazakhstan – International tourism number of arrivals. World Bank. https://tradingeconomics.com/kazakhstan/international-tourism number-of-arrivals-wb-data.html

Trauer, B., & Ryan, C. (2005). Destination image, romance and place experience – An application of intimacy theory in tourism. *Tourism Management, 26*(4), 481–491. https://doi.org/10.1016/j.tourman.2004.02.014

Travellers Worldwide (2022, November 22). Is Albuquerque safe to visit in 2023? | Safety concerns. https://travellersworldwide.com/is-albuquerque-safe/#:~:text= Crime%20in%20Albuquerque,violent%20crimes%20recorded%20in%202021

Tribe, J. (2001). Research paradigms and the tourism curriculum. *Journal of Travel Research, 39*(4), 442–448. https://doi.org/10.1177/004728750103900411

Tribe, J. (2007). Critical tourism: Rules and resistance. In I. Ateljevic, A. Pritchard, & N. Morgan (Eds.), *The critical turn in tourism studies* (pp. 29–38). Elsevier.

Tsartas, P., & Galani-Moutafi, V. (2009). The sociology and anthropology of tourism in Greece. In G. M. S. Dann & G. Liebmann Parrinello (Eds.), *The sociology of tourism* (pp. 299–322). Emerald Publishing Limited.

Tsing, A. (2015). *The mushroom at the end of the world.* Princeton University Press.

Tsing, A. (2017). The Buck, the Bull, and the Dream of the Stag: Some unexpected weeds of the Anthropocene. *Suomen Antropologi, 42*(1), 3–21. http://orcid.org/ 0000-0002-0411-959X

Tuan, Y. F. (1974). *Topophilia.* Columbia University Press.

Tuan, Y. F. (1996). *Space and place.* University of Minnesota Press.

Tuan, Y. F. (2001). *Space and place.* University of Minnesota Press.

Tucker, H., & Akama, J. (2009). Tourism as postcolonialism. In T. Jamal & M. Robinson (Eds.), *Handbook of tourism studies* (pp. 504–520). SAGE.

Tudor, A. (1989). *Monsters and mad scientists.* Blackwell.

Turner, B. (2002). Cosmopolitan virtue, globalization and patriotism. *Theory, Culture & Society, 19*(1), 45–63. https://doi.org/10.1177/026327640201900102

Tzanelli, R. (2007a). Solitary amnesia as national memory: From Habermas to Luhmann. *The International Journal of Humanities, 5*(4), 253–260.

Tzanelli, R. (2007b). *The cinematic tourist.* Routledge.

Tzanelli, R. (2008). *Nation-building and identity in Europe.* Palgrave-Macmillan.

Tzanelli, R. (2011). *Cosmopolitan memory in Europe's 'backwaters'.* Routledge.

Tzanelli, R. (2012). Domesticating sweet sadness: Thessaloniki's glyká as a travel narrative. *Cultural Studies/Critical Methodologies, 12*(2), 159–172. https://doi.org/ 10.1177/1532708611435216

Tzanelli, R. (2013a). *Heritage in the digital era.* Routledge.

Tzanelli, R. (2013b). *Olympic ceremonialism and the performance of national character.* Palgrave Macmillan.

Tzanelli, R. (2015). *Mobility, modernity and the slum.* Routledge.

Tzanelli, R. (2016). *Thanatourism and cinematic representations of risk.* Routledge.

Tzanelli, R. (2018a). *Cinematic tourist mobilities and the plight of development.* Routledge.

Tzanelli, R. (2018b). Schematising hospitality: Ai WeiWei's activist artwork as a form of dark travel. *Mobilities, 13*(4), 520–534. https://doi.org/10.1080/17450101. 2017.1411817

Tzanelli, R. (2020a). Virtual pilgrimage: An irrealist approach. *Tourism Culture & Communication*, *20*(4), 235–240. https://doi.org/10.3727/109830420X1599 1011535517

Tzanelli, R. (2020b). *Magical realist sociologies of belonging and becoming*. Routledge.

Tzanelli, R. (2020c). Virocene imaginaries: Some critical reflections. *The International Journal of Interdisciplinary Global Studies, 20*. ISSN 2324-755X.

Tzanelli, R. (2021a). *Cultural (im)mobilities and the Virocene*. Edward Elgar.

Tzanelli, R. (2021b). Post-viral tourism's antagonistic tourist imaginaries. *Journal of Tourism Futures, 7*(3), 377–389. https://doi.org/10.1108/JTF-07-2020-0105

Tzanelli, R. (2022a). Biopolitics in critical tourism theory: A radical critique of critique [La biopolitique dans la théorie critique du tourisme: Une critique radicale de la critique]. *Via: Tourism Review, 21*. https://doi.org/10.4000/viatourism.8242

Tzanelli, R. (2022b). *Space, mobility and crisis in mega-event organisation*. Routledge.

Tzanelli, R. (2023). Economies of attention and the design of viable tourism futures. *Tourism Recreation Research*. https://doi.org/10.1080/02508281.2023.2188708

Tzanelli, R., & Jayathilaka, G. K. (2021). Worldmaking in Sri Lankan heritage design: The case of travel writers. *Athens Journal of Tourism, 8*(4), 213–232. https://doi.org/10.30958/ajt.8-4-1

Tzanelli, R., & Korstanje, M. (2016). Tourism in the European economic crisis: Mediatised worldmaking and new tourist imaginaries in Greece. *Tourist Studies, 16*(3), 296–314. https://doi.org/10.1177/1468797616648542

Tzanelli, R., & Korstanje, M. E. (2019). On killing the 'toured object': Anti-terrorist fantasy, touristic edgework and morbid consumption in the West Bank. In R. Isaac, R. Butler, & E. Cacmak (Eds.), *Tourism and hospitality in conflict-ridden destinations* (pp. 71–83). Routledge.

Tzanelli, R., & Korstanje, M. E. (2020). Critical thinking in tourism studies. *Tourism, Culture and Communication, 20*(3), 59–69. https://doi.org/10.3727/109830420X158 94802540133

Tzanelli, R., & Koutoulas, D. (2021). Zorba the Greek's tourism worldmaking: Gendering Cretan place identity and Greek memory through film. *Tourism Critiques: Practice and Theory, 2*(2), 170–194. https://doi.org/10.1108/TRC-02-2021-0003

Tzanelli, R., & Yar, M. (2020). Atmospheres of the inhospitable in staged kidnappings. *Consumption, Markets and Culture, 24*(5), 439–455. https://doi.org/10.1080/10253866.2020.1803068

Uriely, N. (2015). Exploring the post-tourist: Guidelines for future research. In T. Ver Singh (Ed.), *Challenges in tourism research* (pp. 33–44). Channel View Publications.

Urry, J. (1990). *The tourist gaze* (1st ed.). SAGE.

Urry, J. (1992). The tourist gaze and the environment. *Theory, Culture & Society, 9*(3), 1–26. https://doi.org/10.1177/026327692009003001

Urry, J. (1995). *Consuming places*. Routledge.

Urry, J. (2000). *Sociology beyond societies*. Routledge.

Urry, J. (2002). *The tourist gaze* (2nd ed.). SAGE.

Urry, J. (2004). Death in Venice. In M. Sheller & J. Urry (Eds.), *Tourism Mobilities* (pp. 205–215). Routledge.

Urry, J. (2007). *Mobilities*. Polity.

Urry, J. (2010). Consuming the planet to excess. *Theory, Culture & Society, 27*(2–3), 191–212. https://doi.org/10.1177/0263276409355999

Urry, J. (2011a). *Climate change and society.* Polity.

Urry, J. (2011b). Excess, fascination and climates. In H. Schmid, W.-D. Sahr, & J. Urry (Eds.), *Cities and fascination* (pp. 209–224). Routledge.

Urry, J. (2014). *Offshoring.* Polity.

Urry, J. (2016). *What is the future?* Polity.

Urry, J. (2017). Accelerating to the future. In J. Wajcman & N. Dodd (Eds.), *The sociology of speed* (pp. 42–51). Oxford University Press.

Urry, J., & Larsen, J. (2011). *The tourist gaze 3.0.* SAGE.

Uyzbayeva, A., Tyo, V., & Ibrayev, N. (2015). Towards achieving energy efficiency in Kazakhstan (World Academy of Science, Engineering and Technology). *International Journal of Environmental, Chemical, Ecological, Geological and Geophysical Engineering, 9*(2), 77–85.

van Dijck, J. (2009). Users like you? Theorizing agency in user-generated content. *Media, Culture & Society, 31*(1), 41–58. https://doi.org/10.1177/0163443708098245

van Dijck, J., & Poell, T. (2013). Understanding social media logic. *Media and Communication, 1*(1), 2–14. https://doi.org/10.17645/mac.v1i1.70

van Es, N., & Reijnders, S. (2018). Making sense of capital crime cities: Getting underneath the urban facade on crime-detective fiction tours. *European Journal of Cultural Studies, 21*(4), 502–520. https://doi.org/10.1177/1367549416656855

Vannini, P., Badalcchino, G., Lorraine, G., & Royle, S. A. (2009). Recontinentalizing Canada: Arctic ice's liquid modernity and the imaging of a Canadian Archipelago. *Island Studies Journal, 4*(2), 121–138.

Vardiabasis, N. (2002). *Istoria mias lexis [Story of a word].* Livani.

Varley, P. (2006). Confecting adventure and playing with meaning: The adventure commodification continuum. *Journal of Sport & Tourism, 11*(2), 173–194. https://doi.org/10.1080/14775080601155217

Vasileiadou, E. (2015). Who speaks for the future of earth? How critical social science can extend the conversation on the Anthropocene. *Global Environmental Change, 32,* 211–218. https://doi.org/10.1016/j.gloenvcha.2015.03.012

Veijola, S., Germann Molz, J., Pyyhtinen, O., Hockert, E., Grit, A., & Höckert, E. (2014). *Disruptive tourism and its untidy guests.* Palgrave Macmillan.

Veijola, S., & Jokinen, E. (1994). The body in tourism. *Theory and Society, 11*(3), 125–151. https://doi.org/10.1177/026327694011003006

Veijola, S., & Valtonen, A. (2007). The body in tourism industry. In A. Pritchard, N. Morgan, I. Ateljevic, & C. Harris (Eds.), *Tourism and gender* (pp. 13–31). CABI.

Verbeek, P.-P. (2005). *What things do.* Pennsylvania State University Press.

Verbeek, P.-P. (2015). Designing the public sphere: Information technologies and the politics of mediation. In L. Floridi (Ed.), *The onlife manifesto* (pp. 217–227). Springer.

Vervoort, J. M., Bendorc, R., Kelliherd, A., Strike, O., & Helfgotta, A. E. R. (2015). Scenarios and the art of worldmaking. *Futures, 74,* 62–70. http://dx.doi.org/10.1016/j.futures.2015.08.009

Vindenes, J., & Wasson, B. (2021). A postphenomenological framework for studying user experience of immersive virtual reality. *Frontiers in Virtual Reality, 2.* https://doi.org/10.3389/frvir.2021.656423

Virilio, P. (2006). *Speed and politics.* Semiotext(e).

Visit Albuquerque. (2014). Film tourism. https://www.visitalbuquerque.org/about-abq/film-tourism/

Vourdoubas, J. (2020). An appraisal of over-tourism on the island of Crete, Greece. *International Journal of Global Sustainability*, *4*(1), 63–77. https://doi.org/10.5296/ijgs.v4i1.17224

Walby, S. (2006). Gender approaches to nations and nationalism. In G. Delanty & K. Kumar (Eds.), *The SAGE handbook of nations and nationalism* (pp. 118–128). SAGE.

Wang, N. (2001). *Tourism and modernity*. Pergamon.

Wang, N. (2010). Logos-modernity, Eros-modernity, and leisure. *Leisure Studies*, *15*(2), 121–135. https://doi.org/10.1080/026143696375666

Wearing, S., McDonald, M., & Pointing, J. (2005). Building a decommodified paradigm in tourism: The contribution of NGOs. *Journal of Sustainable Tourism*, *13*(5), 424–439. https://doi.org/10.1080/09669580508668571

Wearing, S., Stevenson, D., & Young, T. (2010). *Tourist cultures*. SAGE.

Weber, M. (1958). Politics as a vocation. In G. Hans & C. W. Mills (Eds.), *From Max Weber*. Oxford University Press.

Weber, M. (1985). *The protestant ethic and the spirit of capitalism*. Unwin Hyman.

Welk, B. (2020, October 26). 'Borat' sequel promotes 'racism, cultural appropriation and xenophobia' Kazakh American Association says. *The Wrap*. https://www.thewrap.com/borat-sequel-promotes-racism-cultural-appropriation-and-xenophobia-kazakhamerican-association-says/

Wheeler, W. (2021). *Environment and Post-Soviet transformation in Kazakhstan's Aral Sea region*. UCL Press.

Wickens, E. (2002). The sacred and the profane: A tourist typology. *Annals of Tourism Research*, *29*(3), 834–851.

von Wiese, L. (1935). Fremdenverkehr als ziechenmensliche beziehugen [Tourism as an interprersonal relation]. *Archiv für den Fremdenverkehr*, *1*(1), 1–3.

Wilbert, C., & Hansen, R. (2009). Walks in spectral space: East London crime scene tourism. In A. Jansson & A. Lagerkvist (Eds.), *Strange spaces* (pp. 187–203). Ashgate.

Wilson, E., Harris, C., & Small, J. (2008). Furthering critical approaches in tourism and hospitality studies: Perspectives from Australia and New Zealand. *Journal of Hospitality and Tourism Management*, *15*(1), 15–18. https://doi.org/10.1375/jhtm.15.15

Wittel, A. (2001). Toward a network sociality. *Theory, Culture & Society*, *18*(6), 51–76. https://doi.org/10.1177/026327601018006003

Wolf, B. (2007, November 15). Kazakhstan not laughing at 'Ali G'. *ABC*. https://web.archive.org/web/20070219094754/http://www.abcnews.go.com/Entertainment/story?id=1315240

Wolff, J. (1985). The invisible flaneuse: Women and the literature of modernity. *Theory, Culture & Society*, *2*(3), 37–46. https://doi.org/10.1177/0263276485002003005

Wolff, K. H., & Simmel, G. (1959). *Georg Simmel, 1858–1918*. Ohio State University Press.

Wood, A. F. (2005). 'What happens [in Vegas]': Performing the post-tourist flâneur in 'New York' and 'Paris.'. *Text and Performance Quarterly*, *25*(4), 315–333. https://doi.org/10.1080/10462930500362403

Wood, A. F. (2006). A rhetoric of ubiquity: Terminal space as omnitopia. *Communication Theory, 13*(3), 324–344. https://doi.org/10.1111/j.1468-2885. 2003.tb00295.x

World Data Info. (2018). Tourism in Kazakhstan. https://www.worlddata.info/asia/ kazakhstan/tourism.php

World Entertainment News Network. (2005, April 15). Phillips quit Borat after receiving death threats. http://www.contactmusic.com/starsky-and-hutch/news/ phillips-quit-borat-afterreceiving-death-threats

Wray, M., & Croy, W. G. (2015). Film tourism: Integrated strategic tourism and regional economic development planning. *Tourism Analysis, 20*(3), 313–326. https://doi.org/10.3727/108354215X14356694891898

Yar, M. (2010). Screening crime: Cultural criminology goes to the movies. In K. J. Hayward & M. Presdee (Eds.), *Framing crime* (pp. 68–82). Routledge.

Yar, M. (2014). Imaginaries of crime, fantasies of justice: Popular criminology and the figure of the superhero. In M. Hvid-Jacobson (Ed.), *Poetics of crime* (pp. 193–208). Ashgate.

Young, I. M. ([1990] 2011). *Justice and the politics of difference.* Princeton University Press.

Young, I. M. (1998). Impartiality and the civic public: Some implications of feminist critiques of moral and political theory. In J. Landes (Ed.), *Feminism, the public and the private* (pp. 421–447). Oxford University Press.

Young, I. M. (2005). *On female body experience.* Oxford University Press.

Zabortseva, N. Y. (2012). From the 'forgotten region' to the 'great game' region: On the development of geopolitics in Central Asia. *Journal of Eurasian Studies, 3*(2), 168–176. https://doi.org/10.1016/j.euras.2012.03.007

Zakharov, N., Law, I., & Shmidt, M. (2017). Central Asian racisms. In N. Zakharov & I. Law (Eds.), *Post-Soviet Racisms* (pp. 129–183). Springer.

Ziakas, V., Tzanelli, R., & Lundberg, C. (2022). Interscopic fan travelscape: Hybridizing tourism through sport and art. *Tourist Studies, 22*(3), 290–307. https://doi.org/10.1177/14687976221092169

Zinovieff, S. (1991). Hunters and hunted: Kamaki and the ambiguities of sexual predation in a Greek town. In P. Loizos & E. Papataxiarchis (Eds.), *Contested identities* (pp. 203–220). Princeton University Press.

Žižek, S. (1993). *Tarrying with the negative.* Duke University Press.

Žižek, S. (2002). *Welcome to the desert of the real!* Verso.

Žižek, S. (2004). Notes on a debate 'from within the people.' *Criticism, 46*(4), 661–666. https://www.jstor.org/stable/23127251

Žižek, S., & Dolar, M. (2002). *Opera's second death.* Routledge.

Index

Actancy, 7–8, 21
Actant (-s), 5–6, 9, 31, 33, 138
Action, 1–5, 7–10, 15, 19–22, 25,
  27–29, 33, 40–41, 44, 67–69,
  73, 92–94, 116, 133–134, 138
Activism, 20, 29, 65–66, 75
Actor (-s), 5–6, 8, 27, 31, 34–35, 38–39,
  44–45, 67–68, 70, 74–75, 82,
  84, 87, 94, 105, 128,
  134–135, 138
Adiaphorization, 73
Adventure, 31, 40–41, 52, 58–59, 84,
  96, 103–104, 108, 121,
  127–128
Adventurer, 103, 127–128
Advertising, 2–6, 33–34, 63, 66–67,
  76–77, 83, 93, 95–96,
  101–103, 115–116, 125–126
Advocacy, 2, 4, 29–30, 55–56
Aesthetics, 9–10, 13–14, 78, 85, 87,
  106, 117, 127–128
Affect (-s), 3–6, 9–10, 15–16, 28–29,
  32–33, 38, 40–42, 47–48, 54,
  62, 64, 66, 74–76, 79–81, 92,
  110, 113–114, 129–130,
  134–135, 137–138
Agamben, Giorgio, 19, 61–62, 114
Agency, 4, 7–8, 12–13, 19, 21, 24,
  32–35, 37–38, 43, 46–47, 55,
  57, 61, 68–69, 115, 138
Anomie, 107–108
Anthropocene, 5–6, 8, 33, 38, 74,
  77–79, 81–82, 139
Ánthropoi, 5–6
Antisemitism, 82–83, 86
Antiziganism, 82–83
Apparatus (-es), 14–15, 17, 19–20,
  34–35, 78, 91–93, 97–98,
  129–130

Areas (-s), 8, 21–22, 54, 78–79, 84,
  88–89, 97, 110–112, 135–136
Arendt, Hannah, 8–9, 11–12, 66, 78
Artwork, 38, 74
Assemblage (-es), 7–8, 38, 40–42, 53,
  81, 114–115
Ateljevic, Irina, 27–28, 55–56, 76
Atmosphere (-s), 8–10, 21, 42, 47–48,
  52, 54, 68–69, 82, 110, 112
Authenticity (-ies), 2–3, 9, 38, 40–41,
  43, 55, 84, 89–90, 92, 101,
  121, 137–138
Authority, 8–9, 23, 34–35, 42–44, 52,
  61–62, 95
Autonomy, 2, 20–21, 75
Axiology (-ies), 26–28, 52, 98–99

Barad, Karen, 135
Bauman, Zygmunt, 29, 31–32, 62,
  64–65, 73, 103, 139
Benhabib, Sheyla, 92
Biography (-ies), 3, 63, 78, 84, 103,
  111–112, 114, 120–121
Biomedia, 101–102
Biomediations, 101–102
Biopolitics, 6–7, 24–25, 38–40, 60–61,
  64, 70, 76–77, 81, 91, 95,
  97–98, 102, 110–112,
  129–130, 136
Body (-ies), 54, 57–58, 61–62, 64, 74,
  92, 97–98, 124–126
Border (-s), 31, 39–40, 42, 65, 79, 103,
  105, 110–112, 114, 129–130
Bourdieu, Pierre, 46, 134, 137–139

Camp, 38–39, 66, 75–76, 83–84, 86–87,
  91, 96–97, 117
Capital (-s), 9–10, 15–17, 19–20, 22–24,
  27–28, 31–33, 37–39, 51–53,

62, 67–70, 75–77, 80, 87–90, 94, 104, 110, 114–115, 138–139

Capitalism, 10–11, 15–17, 20, 22, 24, 37–38, 53, 65, 70, 75–77, 80–81, 92–93

Captivation, 85

Capture, 23, 47–48

Care, 29, 44–45, 55–56, 58, 61–62, 83–84, 86, 103, 119

Category (-ies), 6, 9, 12–13, 32–33, 56, 63–64, 74, 85, 87–88, 133–134, 136, 138

Character (-s), 74, 76–77, 83–84, 95

Chora, 103–104, 106

Choraster, 106

City (-ies), 5–6, 14–15, 35, 59–60, 88, 94–95, 103, 109–111, 113–114, 116, 129, 131, 133, 135

Civility, 20–21, 39–40, 56, 65–66, 95

Clark, Nigel, 5–6, 74, 129–131

Climate change, 6–7, 17, 27, 78

Coené, 5–6

Community (-ies), 4–9, 21, 28–30, 51–52, 54–56, 64–65, 75, 78–79, 85–86, 90–91, 102, 104, 106, 115, 122

Complexity (-ies), 1–2, 14, 19, 21–22, 25–26, 29–30, 38, 52, 55–56, 63, 74, 81–82, 115

Consciousness, 9, 25, 107–108, 129

Constellation (-s), 9, 26, 85–86, 135

Consumption, 13–15, 24, 29–33, 38, 53–54, 60–61, 73–74, 76–77, 80, 85–87, 101–104, 107–109, 115–117, 121–123, 127–128

Cosmoi, 4–5

Cosmology (-ies), 19–20, 28, 108–109, 114–115

Cosmopolitanism, 8, 31

Creativity, 3, 10–12, 19–20, 34–35, 44, 78, 92–93, 113–114, 138

Crime, 10, 35, 101, 104–105, 112, 122, 130

Crisis (-es), 2, 19, 26, 57–58, 62, 66, 81, 129–130

Critical Zone, 20–21, 101–103, 139

Critique, 7, 10–11, 19–20, 22–24, 26, 29–31, 34–35, 44, 55–57, 84, 90–91, 112, 134–135

Culture, 2, 4, 9–11, 14, 17, 20–21, 27, 29–30, 35, 37–38, 40–41, 44, 47, 53, 56, 61–62, 64–66, 102–103, 111, 116, 123, 127–128, 135

Death, 60, 68–70, 80, 97, 107–108, 112, 116–119, 122–123, 127

De-factualisation, 11–12

Delanty, Gerard, 8, 21, 23, 31, 62

Deleuze, Giles, 7–8, 15–16, 122, 135

De-mediations, 121

Derrida, Jacques, 2–3, 11, 32, 135

Design, 2–12, 14–15, 17, 26–28, 31, 33–35, 41–42, 52, 63–67, 70, 73, 76–77, 81–82, 84–87, 89–94, 96–98, 103–104, 106, 109, 111–112, 114–115, 117–118, 122, 129–131, 136

Designing, 1–2, 5–9, 13–15, 19–20, 35, 73, 76–77, 81–82, 122, 130, 133

De-spiritedness, 12–13

Difference (-s).. *See also* Young, Iris Marion, 7, 11, 24, 63, 66–67, 73, 75, 85–86, 92, 102, 111–112, 121–122, 135

Discourse (-s), 9, 11–13, 16, 20–21, 24, 26, 28–29, 39, 42–43, 58, 61–62, 65–68, 76–78, 80–83, 92–94, 97, 102, 104, 109, 137–138

Distorical, 114–115

Distory (-ies), 114–115

Dussel, Enrique, 27–28

Dystopianism, 14–15

Ecology (-ies), 9–10, 78, 97, 106

Economies, 74–75, 78, 85, 103, 112, 133–134

Ecosystem (-s), 5–6, 64, 78–79
Edgework(-s), 35, 103–104, 112, 119,
 122, 127–128, 130
Edgeworker (-s), 35, 103, 127–128
Elite (-s), 21–22, 64, 78, 85, 88, 91, 131
Embodiment, 50–52
Emotion (-s), 14–15, 19–21, 32–33, 39,
 46–47, 52, 58, 92, 106, 119,
 127, 134
Empowerment, 28–29, 57–58, 61–62,
 104, 127–128
Endangering, 38–39, 78–81, 101–102,
 104, 122, 130–131, 138–140
Engendering, 5–6, 39, 74, 77–78,
 101–102, 138
Entanglement (-s), 11–12, 15–16, 63,
 76, 79, 92–93, 134, 136
Entrepreneur (-s), 7, 41–42, 63, 119,
 135
Enunciation (-s), 8–9, 11–12, 20–21,
 47, 81, 136–139
Environment (-s), 2–7, 11, 15, 23,
 28–29, 31–33, 47, 52, 58–59,
 63–64, 73–78, 80–81, 85, 87,
 91–93, 95–96, 101–102, 104,
 109–112, 134–135, 138
Episteme, 27–28
Epistemology, 28, 32
Eros, 54
Ethics, 13, 21, 26–27, 32, 56, 66–67, 78,
 84–85
Ethno-nationalism, 66–67, 70
Ethnoscapes, 120–121
Evènements, 5, 16–17, 92–93
Event (-s), 1, 4–5, 9–10, 13, 15, 17, 26,
 33–35, 43–44, 52, 78, 86,
 113–117, 122, 129–130, 139
Eventisation, 15–16
Evolutionism, 38–39
Exopolis (-es), 13–15, 17, 62, 110, 112
Exoscapes, 109, 138
Experience, 14, 17, 26, 30–31, 37–38,
 43, 46, 53–55, 58, 63–64,
 66–67, 76, 80, 86–87, 92,
 102, 106–109, 121–122, 127,
 130, 138–139

Fascination, 7, 14–15, 57, 66–67, 74,
 102, 106, 108, 117–118
Fáskō, 76–77
Feminine mystique, 52
Field (-s), 2–5, 7, 19–21, 28–29, 31, 58,
 61, 68–69, 75–76, 80, 85–86,
 89–90, 102–103, 113–114,
 133–135, 138
Flânerie (-s), 63, 88, 96
Flâneur (-s), 103
Form (-s), 1–2, 6–7, 9–12, 15, 20, 24,
 26–27, 29–30, 32–35, 37–41,
 43, 46, 55–56, 61–63, 68–69,
 73, 75–77, 79, 82–84, 92,
 95–99, 102, 106, 111, 114,
 116, 130–131, 134, 138
Freeport (-s), 89–90, 136–138
Frisking, 131
Fuller, Steve, 23, 25, 95, 98–99
Futures, 3, 7–8, 19–21, 31–32,
 101–102, 104, 133, 139

Gaze, 3, 11–12, 14, 24, 31, 33, 40–41,
 52, 66, 81–83, 85, 87–88,
 92–93, 104, 134
Gender, 33–34, 39–41, 45–46, 50–51,
 54–56, 58–61, 67, 81–82, 92,
 96–98, 102–104, 127–128,
 139
Genealogy (-ies), 16, 22, 24–25, 28,
 32–33, 42, 67–68
Genre (-s), 10, 83–84, 88, 91–92, 102,
 124–125, 136–137
Geography (-ies), 19, 58, 64, 81, 106
Geotrauma (-s), 14–15, 65, 82, 89–93,
 101, 104, 109, 121–122, 131
Gesellschaft, 7–8
Glance (-s), 76, 86
Goodman, Nelson, 8–9, 11–13,
 135
Governmobilities, 60–61
Guattari, Felix, 16, 74,
 122
Guest (-s), 6–7, 23, 32–33, 39–40,
 58–59, 61–62, 64, 70, 72, 81,
 95–96, 111–112

Habermas, Jürgen, 15–16, 20–21, 76, 97
Habitude/hexis, 37–38, 46, 60–61
Habitus, 50–52, 63–64, 82, 88, 113–114, 117–118, 134
Hand, Martin, 5–6
Haraway, Dona, 5
Hauntology (-ies), 11
Heritage, 2, 7–11, 13–14, 29–30, 43, 47–48, 51–53, 56, 62–63, 65, 74, 83–89, 94, 97–99, 109, 117, 137–139
Hermeneutics, 32, 121
Heterochronta (-s), 17
Heteroglossic, 8–9
Hierarchy (-ies), 21–22, 24–25, 30, 44, 50, 54–56, 66, 75, 88, 98–99, 111–112, 135
Hollinshead, Keith, 3–4, 8–13, 21, 23–27, 30–31, 37, 39–40, 42–44, 53, 58, 60–61, 63–64, 76, 82, 86–87, 89–90, 92, 98, 104, 114–115, 119, 133–134, 138
Hope, 3, 20, 22, 25, 27, 31, 133
Hope, academy of, 22, 27, 31
Hospitality, 1–3, 5–6, 9–11, 15, 17, 19–21, 25–27, 29–30, 32–34, 38–42, 55, 58, 61, 63, 67, 70, 73, 77, 82, 86–87, 93, 96–98, 101, 111–112, 133–134
Host (-s), 2–3, 5, 7, 23, 29–30, 35, 53–54, 57–58, 60–61, 65, 67, 75, 82, 96, 98–99, 103, 115–116, 135, 138–140
Humanity, 5–6, 10, 31–32
Humanity 2.0, 97–99
Hyperobjects, 77–78, 82

Identity (-ies), 1–2, 8–9, 15, 20–21, 25, 33–34, 37–41, 44, 46–47, 52, 55, 63, 65–67, 75–76, 81–82, 86, 90, 95, 98–99, 106–107, 112
Ideoscapes, 120–121
Imaginary (-ies), 2, 15, 20, 27, 37–38, 42, 44, 47–48, 57, 60, 65–66,

89–91, 93, 96–97, 103–104, 121–122, 131, 138–139
Immobility (-ies), 3, 19–20, 23, 87, 91
Industry (-ies), 2, 5, 25, 27, 30, 35, 37–38, 41, 50, 53–54, 63–64, 73, 75–77, 84, 86–87, 90–91, 96–97, 101–102, 104, 107–109, 112, 114–115, 121–122, 129–131
Installation, 5–7, 58, 73
Instillations. *See also* Habitus; Worldmaking, 6–7, 58
Intermediality, 57
Interpretation, 9–11, 28–29, 39, 42, 46, 54, 60–61, 75, 95, 104, 111–112
Intimacy (-ies), 57–58, 60–61, 92–93
Irony, 24, 75–76, 91, 97
Isomorphism, 4–5, 61–62, 123

Jamal, Tazim, 2, 27, 31, 55–56, 112, 115
Jensen, Ole B., 15–16, 38, 76–77, 82, 92–93, 130–131
Judgement, 1, 4, 17, 21, 26–27, 68–69, 83–84, 137–139
Justice, 1–2, 4, 10–11, 23, 25, 28, 42, 65–66, 76, 88, 90–93, 95, 102–103

Kéfi, 46–48, 50–51
Keyf, 45–46
Kinēma, 74
Kinēmatográphos, 74
Kitsch, 75–76, 91, 129–130

Labour, 3, 9–10, 13–14, 16, 20–22, 25, 33–34, 38–39, 56–59, 61–62, 64, 67–69, 73, 75, 86, 97–98, 130–131, 133–139
Landscape (-s), 6–7, 9–10, 13–14, 25, 33–35, 37, 47–48, 52, 57, 74, 76–77, 81, 87, 89–90, 93, 95, 98, 102, 111, 114, 121–122, 128, 130–131, 133–134, 136
Lanternism, 133–135

Lanterns, 133, 135
Lapointe, Dominic, 3, 28, 39, 60–61, 139
Lifeform (-s), 81
Lyon, David, 73

MacDonaldisation, 84
Map (-s), 5–6, 14–16, 34–35, 38–42, 50, 53, 71, 106, 113–114, 135
Mapping, 15–16, 34–35, 38–39, 114, 134
Market (-s), 3, 6–7, 9–11, 20–21, 23–24, 38–39, 42, 44, 50, 52, 55–56, 59–67, 69–70, 72–73, 75–77, 80, 86–87, 89–95, 98, 101, 112, 121–122
Massumi, Brian, (AU: The Name Massumi, Brian is not found in Chapter Text)
Materialism, 29–30
Matrix, 44, 50–51
Media, 2–5, 9, 13, 15, 34–35, 41, 56–57, 66, 70, 73–75, 84–88, 95–97, 101, 103–104, 109–111, 113–116, 121–123, 127–128, 136, 138–140
Mediation, 2, 57, 127, 137–139
Mémoire-habitude, 37–38, 46
Mémoire souvenir, 37–38, 94–95
Memory (-ies), 37–38, 42, 46, 53–54, 58, 60–61, 70, 72, 74, 78–79, 81–82, 87, 94, 96–97, 117–118, 120–121, 128, 130, 137–138
Metaphor (-s), 5–6, 11–12, 14–15, 17, 21–22, 32–33, 39–40, 64–65, 74, 103, 121–122
Middle class (-es), 27, 62, 64–66, 73, 75–76, 82, 85, 89–90, 96–99, 103, 106–107, 119, 123, 127–129
Minca, Claudio, 61–64, 81
Mobility (-ies), 1–3, 6–8, 10–11, 13–15, 17, 19, 21, 23, 25–27, 29, 31–35, 37–42, 46–47, 56–61,

63–64, 66–70, 72–78, 81–82, 84–88, 91–95, 97–98, 102–104, 106–110, 112–115, 119–121, 128–130, 133–140
Modality. *See also* Modernity, 41, 119, 137–138
Modernity. *See also* Modality, 8–10, 19–21, 27, 29, 47–48, 53–54, 62, 64–66, 78–79, 81, 89–90, 92, 97, 103, 127, 138
Montage, 76–77, 96, 121–122
Morton, Timothy, 5, 78, 81
Movement (-s), 4–5, 16, 26, 28, 41, 53–55, 62, 74–77, 79, 109–110, 137–138
Multitude (-s), 16
Mythomoteur, 11–12, 63–64

Nation-state, 6–7, 10–11, 24, 34–35, 60–62, 75–76, 78–79, 85–88, 90–91, 98
Neoliberalisation, 23
Neoliberalism, 1, 23, 63, 70, 72, 87–88, 135, 138
Netnography, 17
Network (-s), 2–6, 11, 15–16, 19–20, 32–35, 37–39, 51–52, 61, 63–65, 70, 73, 77, 80–82, 86–88, 104–106, 109, 115–117, 119, 128–131
Node, 14–15, 38, 65, 110, 112, 115–116, 129
Nomad, 103
Nomadism, 85
Non-places. *See also* Capitalism; Neoliberalisation; Place; Space (-s), 53, 81–82, 86, 137–138
Nova-us, 5–6

Omnitopia, 114–115
Ontology (-ies), 12, 32–33, 128–129, 134, 139–140
Order (-s), 27, 50–51, 55–56, 105–106, 115, 119, 123–124, 131

Pandemic (-s), 77, 84, 87–88, 93–94,
    139–140
Paradigm (-s), 6–7, 15–16, 22–23, 25,
    27–28, 31–32, 134
  new mobilities, 15–16, 23, 25, 27,
    31–32, 39, 41
Pastiche, 128–129
Pedagogy (-ies), 28, 92–93
Perspectivism, 76–77
Phainomai, 76–77
Phanerology, 29–30
Phantasmagoric, 26–27
Phenomenology, 5–6, 9–10, 29–30, 32,
    106, 138
Picturesque, 109–110
Pilgrim (-s), 121–123
Pilgrimage (-s), 7, 29, 31–32, 43, 94–95,
    101–102, 104, 106–107,
    113–114, 117, 121–123,
    127–131
Place, 2–3, 5–11, 13–14, 16, 25, 27–28,
    31–32, 37–44, 46–47, 50–53,
    55–64, 66–68, 74, 76, 78, 82,
    84–87, 89–92, 95, 101–103,
    106–107, 110–112, 114–117,
    119, 121–122, 127–131,
    134–135, 138–140
Planet, 16, 31, 102, 139–140
Planetary, 3, 5–6, 19–21, 73, 78, 81,
    101–102, 129, 134–135
Planning, 2, 4, 7, 55–56, 65, 78–79,
    92–93, 106, 114, 119,
    128–129, 131
Platformisation, 95, 114–115
Platforms, 2, 30, 34, 95, 138–140
Playscapes, 11–12, 22, 64–66, 109–110,
    127–129, 131, 138
Pluriversality, 4–5
Politics, 2–5, 9–12, 32, 39–40, 58, 62,
    65–66, 69–70, 72, 74–77,
    79–80, 84, 86, 95, 102,
    111–112, 114, 127–128
Post-colonialism, 2–6, 21, 24, 39–40,
    54–55, 76, 84, 95
Post-humanism, 31

Postidentity, 25, 63–64,
    75
Post-modernity, 11–12, 61,
    111
Post-phenomenology, 5–6, 16–17, 106,
    138–139
Post-poles, 5–6
Post-tourism, 75, 84–85, 95–96, 98–99,
    128–129
Post-tourist (-s), 77, 84–85, 95–96, 106
Post-truth, 1, 11, 13, 17, 73–74, 76–77,
    93–95, 121, 137–138
Poverty, 74, 90–91, 110, 123
Power, 2–4, 10–12, 14, 19–21, 23–24,
    27–28, 38–40, 57–58, 60–62,
    64–65, 67–69, 76–77, 80, 85,
    87–88, 92–93, 98, 109–110,
    123, 129–130
Pragmatism, 27
Praxeology, 9–10
Presence, 2, 11, 17, 20–23, 33, 38,
    55–58, 62, 64–66, 70, 72, 76,
    81–82, 85, 90–91, 94, 97,
    102–104, 108–110, 114–115,
    137–139
Privateness, 9, 12–13,
    20–21
Process (-es). *See also* Pragmatism;
    Reflexivity; Worldmaking,
    1–16, 20–23, 32–35, 38–40,
    44, 61–64, 67, 74–75, 92–93,
    95, 98–99, 114, 120–121,
    134, 139
Production, 2–6, 8, 11–14, 19, 24,
    31–32, 41, 43–44, 59, 63–64,
    67, 73, 75–77, 80–83, 86–87,
    89–95, 101–102, 105–108,
    112, 114–116, 122, 128,
    135–136
Property (-ies), 2–3, 5–6, 15, 38, 53, 62,
    69–70, 74, 101–102,
    108–109, 130
Provenance, 138–139
Publicness, 9, 12–13, 17, 19, 26,
    56, 106

Race, 9, 21–22, 57–58, 67–68, 82, 103, 129, 138–139
Racism, 21, 29, 75–76, 82–83
Rationalisation, 10, 22, 139
Realism, 8, 92
  magical, 15
Recognition, 2, 9, 22, 27, 32, 34–35, 52, 55–56, 61–62, 66–67, 75–76, 78–79, 106–109, 130–131
Reflexivity, 23, 26, 31
Refrain (-s). *See also* Trope, 135
Regime (-s), 12–15, 20, 42–43, 55–56, 62, 64, 66–67, 76, 89–90, 133–136, 138
Relationships, 2, 31, 52, 60–61, 92–93, 101–102, 116, 128
Representation (-s), 2–3, 8–9, 11, 13–15, 17, 20, 27, 33, 35, 40–41, 47–48, 55–58, 62–64, 66, 69–70, 74, 76, 83–84, 87, 89–92, 104, 107–108, 116, 121, 123, 127–131, 138–139
Ricoeur, Paul, 10, 37–38, 46, 94–95
Risk, 19, 31, 35, 52, 58, 61–62, 96, 103–104, 108–109, 119, 124–125, 127–128, 130–131
Rorty, Richard, 134–135

Sandywell, Barry, 5–8, 26, 64–65
Script (-s), 42, 52, 60–61, 76–79, 85–86, 89–91, 94–95, 97, 127
Secrecy, 109
Self-care, 58, 62, 88
Sensibility (-ies), 7–8, 39–40, 66–67, 92–93
Sex, 33–34, 38–39, 50–51, 54–61, 64, 67–70, 72–73, 116, 124–125, 127, 135
Sexism, 21, 70, 75–76, 82–83, 86
Sheller, Mimi, 20, 25–26, 57–58, 64–65, 130–131, 135
Sign (-s), 31, 38, 41, 47, 56, 63–64, 73, 85–86, 96–97, 101–102, 107–108, 131, 133–134, 137–138

Simmel, Georg, 15–16, 65, 103, 117–118
Site (-s), 6–7, 9–10, 14–16, 24, 29–30, 35, 41, 43–44, 47–48, 61, 66–67, 79–81, 88, 101–102, 104, 106, 111–119, 124–125, 127–128, 138–139
Sociology, 4, 7–8, 12–13, 17, 19–27, 38, 77, 103
Space (-s), 9–10, 17, 44, 55, 57–58, 61, 63–65, 84, 93, 103–104, 106, 119, 125–126, 128–129, 136–137
Sphere (-s), 10, 20–22, 32, 39–40, 56–58, 61–63, 65–66, 74, 95
  public, 2, 20–22, 39–40, 56, 62, 137–138
Spirit, 2–3, 9–11, 13–14, 19–20, 23–26, 34, 38–39, 46–47, 52, 54, 61, 63, 65–67, 75–77, 82, 98
Spiritedness, 4–5, 10–11, 14–15
Spreadability, 95
Staging, 15–16, 38, 76–78, 89–90, 104, 107–108, 111, 116, 128–129
Stereotyping, 76–77, 83, 89–90, 104, 128–129
Strategy, 7–8, 39, 57–58, 65, 77, 87, 90–91, 95, 97–98, 103–104, 109, 111, 113–114, 129–130, 137–138
Study (-ies), 2–10, 12–13, 15–17, 19–26, 33, 37, 41–42, 54–56, 74, 76, 82, 94–95, 98, 102–103, 115, 133–135, 138–139
Style (-s), 2, 6, 15, 20–21, 23–24, 28, 30, 35, 44, 46–47, 53–54, 57–58, 62, 67, 70, 72–76, 78, 80–82, 84–85, 87, 96, 106, 109–110, 114–115, 125–126, 131, 134, 137–138
Subjectivity (-ies), 62–63, 80–82
Symbolism, 5, 15–16, 64–65
Symbols, 5–6, 9–10, 52, 58, 65, 81, 129–130
Synecdoche, 85, 95

Systems, 2–8, 10–16, 19–22, 31–32, 41,
    44, 47, 57–58, 63, 70, 73–76,
    78–79, 81, 92–93, 96–98,
    101–102, 107, 109, 113–114,
    118, 131
Szerszynski, Bronislaw, 4–6, 74,
    129–131

Technique (-s), 5–6, 15, 26, 33, 76–78,
    81, 85, 92–93, 95–96,
    101–102, 134
Techno-Anthropocene, 6, 8, 33, 38,
    66–67, 136, 138
Technocracy, 6
Technomorphism, 6, 8, 34, 38, 62, 67,
    74, 91–92, 103, 128–129,
    135, 138
Technopoesis, 5–6, 139–140
Temporality (-ies), 16–17
Territoire, 3
Territory, 3, 24, 27, 64, 134
Terrorism, 86, 130
Thanatos, 117–118
Thanatourism, 29,
    117–118
Theory, 2–4, 7–9, 11–12, 15–16, 22, 26,
    28–29, 32–35, 53, 63–64, 81,
    101–103, 107–108
Tiempos mixto. See also Post-
    colonialism, 17
Time (-s), 5, 14–15, 17, 26, 38, 41–42,
    44–45, 47–48, 50, 53–54,
    58–61, 63, 66–67, 75, 83–84,
    87–90, 93–94, 96–97, 105,
    111–112, 117–118, 127, 131
Tópos, 14
Tourism, 1–11, 13–17, 19–26, 33–35,
    37, 42, 52–53, 58, 62, 67,
    72–73, 77–78, 80, 82–99,
    101–104, 108–109, 111–112,
    114–119, 121–124, 128–131,
    133–136, 138–140
Transdisciplinarity, 1, 17, 103, 133, 136
Transmodernism. *See also* Dussel,
    Enrique, 27–28, 76
Travel, 1, 17, 21, 26, 33, 35, 37–38,
    44–45, 47–48, 56–59, 61, 63,
    65–66, 76, 84, 91–92, 94–96,
    116–118, 121–122, 127–128,
    130, 136, 138
Trope (-s). *See also* Refrain(-s), 23, 38,
    55, 58, 61, 104, 114
Trópos, 53–54
Tsing, Anna, 134–135

Urbanism, 7, 111, 138
Urry, John, 6–7, 11–12, 23, 25–27,
    40–41, 85, 109, 130–131
Utopia, 5, 24, 64

Vagabond, 103, 117–118
Violence, 15–16, 31–32, 41–42, 47,
    57–58, 70, 72, 74, 81–82,
    87–88, 102–103, 112, 122,
    129–131
Virtuality (-ies), 16–17, 25, 33, 135
Voluntourists, 92
Vulnerability (-ies), 74, 81–82, 86,
    94–95, 112

Worldmaking, 3–5, 8, 10–13, 17, 26,
    30, 33–34, 37–40, 42–44,
    57–58, 62, 70–72, 76,
    101–102, 104, 134–135

Young, Iris Marion, 61, 92–93,
    102

Zone (-s), 15, 24, 31, 63–64, 78, 82,
    139–140

Printed in the USA
CPSIA information can be obtained
at www.ICGtesting.com
JSHW012112260923
49175JS00002B/7

9 781837 531615